Clara Colby

THE INTERNATIONAL SUFFRAGIST

John Holliday

TALLAI BOOKS

Gold Coast, Australia

Tallai Books
5 Earle Court
Tallai, Qld 4213, Australia
www.tallaibooks.com

Book Layout ©2015 BookDesignTemplates.com

Ordering Information:
Retailers should use Ingram's iPage online search, order and account management platform at https://www.ingramcontent.com/retailers/ordering

Clara Colby; The International Suffrgaist./ John Holliday. —1st ed.
ISBN 978-0-6486848-0-0

CONTENTS

*This book is dedicated to my wife Colleen,
my daughters Alex and Angela and my grand
daughter Grace, who are beneficiaries of the
sacrifices made by people like Clara Colby.*

In all that galaxy of heroic women who have championed the rights of women since 1848, there is not one that has made more personal sacrifices than Mrs. Colby.

—REV. OLYMPIA BROWN

CHAPTER 1

GOODBYE MOTHER

WE MAY NEVER KNOW why three-year-old Clara Dorothy Bewick was left behind in England when her parents and three brothers departed for a new life in America. Her parents, Thomas and Clara Bewick, were migrating to America and the family had been talking about little else in the months leading up to their departure. They were leaving on the sailing ship *Olympus* from Bristol, and little Clara was in tears when she found that she could not join them. She later wrote an essay that revealed how she felt on that day.

> *The very earliest recollection of my life is kissing my mother 'goodbye' at some place, and then riding off with my father somewhere in a great dark house, which afterward I learned was a railway train.[1]*

The year was 1849, and one possible reason why Clara was left behind was that she showed symptoms of an infectious disease. If that were the case, then the most likely suspect would be cholera, for the country was experiencing a cholera epidemic that year. No ship's captain would permit anyone with possible cholera symptoms to board their vessel, which would raise the threat of quarantine on arrival in New York.

With all the family possessions either sold or packed for shipment aboard the *Olympus*, there was no option but to arrange for Clara to stay with her grandparents until she was well and arrange for her to make the journey later. Hence the trip by railway to London, where the grandparents lived.

This part of the story involves three generations with the name Clara, which might confuse you, the reader. To help understand whom the writer is referring to in the text, please refer to Figure 1, which shows the family tree of Clara Bewick. Also, for this first chapter, when mentioning Clara without her husband, her birth name will be used.

Figure 1. Clara Bewick's Family Tree

William and Sarah Medhurst

Married 1819	Married 1826	
Josiah Wllingham Died 1826	**Clara Medhurst** b: 17 April 1801 London d: 1879 Nebraska	**Stephen Chilton** b: 1799 London d: 1876 Nebraska

Rev. Dr. Walter Henry Medhurst

Married 1840

Thomas Bewick b: 25 April 1822 d: 1897 Wisconsin	**Clara Willingham** b: 1821 London d: 18 August 1855 Wisconsin

Married 1871

Leonard Colby b: 25 April 1822 d: 1924 Kansas	**Clara Bewick** b: 5 August 1846 Gloucester UK d: 7 Sept 1916 Palo Alto Ca

Clara Dorothy Bewick was born in Gloucester on August 5, 1846, the third child of Thomas and Clara Bewick.

Thomas was a platelayer, working on the installation of the railways across England. He had a responsible position overseeing several section gangs.[2] In America, Thomas's skills would be in high demand, and so it was that in 1849, the family was preparing to depart England to try their luck in the new world. Thomas Bewick was a hard worker, but he had also shown great academic skills as a young man, and he could well have taken a different direction with the right assistance.

As a young child, he was sent to a private school; each morning he was required to take a penny for his tuition. He made such advancement that at the age of eleven years the teacher sent him home because he had advanced as far in his studies as the teacher could take him. In the following years he became familiar with algebra, geometry, trigonometry, logarithms and the French language. He was known as the most advanced student in his township.[3]

Clara Bewick's maternal grandparents were Stephen and Clara Chilton nee Medhurst. Clara Medhurst's first husband, Josiah Willingham, was the biological parent of Clara Willingham, but he died in 1826, and when Clara married Stephen Chilton, Stephen came to be accepted as her father and the beloved grandfather of the youngest Clara.

Family history has it that Sarah Medhurst, the mother of Clara Medhurst, was a very ambitious woman, someone who thought a great deal of the aristocracy and whose watchword was always to make acquaintances in life above her station. From what we can gather, the ambitions of the mother, Sarah, may have been the cause of her daughter Clara's mishaps.

There seemed an active streak of vanity in the family; Clara was married in her early teens to Josiah Willingham, of an aristocratic family, a family who never acknowledged her. She must have then left home, probably much talked about, and her daughter was born near Bow Bells.[4]

Regardless of Sarah Medhurst's attempts to arrange her daughter's life, the marriage to Josiah Willingham did have two positive outcomes: the birth of a daughter and the financial stability in which she could be raised. Furthermore, Clara Medhurst appeared to retain the benefit of financial independence throughout her life. So perhaps the ambition of Sarah Medhurst in the early 1800s was the first influence we can identify that helped to create a successful suffragist in America almost 100 years later. One strong woman was creating a situation from which another would gain, three generations later.

Clara Medhurst, widowed at age 21, was cast adrift in society. Her first lover, a young man from Gloucester named Stephen Chilton, tracked her down, married her and adopted the child. Fate had it that Clara Medhurst would settle down with her true love and they would spend a lifetime together. Sarah Medhurst was still concerned about keeping up appearances, so she arranged the marriage of Stephen and Clara at St George, Bloomsbury, London on 12 July, 1826. St George was the same church where her mother and father, Sarah and William Medhurst had married in 1791.

In 1849, Stephen and Clara Chilton lived at 11 Waterloo Place in Westminster. So, for little Clara Bewick, this was going to be quite a change of lifestyle, and in fact would be the first significant event that changed her life. The location of

Waterloo Place is close to St James's Park, the royal palaces, and the parliament buildings. The building was composed almost entirely of offices and during 1851, Stephen Chilton, his wife Clara and his granddaughter Clara Bewick were the only residents, so we assume from this that Stephen was employed as something like a caretaker for the building.

Clara Medhurst's brother was Walter Henry Medhurst, a well-known missionary to China whose travels within China were frequently reported in the English newspapers. Grandmother Clara was also a devout Christian, and she was determined to raise her granddaughter in the same way. At the age of five, Clara Bewick could recite all 176 verses of the 119th Psalm, the longest chapter of the Bible.[5]

Stephen and Clara Chilton had traveled to America back in 1842, so they were able to provide their granddaughter with stories of what it would be like for her parents and brothers in their new land. Stephen had heard that there was an opportunity to buy a farm in Royal Town, Ohio and as a result, the Chilton tribe, including Stephen's parents, aged 76 and 82, set off and soon arrived in New York on the *Philadelphia* on May 30, 1842.[6] The plan to operate the farm did not go well. After only a few months, with his money all gone, Stephen let out his farm on a lease for five years and returned to England.

We know this because he lost the title to the farm in the Insolvent Debtors Court in England, as reported in *The Morning Chronicle* in 1846.[7] Stephen's parents also returned; we know that Stephen's mother died in London in 1844, and his father lived on until 1849, when he was also laid to rest in London.

The most significant change for young Clara Bewick would have arisen from the exciting places and people in her grandparents' circle and from the attention she would have received as an only child in the household. Back home in Gloucestershire, the family had lived in a small house with four children under the age of eight, and her father would have often been away on work gangs. There would have been little time for her mother to pay the kind of attention to Clara that her grandmother could provide just for her.

A short walk from her grandparents' home, and they could wander through the royal parks down towards Buckingham Palace, in the hope of seeing Queen Victoria. St James's Palace was even closer, and grandmother would point out the Palace as the place where her nephew, Walter Medhurst Jnr, met Her Majesty at the Queen's Levee in February, two years previously.

Walter Medhurst Jnr was then on leave from his position with the British government in Hong Kong. Later that year, Walter was married at St John's Church, Notting Hill, to Ellen Cooper in a double ceremony, where Ellen's sister was marrying Walter's cousin Charles. So young Clara was beginning to understand how well connected she was to London.

On select days, grandmother would take Clara for a walk across to Horse Guards Parade to watch the Changing of the Guard and other ceremonial military spectacles.

The River Thames in those days was a busy thoroughfare of commercial boats of all sizes. A short walk along the river was the New Hungerford Market, one of London's biggest produce markets, located on the site of what is now Charing Cross Station. Other parts of London were easily explored using a short carriage ride and often that meant visiting grandmother's friends and family.

Clara Chilton's sister, Mary, lived on Great Russell Street by the British Museum, and her husband was head accountant. Their son, Charles Baker, who married his wife Harriet in the double ceremony mentioned above, had recently had a new baby, which made their home a favorite place for young Clara to visit.

Living in London meant that Clara experienced all that was going on in the world. Clara would not necessarily read the newspapers, but she could not help to be influenced by what was going on in the conversations of the adults. In 1851, the Great Exhibition, often referred to as the Crystal Palace Exhibition, opened in Hyde Park. It was attended by famous people of the time, including Charles Darwin, Samuel Colt and the writers Charlotte Brontë, Charles Dickens, Lewis Carroll, George Eliot, Alfred Tennyson, and William Makepeace Thackeray. As a role model who might inspire her of what she could be when she grew up, she would often hear about Florence Nightingale, the founder of modern nursing, whose name was famous throughout England in the mid-fifties.

The most massive construction projects of the day in London were the new railway stations that were taking shape all over the city. Waterloo, Kings Cross, and Paddington all opened during the time that Clara lived in London. When Clara's grandmother took her on her first train journey, the little girl jumped for joy, later recalling her trip in an essay, 'Riding the Cars.'[8]

My next ride on the cars made me about as happy as a child is capable of being: and that is saying a good deal. I well recollect standing at the window jumping, and clapping my hands, with great delight at seeing houses and fences and men go by so quickly. As I turned to the person who had charge of me, she told me my eyes looked like diamonds: a remark which left a greater impression, as I do not think it was ever made at any other time.

Other events included the opening of the new department store, Harrods, in Knightsbridge. For Clara, that probably did not compare to the excitement of visiting the oldest toy shop in the world, Hamleys, in High Holborn, which as today's readers would know, has moved to Regent Street. London was an exciting and educational place for a young girl. Her recollections of a visit to the British Museum illustrate the influence that early life in London had upon her.

A long time ago, when seven or eight years old, I was taken to the British Museum. Since then I have read no account of it, and if I remember rightly, have heard no one speak of it: therefore my ideas of that noble structure are somewhat obscure, and I cannot hope to give you any description of it. But the memory of that visit cannot ever be lost: it is more vivid now than at first. If I had at that time any idea of the value of that magnificent collection of the nations and ages represented there, or any thought that the time was coming when I could no longer go there as I pleased, perhaps, child as I was, I might have learned more of it. I will endeavor to recall for you from memory the impressions made by that event.

The first object that attracted my attention was the peculiar carving over the door: then I remember nothing more until I find myself standing by long tables on which are arranged precious stones sparkling with un-dreamed of glory. Then the fossils: ....Perhaps that huge wonder on the wall is the great Mastadon, the dreaded monster of the older world.

Next on memory's tablet is the collection of birds: every imaginable variety of the feathered tribe, other tropical birds all glorious in their attire. Now to the library: here to find books of every size, on every subject, and in every tongue. As I saw them then, I thought what pretty stories must be there.

But leave this side of the building and come with me to view that which always stands out distinct from other things seen there. Come and gaze with me at those who have come up to us from the grave of centuries to show us the insignificance of earthly fame. Here are the honored dead of the ancient world: kings and queens perhaps, to whom no token of their former greatness remains, save a mass of smoldering ruin. The land which once they proudly called their own is now given to the oppressor, until they shall no more have respect to that which their own hands have made, but shall turn unto the Lord their God.[9]

We don't know whether Clara had any formal education during the six years that she lived in England, but we know she received a level of home schooling from her grandparents that would have surpassed what most young people experienced in those days. They were regular churchgoers, and Clara would have indeed gone to Sunday school, since Sunday schools were the forerunner of the state school system in England. Sunday schools were founded by a fellow native from Gloucester, Robert Raikes. His statue now stands on the Victoria Embankment in London, not far from Clara's home in Westminster.

I am sure the topic of China would have been raised in the Chilton household on a frequent basis, with the letters received from family members and the often reported adventures of Walter Medhurst in the London newspapers. In

1852, Walter's daughter Eliza and her husband Charles visited England from Hong Kong, along with two sons, aged 4 and 18 months. With the distance traveled being so far, Eliza and her boys would be staying for a year in Bedford, just north of London. Charles returned almost immediately to his position as Chief Magistrate of Hong Kong, but Clara relished the opportunities to visit with her Aunt Eliza and the two boys.

The other topic of conversation, raised almost daily, would be America. The year after Clara's parents left England, news came of the birth of a new brother, Ebenezer, and two years later another brother, John, was born, and finally, a sister named Mary was born on January 1, 1854.

Young Clara's parents wanted to know when she would be joining them, but her grandmother thought she was too young to make such a journey on her own. Stephen and Clara Chilton anguished over the decision, but eventually they decided to return with Clara to America and set up home with, or close to, their family in Wisconsin.

Clara looked forward with great excitement to her impending move to America. She could not have known what a change this would mean to her life; she only knew how much she wanted to follow the same journey that her parents and siblings had made in 1849.

CHAPTER 2

THE PIONEERS

THE JOURNEY THAT THOMAS (her father) and Clara Bewick took started in Bristol, England, on August 10, 1849, when they set sail on the sailing ship *Olympus*. Steamships were beginning to appear on the Atlantic route, and although they made a faster passage, the fares were more expensive than the sailing vessels. Thomas and Clara were on a tight budget, so they had no choice but to go by sail. Sailing vessels were also safer, since steamships were new and subject to breakdowns.

They arrived in New York on September 11, 1849,[1] making a faster-than-average journey, in just over four weeks. New York was only a place to change from one ship to another, however, because the Bewicks were heading to Milwaukee. Thomas hoped to get work on the new Milwaukee and Mississippi Railroad, which was under construction. Thomas made sure that when they arrived in New York, they should proceed directly to the next ship because an industry of abuse and exploitation thrived at the port areas where immigrants disembarked. There were sellers of forged tickets, people who would steal their luggage, and human traffickers posing as good Samaritans. He was told to go straight to the departure pier of the river steamer and purchase tickets at the ship.

From New York, the Bewicks took a steamer up to Albany, then transferred to a canal boat which took them to join Lake Erie at Buffalo. From there, another ship took them across Lake Erie, through Lake St Clair, Lake Huron, and Lake Michigan to Milwaukee. This route would typically involve a journey of another two to three weeks. So, about two months after leaving Bristol, they arrived at what was planned to be their new home.

The Bewicks spent their first winter in Milwaukee, where they rented a room while they planned where they could set up a proper home. Work was scarce and the prospects for Thomas to find success in the railway construction industry were bleak. For a time, he found employment dressing millstones, but this was not why he had come to America.

As with many emigrants to new lands, plans changed, and at some stage, Thomas decided to change his career: to leave his work with the railways and start a new life as a farmer. To newcomers like the Bewicks, America offered the opportunity to become members, in both economic and social equality, of a new society. In Wisconsin, virgin prairie land was available at a nominal charge to anyone who dared to clear and cultivate the land on which they would build a future investment for their family. This was the dream that Thomas and Clara shared and so they accepted the challenge to make the dream come true.

It did not take Thomas long to find out where land was available – on the border of the settled part of the country – and to find someone who knew the section-lines where he might find a good location for a farm. Thomas and Clara were not wealthy, but they were smart enough to maximize any opportunity to finance the purchase of land and to set up the farm. Perhaps Clara asked her mother to help out by loaning them money, and although that seemed likely, we do not have any record of that.

Thomas found 80 acres of land for $5 an acre, about 15 miles north of Madison, near the new settlement of Windsor. Here they would face many hardships, not having sufficient capital to buy teams and machinery with which to equip the farm. The family lived in a small stone house that Thomas built himself. By comparison to some of their neighbors, they were lucky... since many had resorted to living in a 'dugout,' a home excavated from the ground, overlaid with a wooden framework that would support a sod roof.

What stock he could afford would have to roam freely, since they didn't have the materials with which to build the fences needed to protect their crops. Most fences were made of earth, with a deep ditch on both sides.[2]

Every task involved significant manual labor and everyone in the family was involved. Little children fetched water, the older boys had to help their father in the fields, and Clara had to manage the house alone and look after the chickens and pigs that surrounded the homestead. Thomas plowed the land with the neighbor's oxen; the animals traded on one day's loan for one day of Thomas's labor. The oxen were required for the initial breaking of the ground. Later this was achieved by horses, which the Bewicks had to purchase and look after.

The frustration of hard work that achieved nothing must have been overwhelming. Thomas dug an open well down to 50 feet, complete with a rock wall lining. At 50 feet he hit the hard rock, which was impervious to his tools, so he gave up. For eighteen months they had to carry water for three-quarters of a mile, but after that, Thomas attacked the rock with a hand drill and as a result found water, just less than two feet deeper. That supply lasted 20 years before he had to deepen the well.

The climate was extreme by comparison to the places where they had grown up in England. The winters would have at least four months of below freezing temperatures and three months in the summer when the temperatures would exceed those which they knew back home.

Throughout the time of this constant struggle to build a farm and a home for the family, Clara was almost always pregnant or looking after a young baby. In the fifteen years that they were married, Clara experienced ten pregnancies, from which seven children survived. During the first nine years of their marriage, they lived a reasonably comfortable life in London and Gloucestershire, and the comparison to the life they were living in Wisconsin was extreme. They endured this struggle for the sake of their children; ultimately it was proven correct that the children were the beneficiaries of the migration and not Thomas and Clara.

Thomas Stephen was the eldest son at the time they settled in Wisconsin, and being only nine years old did not excuse him from sharing with his father the constant toil of pioneering in a new country. According to the family history, he grew up rugged and sturdy and went on to become a farmer himself. William Bewick was the next son, one who took a large share in the labor and responsibility of caring for his younger brothers and sisters. He was the one who his mother selected to be her special helper.[3]

While the father demanded strict obedience, he was said to have had an affectionate and sympathetic nature. During all the years of adversity and prosperity, Thomas held family worship, with scripture reading every morning and evening, and for many years a service of prayer was conducted by the father in their home on Sundays.[4] Thomas was very much an early fundamental Christian who rejected theological modernism, which he saw the established churches teaching. He wanted to raise his family according to a literal interpretation of the Bible, and he passed on a lot of his beliefs to his sons.

Back in London, the Chiltons made a decision. Stephen and Clara Chilton would travel with their granddaughter Clara to America, and they would sail in the spring of 1855, when they might get a smooth crossing of the Atlantic Ocean. They would head for Wisconsin and set up home for themselves in Madison, not too far from the Bewick farm. Wisconsin would be a significant change for Clara. Her only memories were of London, where her life had been full of exciting educational experiences. She would look back on those years as the only pleasant times of her childhood.

The Chiltons booked a passage on *The Robena*, a clipper ship of the United States Line, which was leaving London for New York on April 24, 1855, under the command of C.W.

Bartlett. *The Robena* was a packet ship of 825 tons that regularly made the Atlantic crossing. According to the advertisements she was, 'Fitted up expressly for the convenience of passengers and the Between Decks are spacious, well aired and ventilated, and from 7 to 9 feet in height.' The Chiltons would need all the space they could get, for, according to the arrival documents, there were 184 souls on *The Robena* in the Between Decks space. There were also four passengers in cabins, but the Chiltons traveled, like many of their peers, between decks, commonly known as steerage.

Travel by sail could be a prolonged process. The first hurdle to cross would be getting from London, down the Thames and out to 'the Roads', an anchorage near Deal, where ships would wait for favorable winds to carry them down the English Channel and out into the Atlantic Ocean. According to the Deal Maritime Museum, as many as 800 sailing ships were at anchor at one time. So it would be many days before the Chiltons lost sight of England and then several weeks of open ocean before they sighted America. Clara wrote of her experience in an essay which looked back at the journey.

We have been tossing on the ocean for three weeks. Most of our number have become heartily tired of it during that time, but I, possessing a natural fondness for the water, and having escaped the disagreeable sensations generally attendant upon sea-life, have thought every day too short.

The boundless expanse of water was a mystery to me, and children love mysteries. So with a feeling something akin to that with which, in our pensive moods, we gaze towards the horizon, I have stolen away from my companions, and leaning far over one side of the ship, tried to learn the secret of the deep. We became pretty well acquainted in those days, the old ocean and I, considering the disparity of our years; my aged friend would listen patiently to the story of my childish griefs, and soothe my troubled spirit.

But most of all I loved the ocean in a storm. Setting aside the gratification of tumbling from one side of the ship to the other, of watching the terror-stricken faces, of listening to the noise and confusion of those running hither and thither there is something awe-inspiring in the manifestation of so much power. For even at this moment, I hear a sailor from his look-out cry, 'Land aho.' The words are echoed by every tongue, and all eagerly strain their eyes to catch a glimpse of the desired heaven. ...We go on deck, and we can see, faintly looming up before us, as a cloud in the horizon, the lovely island of Staten.

The air is balmy this morning; it is like the breath of sweet-tempered June, rather than that of impulsive, irritable May. We have suffered very much with the cold while passing the banks of Newfoundland. Only a few mornings ago, we could hardly stand on the deck for the ice; and now, how changed the face of the great ocean sparkles with joy, and reflects undimmed the radiance of the sun. I can not tell how Staten Island may appear on nearer examination, but certainly, it is of surpassing beauty as the first object which welcomes us to the new world.[5]

The Chiltons disembarked from the ship on May 21, 1855, at the Port of New York. Interestingly, according to the Manifest of Passengers, Clara and Stephen Chilton had taken a few years off their real ages and had recorded little Clara as their daughter. Perhaps they were trying to avoid any potential problem with US Immigration officials. These were the days before Ellis Island, and so the procedures for qualifying and screening new arrivals were quite informal.

During the six years since the Bewicks had made the trip from New York to Milwaukee, the railroads had expanded, providing more convenient transportation options than the canal and lake steamers. The New York Central System, along with several affiliated rail lines, opened a route to Chicago in January 1853, so this is the way that the Chiltons traveled. From Chicago, they took what was to become the Chicago, Milwaukee and St Paul railroad to Madison, Wisconsin. The final 15 miles from Madison to Windsor were traveled by horse and buggy. Referring back to Clara's essay on Riding the Cars, she compounds her train memories thus:

> *A few more pleasant trips on the cars and then I was on a western prairie and did not enter them again for many years, but often I went to the depot or track to catch a glimpse of them.*
>
> *I have watched them coming in with their human freight, bringing friends for everybody; stopping just a minute, then, like some huge monster seizing his prey, bearing away everybody's friends, before the last farewell had been said. And, how I wanted to go too: no matter where; only somewhere.*[6]

So, at the end of May in 1855, Stephen and Clara Chilton, with their granddaughter Clara, arrived at the Bewick farm just outside of Windsor, six years after their tearful goodbyes in England. For the adult members of the family, this was a joyful time to exchange experiences, recall happy, shared times together and to give thanks to God for bringing their family together again.

For young Clara, it was time to meet five brothers and one sister and meet the mother and father that she hardly remembered. Grandmother had been her mother as far as she could remember, but Clara Chilton had left no doubt that she was handing her back to her birth mother, whom she assured Clara, would love her dearly.

Mother and daughter bonded quickly, and they enjoyed their first weeks together in great joy, especially since the grandparents were there to relieve mother of some of the work that she faced in running the home.

CHAPTER 3

WISCONSIN

CONTRASTING WITH THE JOY of reuniting with her mother was the rude awakening of the life that Clara had to now face, of eking out a living in this harsh new country. What she knew about farming had come from England, where farms had existed for more than a thousand years, and she had no preconception of what life as a pioneer would entail. She would later write a paper that described what a Western farmer's wife endured:

The houses are small, inconvenient, and finished only by degrees. She has few facilities to make easy the care of her household, her cows and her poultry. The fuel is not under-cover, the water is hard to draw. Her work is heavy through lack of conveniences. The husband has no time to 'potter' in the garden, and she must plant, hoe, and gather such vegetables as she needs for the table. Even the cooking is a task of magnitude, for farm folk are the hungriest in the world, and the meals must be ready at the moment, lest the hands have to be idle. All these varied cares keep her constantly weary and unprepared to endure any extra strain on her system.[1]

August 17, 1855, was like any other day on the Bewick farm. As Clara's diary notes retell, Mother was working, getting ready to do a colossal washing, with young Clara and William helping to pull bucket by bucket to fill the great boiler on the wood stove. 'How tiny Mother looks,' thought Clara. 'What beautiful auburn curly hair – gold brown and blue eyes – tiny hands and feet. And yet – an unhappy face.'

Mother called Clara to come to help her lift the boiler off the stove. Clara tried her best, but she struggled and found it far too heavy. 'I am sorry child. It is more than you can lift.' Tears came to her eyes. She was numb with weariness. Impatiently she lifted the boiler herself, seizing it with both tiny arms. She began to rub the heavy clothes. Clara helped her wring the bulky shirts and trousers.

By the time Thomas and his four sons came in from the field, the girls had covered the big pine table with a white cloth, and there were heaping plates of food waiting. Thomas lowered his head and said grace.

After supper, Thomas picked up a book and was turning a few familiar pages when he heard his wife give a sharp little cry. She had sat down, her head resting on the table. Thomas went to her side. 'What is it, Clara?'

She clutched at the edge of the table. 'The pain,' she whispered. 'The unmistakable pain.'

With a stern voice, he said, 'Brace up, Clara.'

She went to bed in agonizing pain. The three older boys knew what it meant. Thomas Jnr and his father hitched the horses to go for the doctor. The younger children went to bed and dropped off, only to be wakened by piercing cries. The doctor finally arrived. William prayed to God for help; alas, peeking through the door, he saw that the doctor was drunk. Screams stopped in silence. She was unconscious. The boys waited, wondering.

The doctor sat there, now sober, and tried to keep her from bleeding to death. Around three or four in the morning, she died. Thomas in his own heart knew that he had worked her to death. He sobbed, laying his head on the table. They took her to the lonely cemetery. Goodbye, Mother. Clara had known her mother for less than two months.

Grandmother had one lingering thought... 'how Thomas had treated her daughter.' After a week, she and Thomas had a bitter quarrel. Thomas erupted in anger. Grandmother took little Clara to one side and placed her arm around her. *Thomas could not kill Clara as he had killed his wife.*

It was the men and boys who must be served: the food for them and their beasts. Their meals must be cooked, their clothes made, washed, mended. All their house must be made comfortable. Yes, and more boys must be born to help in the fields.[2]

The experience of watching her mother's death in childbirth had a far-reaching effect on Clara. She would have constant apprehension about becoming pregnant herself, and she would forever be wary of the medical profession. She later saw the inequity of the woman's role in life, which became a foundation for her future activism for change.

Thomas Bewick was now left with seven children to support and a farm to run. Clara and Stephen Chilton felt compelled to stick with him and provide what support they could for the family, even though they were now in their mid-fifties. Clara Chilton's priority would soon turn to finding Thomas a new wife, one who would be able to take over their duties. The grandparents were very dear to all the children, and for more than a year they cared for the home.

About a year after Thomas was widowed, he married again. Jane Boynton Cox was a widow with five children. They all came to live at the farm just at the time when a new larger home had been completed to replace the old one. The larger home was essential, because with the Chiltons still living there, this meant that a total of sixteen people would be living in the new house. Thomas would go on to father five more children with his new wife, Jane.

None of the Bewick children liked their stepmother very much, but Thomas demanded strict obedience, and he was determined to control and regulate the varied interests of his mixed family. By comparison to his refined and feminine mother, young Stephenson Bewick was not impressed with his new stepmother and her brood. The Bewick children had all been encouraged by their father to read books, many of which they had brought from England, and yet, the Cox children showed no interest or ability to read anything. In his later history of the Bewick family, Stephenson wrote:

If I should say they (the Cox children) were regarded as undesirable, it would be but giving expression to our feelings at that time. Yes, there was some friction, but father's stern attitude toward any offenders, who were guilty of dis-

respect towards the wife, kept any such manifestations in the background. It may have appeared to some outsiders that our father was at times unduly strict, and even severe. It was only the successful course to pursue under such trying circumstances. A less capable man could not have controlled the situation for a day. He was a most affectionate man, who his children loved very dearly, and whom all his neighbors respected and honored.[3]

With Jane Bewick now able to take over all the household duties, with the assistance of the children, especially Clara, the grandparents decided that it was time for them to move on. Once more, they were unsure about when and where to go. At last, they decided that they should return to London and leave young Clara with her new family. For Clara, this was the start of a new chapter in her life.

From a privileged life in London, Clara found no pleasure in an arduous existence on a pioneer farm, where the family suffered many privations. For the past year, Clara still had her grandmother to keep her company, such that she did not have to adapt to the changes alone. Now, with grandmother leaving, and Clara being the oldest daughter in a household of eleven children -- with five of them under the age of five and the three eldest boys doing work out in the fields -- stepmother Jane insisted that Clara help her in running the home and caring for the little ones.

Clara did attend the one-room district school, but she had already surpassed the levels to which that school was teaching, and the teacher soon relied upon Clara to assist some of the other students. Her studies were cut short, however, when her father and stepmother asked her to care for their firstborn child, Sarah Elizabeth.

Clara developed a special bond with her step-sister Sarah, and this became a role which she cherished. Sadly, at the age of five, Sarah caught typhoid fever and died.[4] Sarah's death was another sad milestone for seventeen-year-old Clara; first, her mother died, then her grandmother left, and now her special friend Sarah had died.

The loss hit Clara very hard. The arrival of a letter from England was the one thing that lifted her out of grief: a message which included the good news that her grandparents were returning to the Windsor farm.

Stephen and Clara Chilton had not settled well back in London and were missing their family, especially the girl they viewed as their daughter. During the time they lived at the farm, they had made many friends with neighbors, and they had regularly attended church in Windsor. They had started to regard Wisconsin as home.

Thomas Bewick, meanwhile, had additional work in managing the 80 acres that he had inherited when he married Jane Cox. There were 30 acres of timber on the property, which Thomas rented out. Thomas offered the vacant log house in which the Cox family had lived to the Chiltons on their return to Wisconsin. Thomas arranged for his son Ebenezer to help out on the farm. Clara and her sister Mary soon moved in with them, which was an excellent thing for Mary because she was getting better training than she had at home.[5]

Life in the log cabin was rather primitive, and after lightning struck the stove pipe on the roof, killing their dog sleeping by the stove, the Chiltons decided that they should find their own house and property. They soon found their own 80 acres of land in Windsor, to which they moved.

Clara was ready to find the first job in her young life. Her opportunity came when she was asked to go back to the district school as a teacher. She did find this to be quite a challenge and later wrote in her diary, 'It is hard to keep 54 pairs of hands and feet and 54 little tongues in perfect order.'[6]

The location of the school was not far from the house that her grandparents had moved into and it was soon to be her new home. Traveling from the farm each day was time-consuming, and during bad weather, difficult or impossible, so the obvious solution was to move in with them. No doubt, her father was not too happy about this, but he had many other issues to face in running the home and the farm, and at least Clara would be with a family member; someone who was a good Christian. For Clara, this was an excellent solution, and for years afterward, in letters to her grandparents, she always referred to this house as her home.

CHAPTER 4

UNIVERSITY

Clara yearned for more than being a teacher in a country school, so she asked her father about enrolling in the Wisconsin State University in nearby Madison. Father was opposed to the idea, primarily because he believed that attendance at university would expose Clara to too many irreligious ideas. She was not put off, however, and so sought the advice of her grandmother. She of course loved the idea and encouraged Clara to apply. Father was asked to support her goal and, thinking back to his early academic prowess and the opportunity that he had missed, he eventually came around.

So, in 1865, at the age of nineteen, Clara entered Wisconsin University. Then in its infancy and like many state universities at that time, the institution was struggling with the question of co-education. Her brilliance and determination as a student, however, enabled her to exert a marked influence in securing the future admission of women to the University and eventually, adoption of the principles of co-education in Wisconsin.[1]

Clara took to the university like a duck to water. A letter from Miss Ellen C. Sabin, President of Milwaukee-Downer College, a contemporary student of Clara, gives us a picture of Clara's college days:

> *She simply devoured her studies and her mastery of each subject presented to her mind, languages, mathematics, philosophy, was the admiration and wonder of her fellow students.*
>
> *Yet Clara was never a somber grind. No one else origi-nated so many college enterprises. The literary society, Castalia, took on a new life when she entered it. Debate was her delight, and she always organized every effort of a forensic character, leading one side – generally to vic-tory. The drama was especially dear to her, and scenes from the great dramatists were constantly a feature of the programs.*
>
> *In all the valiant struggles of those days to secure for girls in the University opportunities and privileges equal to those that the men enjoyed, Clara was a dauntless leader. The suggestion of injustice or lack of fairness was to her a bugle call to action.[2]*

Clara's letters to her grandparents show how determined she was to take as much responsibility as she could, plus they show what a close relationship they held. By comparison, there are no letters between Clara and her father in the collection of Clara's papers held at the Wisconsin Historical Society, since Clara and her father were estranged for the whole time she studied at university.[3] The following letter was written as Clara went into her senior year:

Wisconsin University
April 14, 1867

My dear Grandfather and Grandmother,
I know you will want me to tell you all about myself, so I am going to begin. I have at last got my studies arranged, though I have had some difficulty about it. I had Latin, Mental Philosophy and geometry; only three studies. I asked Prof. Pickard what else I should take and he said, 'Nothing' but I felt as if I ought to do more, so I decided to go into the advanced Latin class which was reading Cicero. I did so; and though I find it rather hard, I think I shall be able to remain in it.

I find it very pleasant here this term. Ella and Maggie are very good company. I went down town yesterday to buy a hat. When I was walking up the street, I saw someone that looked familiar, but as she was close to me before I saw her, I did not think who it was till she had passed. Then I turned instantly and called out, 'Mrs. Bartlett'. She said I passed her so scornfully in Findlay's that she thought I wouldn't know her. I suppose most of the Windsorites think that I must be proud as Lucifer as the inevitable result of going to school.

As you will see from the account I send you, I shall no doubt get along very well. And now let me say for the fiftieth time, 'Do not under any circumstances worry about me.' Oh! I was so angry with myself when I found I had forgotten to take the kindling out of the buggy, the more so as the other girls had forgotten to bring any; but we have gotten along very well, having found some down the cellar.

Don't get lonesome and don't worry about me. And may God bless and keep us for each other. With 1,000 kisses I remain your loving granddaughter,
Clara Bewick.

Attached to the letter was a list of expenses amounting to a sum total of $15.00, with cash in hand of 10 cents. She also highlighted the steps taken by the university to keep the boys and girls apart, probably told to ease concerns that she knew her grandmother had.

August 31, 1867
Dearest Beloved Grandfather and Grandmother,
I write to you this Saturday afternoon because I want to talk to you a little, and because I wish I was at home and because I'm sleepy and because I know you will want to hear from me. Now don't scold because I write so dreadfully, for I can't write any other way.
Lizzie Spencer and I have got No. 52 and we are to room all alone as there is only one bedroom in this suite. Isn't that splendid? Lizzie says we must have a carpet and that it is a natural impossibility for Seniors to do without a carpet. Lizzie is a pattern of neatness, so I suppose I must be careful and not leave anything lying around. I want you to come and see me just as soon as you can. I want to come home one week from next Friday. If I feel as I do now, I'm sure I shall walk if I can't get home any other way.
We all like the Preceptress very much, but I do not like the new arrangement yet. We do not go up to school until a quarter of ten. (That's so we shan't meet the young gentlemen; they go at nine.) and then we can't come down till one o'clock. ..... We (Seniors) attend Chemistry lectures with the young gentlemen but then a teach-

er goes with us to see that we don't come to any harm.
Now, please write to me as soon as you get this. Believe
me to be now as ever your most affectionate granddaughter.
Clara D. Bewick

How did Clara see herself in those formative years? An essay written while at university gives us some insight into that
question. It was titled 'A Plea for the English Government',
but it reads more like it should be 'A Plea for the English', and
it reveals an author who feels part English and part American.
It also shows that she was a proficient writer with a good com-
prehension of history.

God forbid that I write one word which may have a ten-
dency to estrange the individuals of England and America,
to add one more bitter feeling to the host of those throng-
ing the ignorant mind, to increase a prejudice, already so
widespread and disastrous.
While I sympathize most truly with my adopted coun-
trymen, in all their struggles for liberty, in all their battles
for the right, in all their aspirations and determinations
for the future, I can but see that there are two sides to the
questions that are everlastingly brought up before. ...
So far I weep with Americans; rejoice with them; am
injured and insulted with them and am proud with them.
But I want to know what causes influenced the Americans
and made them what they are. It is not enough that the
words, 'Freedom, Liberty, and Equality' be sounded in the
people's ears until they forget that they are under any law,
even that of their own nature and that there may be some
who are superior to themselves. It is not enough that they be
told of oppression, and tyranny, and abject slavery, across
the seas until they imagine they constitute the only free

and enlightened people in the world, and pity and despise all those so unfortunate as not to be Americans. 'Freedom, Liberty, and Equality' will not solve the difficulty. Before ever the Americans possessed these as commonly understood, while yet they boasted in the name of Britons, they manifested the same traits and held the same principles as now. So far from having gained anything in a moral point of view since July 4, 1776, they have rushed from the extreme of honesty, virtue, and earnest Christianity, until a recent law prohibited devotional exercises in the Madison schools. Compare the first congress of the united colonies of which Pitt said that in the solidity of reasoning, force of sagacity, and wisdom of conclusion, it was surpassed by no other body of men; compare it with that of today. Will it suffer by the comparison? No. Its members were some of the men whom America is justly so proud. Yet, these were English; with minds perhaps a little enlarged after the type of the broad, new world, but still English: imbued with English principles; with all the English love and respect for hereditary sovereignty, until they were trampled out of them by the tyranny of a government which showed only its worst side to its far-away subjects. Can despotism and servility foster and develop such men as peopled the new world?[4]

Clara's letters reveal what an active social life she led in Madison. She was rooming with other students and frequently went home to Windsor whenever the opportunity arose. Also, her grandparents and her siblings occasionally visited her in Madison. But no reports were found of any visits from her father. The students went home for the Thanksgiving vacation but were back in Madison for Christmas of 1867, which Clara wrote about on December 29.

Dearest Grandfather and mother.

This is the last letter I shall write to you dated 1867. How strange it is that the years fly so quickly by! The close of each year brings us to a stopping place, where just for a moment we may tarry and glance back over the road we have passed; a milestone measuring off for us the past from the future, the actual from the ideal. The New Year is always pleasant, always sad. It is sad to think of broken resolutions, lost opportunities, miserable failures, and more miserable successes; but it is very pleasant to turn from this blotted and blurred page of our life's history to a new leaf, as yet clear and bright. So 'forgetting the things which are behind' we will 'run with patience the race set before us.'

Our Christmas was a glorious success. The tree was festooned with strung popcorn, and trimmed with small pretty apples. There was a cornucopia for each and a present for each, and more for some. I had two nice drawings which Mary C. made for me and a pair of sleeve buttons and some green chenille. The janitors were over, and there was a cornucopia full of candy and a comforter for each. One of them has a little girl. We put a lace stocking full of candy on for her, and Mrs. Perry slipped a dollar in at the top. Pat was delighted. The servant-girl also had a cornucopia and a work basket.

In the afternoon at about two o'clock, just as we got it trimmed, the tree fell over, but one of the girls was near and caught it, so the beauties did not fall off. What was to be done? At length, I volunteered to go to the carpenter's and ask him to come and fix it. You know what a bad day underfoot it was. There was no sidewalk leading to the house, and the road was full of water. I was just preparing to make a desperate plunge when someone called out, 'You'll have a wet walk, Miss Bewick!' I turned and saw

*two of the young Methodist minister students, Messrs. Da-
mon and Teal. After passing the compliments of the season, Mr. D. very kindly did my errand. All came out right at
last, but it took us all day to fix it, and it made me so tired.*

*Last Saturday Carrie Adams and I called on Mrs. Lew-
is and had quite a pleasant little visit. We then called on
Mrs. Pickard. The Prof. was quite jolly. He asked me what I
was going to do when I got through. I told him I expected to
teach and asked him if he didn't want a teacher down there.
He laughed and said, 'I guess so.' He told me Anna McAr-
thur was in Chicago waiting for a school. There had been
15 examined, only seven passed, and Anna stood second.*

*The picture enclosed is for Cousin W. Maskell. Give
it to Brother William. I think it is the best I ever had
taken. I am making you a New Year's present, but I cannot send it by letter. Don't send any bread. I made some
last week splendiferous. I may yet be able to come home
in 2 weeks from next Friday, but I will write and let you
know. Good-by dear ones, I wish you a happy New Year.
Your loving Clara.*

On February 16, 1868, she wrote the following letter to her
grandparents, which revealed some changes in her plans.

*Very Dear G. F. and M.
I have some news for you, very important indeed; now,
don't be alarmed, but I am not going to graduate.
Nellie Chynoweth, the young lady I spoke to you of, has
decided not to come to school anymore, so that reduced
our class to four. One of those four, it is very probable
and almost certain, could not pass the examination.
Then Lizzie's health is not very good, and she thinks she
ought not to come next term. So that would leave just
two of us, and it would be neither pleasant nor profit-*

able to have such a class graduate. Now, I want you to distinctly understand that I could graduate if I wanted to, for the President said he would never have proposed such a thing. But they all think it will be so much better for us to graduate next year, and meanwhile, we can teach school. The class next year will be really nice, and we shall have more experience and graduate more worthily then.

This alteration of my plans need not interfere with yours, only to make it more urgent that you come into Madison. I feel pretty sure I can get a school within walking distance of the city for summer, and I would stay here next term till it was necessary to leave. Then, if I am near here to look after my interests, I think I can get a school in the city for the fall term, and perhaps come back here. This will cost you but little, as I should not have to work so very hard next term and could live at home, and there would be no graduating finery to buy.

But we can talk of these things when I come home at vacation. It need not make any difference in our arrangements as I can live up here till you come in. One thing I want to say: I think it will be much better that I should not teach out there, and nearer here the better for me. With very much love, I am your
Clara D. Bewick[5]

Clara decided that her graduation would be put off until 1869 and in the meantime, she felt confident of finding teaching positions in and around Madison to fill in what would be a gap year. Clara Chilton was more concerned about the lack of a suitable arrangement to chaperone the girls at university, and so she persuaded Clara to move back with her and her grandfather. The Chiltons had by this time invested in a rooming house in Madison, and Clara was pleased to accept the live-in arrangement, remembering fondly her early childhood with them.

The rooming house was located in the center of Madison, close to the University, her residence situated at State Street between Francis and Gilman.[6] The 1868 Madison City Directory showed the residential address of Stephen Chilton to be the same. So, once more, Clara was living at home with her grandparents, continuing the relationship which was more like that of a daughter than a granddaughter.

Family life continued back on the farm in Windsor, where Thomas Bewick was making significant progress. In 1868, he purchased the adjoining 80 acres for $3,600,[7] plus he had another 80 acres, which had belonged to his wife, Jane. Younger brother Stephenson had taken over Clara's former teaching role at the Windsor school, and her older brother William had assumed the responsibility of pastor at the local Baptist Church.

The Madison newspaper kept the locals informed about Clara's extra-curricular activities around town:

On January 5, 1869, a full meeting of the Young People's Association met at the Congregational Church. Following the singing of 'Guide me O Thou Great Jehovah,' Miss Clara Bewick read Tennyson's New Year's Poem 'Ring out Wild Bells.' On June 5, 1869, the State Journal reported on the fourth anniversary of the dedication of the Castalian Society Hall, where they said of the essay, 'The Two Lives' by Miss Clara D. Bewick was the 'gem' of the evening, and 'it would be a great injustice to Miss B. to even attempt a synopsis of her essay.' [8]

CHAPTER 5

THE GRADUATE

In September 1869, Clara took up her new role as a lecturer at the University of Wisconsin, teaching history and Latin. She was beloved by both students and her fellow faculty members, and she exhibited a quality that had her remembered as a remarkable teacher.[1]

One concern that continued to pray on her mind, however, was the fact that the university paid her less money than the male teachers for doing the same job. Since Dr. Chadbourne had indicated she could expect an increase in her starting salary, and time was drifting by unchanged, in the summer of 1870, she wrote to the University Executive Committee to request an increase.[2]

Madison Wisconsin
September 30, 1870
Gentlemen of the Executive Committee
The following is respectfully submitted for your consideration.

When first engaged by Dr. Chadbourne to teach at the University, he agreed to pay me for the first year $400.00 for teaching four classes and $100.00 for each additional class it might be necessary to assign to me: with the intimation that in the future my salary would be raised.

Early last spring, Dr. Chadbourne asked me if I wished to teach here another year, and whether I wanted more money. I told him I did, and no more was said at that time.

As Vice President Sterling told me in the vacation that he did not know anything about the matter, I went to see Dr. Chadbourne after his return from Cal. He told me that if he had remained here another year, he intended to pay me $500.00 for four classes and for additional ones in proportion. He said I might state this to the Vice President: and that he himself if questioned, would inform Prof. Sterling or Mr. Van Slyke what his intentions had been.

Having learned that no mention of this has been made to the Executive Committee, and relying on the encouragement given me by Dr. Chadbourne, I take the liberty of requesting an increase of salary.

Very respectfully
Clara D. Bewick

Initially, there was no response, but she continued to press for an answer, and in November she received a reply from one of the vice presidents.

November 7, 1870

Miss Clara D. Bewick
Lest there should be any misunderstanding between us in regard to the matter of our recent conversation, I deem it best to repeat what in substance, I said at that time.

1.   *I feel averse to giving more than four recitations to any teacher in the University, and should be unwilling to do it, except in case of special exigency.*

2.   *There is very little probability that such an exigency will occur next term.*

3.   *Should there be occasion to assign a fifth recitation to anyone in the Female Dept. I prefer you should take it, in that case, I should recommend that your salary be increased proportionately. Whether the Ex Committee would allow it, I am not able to say.*

   It is important that I should know immediately what, in this state of the case, your decision is.
Cordially
J.M.Sterling
Vice President

Sterling's letter was followed three days later by a letter signed by the Regents of the University.

> *The Regents of the University of Wisconsin*
> *Executive Committee Rooms*
> *Madison*
> *Nov 10, 1870*

Miss Clara Bewick
Your resignation under date of 8th inst. received. It will be regarded as taking effect at the close of this term as we presume you intend to be understood.
   Regretting the necessity of you thus terminating your connection with our institution.
   I remain your obedient servant.

It sounds like she had backed herself into a corner. Perhaps she did not understand her negotiating strength significantly, resulting in the response from Sterling demanding to know what her decision was.

Having taken a stand on the principle of being paid less because of her gender, Clara decided to submit her resignation to the university. Although this showed that Clara held strong beliefs, which would cause her to take a stand whenever she saw them compromised, it also revealed that she could act impulsively without thinking through all the consequences.

Both parties were to lose out in this decision because it was clear that Clara was a very successful teacher. Olympia Brown believed that had Clara chosen to devote herself to teaching, she would have become noteworthy as a professor of literature, history, economics or philosophy.[3] Her students shared that view, as was evident from the report in the *State Journal*:

> PRESENTATION AT THE UNIVERSITY
> TO A TEACHER IN THE FEMALE COLLEGE.
> *During the examination at the University on Saturday last, the class in modern history, consisting of young ladies from the several classes of the female college, presented their teacher, Miss Clara D. Bewick, with a beautiful memorial of their affection and respect. The present was an elegant rosewood writing desk, adorned with silver and velvet, and having the name of the teacher and the date of the gift gracefully engraved upon the lid.[4]*

Not one to sit around and feel sorry for herself, Clara looked for another opportunity, and she was soon offered a teaching position at Fort Atkinson, about 45 miles from Madison, starting in January 1871. The letter of offer from Professor Purdy, dated November 29, asked for an immediate response as there were other applicants awaiting replies. Most people had high regard for Clara's reputation as a teacher; indeed, the school at Fort Atkinson was eager to recruit her.

The Chiltons were not happy about Clara moving away, and they wrote regularly to each other as soon as they were apart.

January 9, 1871

My Beloved Child,
After you left, I felt as if someone had beat me. ...GF would not trust himself to speak of you at first, but now almost every meal he has something to say. 'I wonder how Pie is getting on!' I think of you as usual almost every hour in the day. I need not say as times are hard, be careful of your money. You need not fear we shall easily neglect or forget you, so cheer up.

Grandmother[5]

(Pie was the nickname which Stephen Chilton called his granddaughter)

January 22, 1871

My Beloved Child,
Today at dinner Jones (a lodger) said, 'Let me see, Clara has been gone two weeks.' 'Yes,' I said. 'It seems more like three months.'
C looked as if he would shove his plate over the table. GF said he would like to take a sleigh and go to see you. I said if he did, I must (looking down the table) enlist Mr. C to take care of him which, in spite of his solemn face, made him laugh – the others too. I think C might be a little more sociable.
God bless you, my Dear Child.[6]

(C was Leonard Colby, still a boarder at the Chiltons)

Colby was missing Clara deeply, but he could not find it in himself to discuss the matter with her grandparents. He was very much cheered up when Clara sent a poem that she had written about him.

> *When I talk with other men*
> *I always think of you*
> *Your words are keener than their words*
> *And they are gentler too.*
> *When I look at other men*
> *I wish your face was there*
> *With its grey eyes and dark skin*
> *And tossed black hair.*
> *When I think of other men*
> *Dreaming alone all day*
> *The thought of you like a strong wind*
> *Blows the dreams away.*

Colby had written to ask her to come home, but unfortunately, we don't have copies of his letters. Exerpts from some of Grandmother's letters follow;

January 25, 1871

My Beloved Child,
I was glad when C said he should write and ask you to come home. I should like to have asked C to go to church for I wish he would, but I did not like to appear to use my influence, and he is not very communicative. Perhaps 'tis bashfulness, perhaps 'tis fear.[7]

January 29
... my dear child, we do think of you as our own dear little girl and hope tho' now for the present separated it

may not be for long. There is nothing here worth living for if we cannot be with those we love. I am sorry GF is so poorly and is obliged to go to bed. He says he feels as if all his limbs fail him. God is our refuge and our strength.[8]

February 8

... C has stayed an hour tonight. His cough is rather bad, so I have prescribed for him. I told C if he was not so much engaged I should wish him to read it. (Bible teachings) He said he would. I believe it would do him good, it appears to me the right way to get the gospel before the sinner and to leave the Spirit to work His own work in the heart.[9]

February 12

My Beloved Child

What is the reason you did not send my usual letter on Saturday? Also there is another disappointed as well as myself for he came to me in the kitchen this morning to ask if I had had a letter. When I said no, he said, neither have I since Monday. GF coughed full an hour last night. I thought he would be choked. I hope he will be spared until you come home to stay. C has been bad too. All my doctoring failed, although I think he took it faithfully. He has a constant hacking cough, so yesterday he stayed for prayers and wrote your letter. GF prescribed camphor for he saw the lungs needed warming and that did him good. After he came from the post office, we persuaded him to lie down, and I gave him some broth. He was much better and remained so today. C gave me $20 last week, and I have been able to lower my heavy bills.[10]

Leonard Colby was frequently absent from Madison over the next few months, no doubt visiting Fort Atkinson, but true to his nature, he did not discuss the fact with the Chiltons or anyone else back in Madison. The truth was not missed by Grandmother though, and on March 17, 1871, she wrote::

> *I suppose you were very pleased at your visitor. Mr. Colby is yet arrived, but we guess you know. ...you cannot make a Christian of him, you may as well try to change the Leopard's spots. I should like to have some talk with C about his and your future, but unless he begins I have no right to interfere tho' I have many thoughts about you. Be careful of yourself.*[11]

Leonard Colby graduated as the valedictorian of his class in June 1871 with a Bachelor of Arts and a Civil Engineering degree.[12]   He held the rank of Captain in the university cadets and then received a recommendation for a lieutenant's commission in the United States Army.

He remained as a postgraduate student. By the middle of 1872, he had added a Bachelor of Law to his qualifications, which gained his admittance to the bar of the Supreme Court of Wisconsin. The *State Journal* printed his valedictorian address at the Commencement, and the journalist commented that although the orations of the young gentlemen were highly credible, in merit it fell below those of the young ladies. Colby's address displayed his military background and his way of looking at life's challenges that lay before him.

It now becomes my duty, on behalf of the graduating class, to speak a few farewell words.

Gentlemen of the Board of Regents, as students we desire to publicly acknowledge the efficient services which you have rendered to us and our alma mater. .....The University has lived through some dark days. Its ranks of students were thinned by the war for the Union. Its affairs of administration and finance at times have been sadly disordered. But all those days of trouble have passed away, and now the foundations of its prosperity are firmly settled. With a popularity daily increasing; with an ample revenue; a talented corps of professors, and a friend in the executive chair of the State, whose generous and manly course has gained for him the highest respect of an enlightened people, we may expect that the University, under your guidance, will soon stand in its proper place among the honored institutions of our land, a throne of power and a crown of glory to the State whose motto is 'Forward.'

Beloved Classmates, soon to be companions no more – our time has at last come. Together we have wandered in the mazes of science; hand in hand plucked flowers in the fields of languages; groped our way in the enchanting mists of metaphysics; and peered into the invisible. We stand at the portal of manhood; our powers and attainments are to be tested in the laboratory of life. ...No more dull foils, but weapons keen and glittering as the Damascus steel. No more sham fights, but stern, rough struggles in which many a blow and thrust must be given for principles; many a painful wound endured for truth. ....Thus shall our manhood blossom and yield its ripened fruit.[13]

CHAPTER 6

THE PARTNERSHIP

THE RELATIONSHIP BETWEEN LEONARD and Clara was getting serious, so the family expressed concern that this should lead to a union blessed by God. Brother William had heard that Colby had been making secret visits to Clara in Fort Atkinson and, like his father, he took a stringent Christian view towards marriage. William decided to take matters to hand and visit with Colby at his grandmother's house, which we see from Grandmother's letter to Clara, dated February 15, 1871.

William came in yesterday in order to have some under-standing with Colby as he had heard you were engaged, etc., and they had a long conversation on the subject. William spoke pretty freely to him, and as a Christian brother should do. Mr. C said his intentions were perfectly honor-able etc. and that when the time arrived to be married they would all know it; he went away early this morning, you know my dear child my thoughts on this subject and how much I had hoped you would not be unequally yoked however strong the natural affections are, it is but natural and there must be separation and sorrow sooner or later will attend the union – but I spare you, I should be sorry not to treat with kindness him you intend to marry for your sake but rather pray the Lord would open his blind eyes, to see himself as he is before God – and now may the Lord have compassion on you both and for Jesus sake forgive. From your affectionate GM, Clara Chilton.

William also followed up his meeting with Colby in a letter to Clara:

Windsor, Dane Co. Wis.
February 24 1871
Dear Sister Clara
I was in Madison last Monday and stopped all night. I was sorry to find Grandfather so poorly. ...I must tell you that Thomas and I are here alone this evening. Stephen has gone down home, and the 'old lady' (their stepmother) has gone to a Mite Society at Mr. Spencer's and left me to clear the supper table and work up the bread and bake it, which I shall have to leave off writing shortly, to do....

Clara, there is a rumor afloat that you are married, but of course, I don't believe it. Unless you told me yourself I would not believe that you would consent to a clandestine marriage but one thing I do believe that you and Colby are engaged, but why are you so opposed to saying a word about it to me I have yet to learn. Now if you will bear with me and hear a little of what I must say I shall feel better and seeing it is down in black and white, you will have to hear it or throw this letter in the fire.

First I will call to you remembering what you said about May Cole when there was no fear of me marrying her, 'that she had been brought up in an ungodly family taught to scoff at anything of a religious nature,' and is not this the case with Mr. Colby? ...

Perhaps you think this is strong language, but I cannot find language strong enough to suit my thoughts. ...

You surely expect that he will be saved at some time, and why not now? Does this seem too hard a thing for the Lord? Is not your love for him strong enough that the thought of him being eternally damned is harder to bear than that of losing him in this life? ....

I do not wish to say anything against Mr. Colby, for I know nothing against him as a man. The objection I have is that one should be joined to a man who does not believe the Bible, which is making God out a liar. ... this one flesh which was formerly two is going where? Part of it to heaven and part to hell? Can it be possible? Is not the one sure to drag the other with it? ...

For the present goodbye. God bless you and keep you near to himself ever subject to his mind and will.

I am as ever your very affectionate and loving Brother
William Bewick[1]

The letters were flying back and forth between Madison and Fort Atkinson, and not all mentioned concerns about Clara's relationship with Colby. Grandmother wrote more than twice a week, and her letters referred to letters from Clara, although we don't have copies of those. Clara's younger brother Ebenezer was apparently studying at the university while living with his grandparents, as Grandmother commented that he would never study when there was a girl around. Their father was still decidedly opposed to any of them studying at the university; at one point, Eby (Ebenezer) had to go home to get permission to stay for another term. At least his grandmother was taking him to church. She said he was 'such a fidget' and could not sit still for one moment. He sat next to her at church that morning, but she said he wouldn't do that again.

Two of Clara's students from the previous year called and asked after her. They said that the Ladies Dept. was very low in numbers, and many did not intend to come back next term. They said that if they asked a question, a reason, or meaning, they could not get an answer. Grandmother told them she hoped it would be better when they got a new President, but the girls said if Clara were there, there would have been some life and spirit in the classes.

A week later, Grandmother wrote to Clara concerning another problem that the Senior girls were facing, from which it arose that some of the girls would have to leave. In her opinion, she said that the pit that 'they' had dug for Clara, they had fallen into. One assumes 'they' means the University.

Grandmother was warming to Colby, as she wrote, 'Colby a dear good fellow as he is, has just been up to the PO, and brought our letter.... I must say he is far from well and from what I can understand desires only your happiness.' Confused, she wrote, 'as it regards you, I am more in the dark than ever, but three weeks more and then I suppose Mr. C. will explain.'

She yearns for a discussion with Clara and Colby about their future, and she confesses, 'you see the Old Lady feels her pride wounded – and alas what am I – in a little while the place which knows me now will know me no more. I shall be numbered with the dust – I hope he will love and care for you as I have, then I will willingly give up my charge to his care – and say my work is done.'[2]

There must have been much talk around Madison about the possible nature of Clara's relationship with Colby, for on May 29, even the minister of her church in Madison wrote to her to express his concerns.

> *Madison, Wisconsin*
> *May 29, 1871*
>
> *Dear Friend Clara Bewick*
> *I wonder if you will forgive me if I say a word about something which is 'none of my business?' Of course you will, for you know me well enough to trust me, I hope, and to believe that I am no meddlesome gossip and am only anxious for your welfare. All I am going to say is this: why don't you tell me all about a certain matter (which I need not name), and let me advise and help you? I wish you would, for I have seen that you have fought trouble enough alone in your own mind, and I think you would find relief and help in sympathy and counsel. I am not curious and I know how to hold my tongue. I suppose I know of the matter sooner than anyone in town, perhaps being told by a gentleman abroad who was anxious for you. But I said nothing to you, nor to anyone about it because I thought it was your private affair, and if you choose to keep it entirely a secret, I would not seem to intrude. For had you then (I think) felt any special need of sympathy or advice, I thought I would wait till you should say something of it to me yourself. But now, as you are aware, it has become generally known and the inquisitive, pigheaded, critical public has no doubt been giving you some annoyance. It is no longer a secret: although I had not lisped a syllable of it till it became publicly spoken of. I have since done what*

I could privately to stand up for you and stop the tongues. Now I am only anxious in the future for your happiness, usefulness and success. And if you want to talk with me about it, I think I can help you, in your own feeling at any rate, but not unless you choose. I am no priestly confessor, only your Pastor and friend. Think it over and let me know, by letter or when you come home.

    Mrs. R follows you with her constant good wishes and prayer. All your Madison friends miss you, and waft kind thoughts your way.

Ever cordially,
your Pastor,
C.H. Richards.[3]

Just over three weeks later, the following report appeared in the *State Journal* of June 24, 1871

A UNIVERSITY WEDDING
Last evening a few friends gathered at the Congregational Church to witness the marriage of Mr. L. W. Colby, valedictorian of the recent graduating class of the State University, to Miss Clara D. Bewick, a graduate of the institution, and valedictorian of her class. Messrs. Bassett, Jones and Frankenburger, were groomsmen, and Misses Overton, Hardenberg and Adams were bridesmaids, all fellow graduates. The groom and bride made their pledges to each other in beautiful language of their own, and Rev. C. H. Richards pronounced them man and wife. After the ceremony, the bride and groom held a pleasant reception for an hour at the home of the bride's grandfather, and then started for the home of the husband at Freeport, Illinois. A few classmates and friends attended them to the depot, sending after them, their heartfelt 'God speed.'

A lady graduate friend, in a note from which we take most of the above particulars, writes us:

'Miss B., lately teaching at Fort Atkinson, was for some time a teacher in the Ladies department of the University, and by her unwearied efforts in the class room, greatly endeared herself to her pupils. Mr. C. and his bride, for so long time connected with the University, will carry with them the sincere esteem and warmest well wishes of all who, as fellow students or as pupils, have associated with them.'

What was the basis of the widespread concerns of Clara's family and friends regarding her relationship with Leonard Colby, and why did the marriage take place in such haste, without her father and siblings being present? Could it have been the case that Clara had become pregnant and subsequently had a miscarriage, or the baby died? That would be a far more reasonable explanation for the reference by Rev. Richards to the 'matter' which he need not name. No records exist for the year following the wedding, so there is no way to confirm the existence (or not) of a baby or miscarriage. To add to the mystery, there is an unexplained reference to an adoption in the Bewick Family history.

According to that History, Leonard and Clara Colby adopted a baby named Ada May, who lived less than six months. Ada May has no record of birth, adoption or death, and the frequent correspondence between Grandmother and Clara, at times as often as twice a week, made no mention of a child. Neither did Clara ever mention such a child in her extensive, subsequent writing. Stephenson Bewick wrote the Bewick Family History some 52 years later, during which time he had little contact with Clara, so perhaps the story results from a confused memory of a 'cover story' rather than a real adoption. An internet search reveals a family tree which shows Leonard and Clara as the parents of the child Ada May, who was born and died on the same day, but the records have no source for the information.

Following the wedding, the happy couple departed for Freeport, Illinois, about 70 miles from Madison, where Clara could meet Leonard's parents, his sister Abigail and his brothers, Edward, Albert and David. Leonard and Clara stayed away in Freeport for approximately four weeks, according to Grandmother's letter to them of July 11, 1871. We also see that Leonard had left Clara at his parent's home to travel somewhere, for a purpose unknown.

Madison Wis.
Tuesday, July 11, 1871

My Beloved Children
I suppose you will be expecting to hear from us once before you come home and you wish me to gather up all the news to send. First a notice in last night's paper tells us that Sarah has been appointed to the school, etc. We had a burning hot day yesterday. I Hope you got home safe. We thought you would about four o'clock, and how glad Clara was to see you, and we pray that love and care for each other will bring you closer and closer still......

I suppose you will not get this before Tuesday or Wednesday and by that time you will be preparing to return home and we shall be getting ready to receive you.
Your affectionate G. Mother Clara Chilton.[4]

Following this letter, there is a gap in the records of about a year, and the next letter found in Clara's records is dated June 17, 1872. It's from the Principal of the First Ward school in Madison. It refers to the examination papers of the children in a class that Clara had been teaching. He complements Clara on her careful instruction of the children, and observes how the documents are far better than those written previously.

About this time, Leonard was awarded a Bachelor of Law at the commencement on June 19, 1872. The *State Journal* reported that the Law Department was accorded only one representative among the speakers and this was Leonard W. Colby. His oration was about twenty minutes in length and was a defense of the profession of law. The article continued, 'Mr. Colby has a fine presence, and while the profession of law has such defenders and representatives, it cannot fall into disrepute.'

From these frequent letters, Clara showed how much she missed her grandparents, who she viewed more like her mother and father. She knew that they were becoming old and frail, and she exhibited a desire to have them close, where she could care for them as they had done for her. She had discussed this with Leonard and he supported the idea. In the next letter, she again showed her positive attitude; 'Buying a nice house will not be difficult, and the journey from Wisconsin will be easy.' The Chiltons still had six other grandchildren in Wisconsin, but none of them had as close a relationship with their grandparents as Clara had.

Oct 27, 1872

Dear Grandparents
I think you had better come here and live. If you could sell your house for $2200 you could put up a house here for $1000 – a splendid one (Ours only cost $600 and is real nice) on those lots near ours that Leonard will get for you, and allowing a wide margin for expenses you would have $1000 left for Leonard to invest for you in tax-titles at 40 percent. ....

Leonard has not yet got an office... He has engaged one for $14 a month. It is now in use as a barber's shop, but I suppose the occupants will leave tomorrow. The new firm will print their letter-heads and enter upon business right away.

What arrangements shall we make for Harpers next year? I cannot get along without it and it seems too bad for us both to buy it.... I expect to see you soon. The journey on the C.B.& Q. (railroad) is nothing. I don't feel as if I went out West at all.

Yours lovingly, Clara B. Colby

Beatrice, Ne.
Nov 3, 1872

Dear Grandparents

Today is a regular autumn day: when the sun don't peep out once and the wind blows cold and chill. We three are sitting round the stove in our un-plastered kitchen and the wind comes in at the crevices. In the distance, as I glance up, I can see one building on the hill with the rafters up but the roof not yet on. We have not got a parlor stove, because we thought we could do without it the little while we stay and it would be so much less to transport and I should not wonder if the owner of the house will plaster the kitchen this week and then I shall have to transfer kitchen furniture to the parlor, then an extra stove would only be a nuisance. Yesterday, for the first time I went out calling and made 10 calls in the afternoon, some of the ladies fortunately being out. I like the people here very much...... The new firm have not yet opened shop. It is a good deal more of an undertaking than you might imagine. The first three days of the week were stormy so they could not do anything but make plans. After being twice disappointed, they have finally engaged an office at $8, but they have to fix it up themselves, paper it, etc.. They have sent to Chicago for books, paper, envelopes, etc.. They are busy about advertising, getting out cards, etc. Yesterday they made an office table with 2 drawers in it.[4]

Nov 26, 1872

Dear Grandfather and Grandmother

I received your note this morning with its welcome contents..... your kind loan will keep our heads above water,

*enable us to go to Thanksgiving Supper, etc. We expect
to move on Saturday. Friday I clean up. It has frozen just
enough to render it unwise to put any more plastering. We
expect this will be loose and have to come off before any
more can be put on. We have a fire there night and day and
when we go in we shall have a fire in my bedroom, so you
must not worry about my taking cold.*

By her next letter, Clara reported that they had moved into
their new unfinished home, although it sounded as if it required a lot of work. It was also the first letter which Clara
wrote on the letterhead of the new company.

*Office of Colby and Sale, Attorneys and Counselors at
Law and Real Estate Agents.*
December 2, 1872
Dear Grandfather and Mother
*We moved in on Saturday and of course did not get much
straightened. I went to Church yesterday morning and that
with my necessary work took up most of the day. At night
our gentlemen took advantage of the privacy which bed-
rooms afford to clean up, but we had only one lamp. ...*[5]

Significant activity for newcomers to pioneer communities
like Beatrice in those days was to go 'calling.' We see lots of
references within Clara's letters to people's houses she had
called on and the number of people who had called on her.
A young, well-educated couple like Leonard and Clara Colby
made a very positive impression on the residents as new arrivals who could contribute to the growth and prosperity of
the town. Their regular attendance at Church would be another way in which the Colbys would increase their fellowship

with some of the influential leaders of Beatrice. The results of these social interactions would greatly benefit the business of the new law firm, Colby and Sale, and for Clara, they would open up new challenges in which she could engage

It was from this activity that Clara was invited to join a group of wives to discuss the formation of a public library for Beatrice. The ladies met at the home of J. E. Smith, President of Smith Brothers Bank, and established a group known as the 'Ladies Library Association of Beatrice.' Clara was appointed the secretary of the new group and co-wrote the association's constitution and by-laws. The association was approved within two weeks of that first meeting.[6] She became actively involved in soliciting donations of money and materials, plus membership subscriptions for the new library, thus gaining the support of the local newspaper, the *Beatrice Express*. The objective of the association was to establish a library and reading room, with access to newspapers and periodicals, and to promote cultural activities and lectures

Clara regularly updated Grandmother on the progress of the library, and in return Grandmother added her advice on the selection of books, which she hoped would avoid any volumes that could 'corrupt and lead the mind from God and not for his Glory.' There is no evidence that Clara took her grandmother's advice on the selection of books.

Clara's report to the *Express* noted the library's original collection included 'many of the most popular and high-toned works of fiction of the day,' including fourteen volumes of works by Charles Dickens; another fourteen volumes of Sir Walter Scott; biographies on George Washington, Christopher Columbus and Mohammed; as well as Charles Darwin's

The Origin of Species. Grandmother wrote about the addition of Darwin's volume, stating, 'Darwin, for instance, is not so dangerous (at least not to me) because no person with any sense would believe his dogmas.'

Within 12 months of Clara arriving in Nebraska, the new library opened in the offices of Colby & Sale, with Clara Colby as the librarian. From the very beginning, the association intended support of the library to be by members' subscriptions and overdue fees, and it not to be regarded as a charity for the community. With this in mind, the management plan was based upon sufficient members' fees to cover the expenses of the library. One of the other objectives of the library association was to lead to another challenge for Clara, one which would occupy her for the rest of her life, and that was the matter of woman suffrage. But more on that later.

Leonard was also making the most of his new connections around Beatrice and indeed, around Nebraska. His induction into the Ancient, Free and Accepted Masons occurred in 1878, and he was appointed the Grand Orator of the Nebraska Lodge. A close friend was Algernon Paddock, who had been the first acting Governor of Nebraska, and who became a United States Senator in 1875.

The law firm was doing well, and although he dissolved the partnership of Colby & Sale in 1874, Leonard continued in sole practice until he formed another business in 1876 as Colby & Hazlett. Leonard's cases took him to district courts throughout Nebraska, resulting in his frequent absence from home.

In 1874, Leonard was commissioned first lieutenant in a company of state militia at Beatrice, designated the Paddock

Guards, and in 1877 he was appointed captain by the Governor of Nebraska and placed in command of four companies of mounted rifles. He marched his battalion from Beatrice to Red Cloud, thence to northern Nebraska and Wyoming in pursuit of bands of marauding Indians. In November 1876, Leonard was elected to the state senate, representing Gage and Jefferson Counties.

The correspondence from the Chiltons continued to reveal their plans to move to Nebraska. An opportunity to rent the rooming house in 1873 fell through, but they were still hopeful of a sale. Grandfather wrote to tell them that they had sold the farm to brother William, which provided some income for their retirement to Beatrice.

Madison
May 31, 1874

My dear Children

I am once more put into harness as my partner, after long practice finds herself unable to use her finger so that you might enjoy her pictures of life around us......

William has been this weekend. The farm has been made over to him on the condition he gives us a mortgage for the balance due us – Eighteen hundred dollars with a Bond to pay two hundred and fifty yearly until the whole principal and interest be paid..... If we can dispose of this house that will furnish some addition and will allow us to turn Travellers in our old days. .....

Very truly yours
Stephen and C. Chilton[7]

The Chiltons must have made a move to Beatrice soon after this because a friend who wrote to Clara in February of 1875 hoped that Clara's grandparents were enjoying their new home. Stephen was by now 76 years old, and Clara was 74.

Many of the letters between the family members at that time spoke of a period of significant sickness. Diphtheria sounded quite common, as was influenza and pneumonia and sister Mary even suffered from cholera. We don't know what ailment Stephen suffered from, but his retirement was short, for in February of 1876 he became sick and died. It had been almost 50 years since the marriage of Stephen and Clara at St George's Church in London, and they had enjoyed a full and loving life together. Grandmother accepted her loss as a temporary parting, but without doubt, she missed her long-term partner. They buried Stephen in the cemetery, and in May, Clara wrote that 'Leonard has planted a cottonwood in the center of the lot at the cemetery and a cedar at the head and one at the foot of dear Grandfather's grave.'

Grandmother Clara returned to Madison in August of 1876 to visit her family and friends, staying with Clara's brother Thomas, his wife Eliza, and their nine children. Clara wrote that she could not wait to get her back again; meanwhile Grandmother must have looked forward to getting back to the peace and quiet of Beatrice.

Clara continued with her role as Beatrice librarian and also became involved in organizing lectures for the Ladies Literary Association; she served as the principal of the Beatrice Public School District, and she wrote articles for the *Western Woman's Journal*, a publication of the Hebron Journal, published by Erasmus Correll. Correll's wife Lucy was instrumental in establishing the first permanent suffrage association in Nebraska, and she quickly recruited Clara to be involved in the movement. Also in 1876, Leonard acquired the local newspaper, *The Beatrice Express*, to which Clara contributed columns.

In October of 1877, Lucy Erasmus was arranging for one of the national leaders of the suffrage movement, Susan B. Anthony, to visit Hebron to give a lecture on woman's rights. Clara planned another address for Lincoln, and she invited Ms. Anthony to stay with them in Beatrice. Since Leonard had now taken up his role as a State Senator and owned the local newspaper, this would have been an excellent connection for the suffrage leader. By the end of the visit, however, it was the connection with Clara that would make the best impression on the visitor. The next day, while waiting for the train in Lincoln, Susan B. Anthony wrote a four-page letter to Clara, sharing her opinions and feelings about the visit.

> *Lincoln Neb.*
> *Nov. 2nd 1877*
>
> *My Dear Mrs. Colby*
> *.... Such women as you... have individual work to do – to lift the world into better conditions – and I hope you will not allow anything to stop you from doing what seems to be your duty.*
>
> *I long to see women be themselves - not the mere echoes of men.... Did your non-believing husband tell you the 'mission' I laid upon him for the coming session of the legislature? Now don't you insist that your husband shall act for you – represent you – in the Senate – just push the 16th amendment resolution to a discussion and vote.....*
>
> *Mrs. Colby – do, please, write a brief letter of your library work – and lecture course. In the December number*

of the Ballot Box – it goes to press about the 25th of each month.... For you and every woman to tell what you are do-ing – helps to rouse other women to do likewise. Women want to be helped with the feeling that they can help on the good works they like to see done. We have been told we <u>couldn't do anything but help</u> the individual man or men in our families.

I hope I shall hear from you after, <u>through the Ballot Box</u> if no other way. Give my kind regards to dear Grand Mother, husband, brother, wife and Miss Coleman - I sel-dom liked the people I see so little of, so much. As with love and hope that you will keep up....

I am truly yours,
Susan B. Anthony[8]

Receiving Susan Anthony's encouragement must have been a critical moment in Clara's life, one when she identified a part that she could play in the future. It must have been tough to imagine herself taking an active national role from a small, mid-western pioneer town, but she did, and this would be the time when she made that decision. The only problem, however, was that another family issue arose that had to take priority.

Clara's sister Mary had married Alanson Bridges in Madi-son in 1875, and they had two daughters, Sadie and Eva. In September of 1877, her husband died, leaving Mary and the two daughters without any means of support. Clara arranged for them to move to Beatrice to live with them, where she and Grandmother could assist with raising the girls.

Mary was a qualified nurse, but she had ambitions to be-come a doctor. Clara was quick to encourage her to take up the challenge: enroll as a student and work towards her goal.

Mary enrolled in the Chicago Homeopathic Medical College, while Clara took on the role of looking after the two girls. Fortunately, by this time Leonard's law firm was doing well, plus he enjoyed a salary as a State Senator, sufficient for Clara to employ a fulltime housemaid.

By 1878, Grandmother's health was deteriorating, and the doctors diagnosed cancer of the stomach, for which there was no cure. Having been informed by William that she was sick, Grandson Thomas wrote to his grandmother in February 1879, wishing her blessings, with mention of her 'last days.' Then, in August, with William and Ebenezer visiting their grandmother in Beatrice, their father, Thomas Bewick Senior, wrote to them to say, 'poor grandmother is fast passing away. I hope you, William, were able to stay till the close, which cannot be long.' A fighter all her life, Clara Chilton held on to life for most of that year, eventually passing away in September 1879, at 78 years of age.

Without a doubt, the achievements of Clara Chilton née Medhurst were a significant influence on Clara Colby. She and her husband Stephen made at least five crossings of the Atlantic by sailing ship, traveled halfway across America on several occasions, and started running a boarding house when she was 64 and Stephen was 66. Although grandmother and mother to Clara, at various times she also looked after William, Mary, and Ebenezer. From her letters, we can see how active she was in the church, and she always had an extensive network of friends that she called on or those who called on her.

Save for the problem of being unable to board the ship in Bristol in 1849, life would have been very different for young

Clara. She would have grown up on a pioneer homestead in Wisconsin and likely have gone on to be a farmer's wife and raised a family. Grandmother opened Clara's eyes to a broader, more sophisticated world and encouraged her to go out and become someone in it, from the time she arrived in London at three years of age until September 1879, when grandmother passed away.

The other grandchildren benefitted from Clara Chilton's influence also. Mary went on to be a doctor, and Ebenezer became a Southern Baptist pastor, both of them having been strongly influenced from their grandmother. One of the grandsons wrote the following, which became a part of the eulogy.

> *Had Dickens met grandmother he would have made her all his own. Her clear intellect, her determination, her brusque comments on the follies and vices of the day, her wit.... would have delighted the great student and painter of character.... It would be impossible to associate with such traits, the faintest shadow of hypocrisy. She ever bore with her the pure diamond of truth.*[9]

The passing of Grandmother would have filled Clara's concentration to the point that she may have closed her mind to a problem in which Leonard was embroiled. Under a headline 'BEATRICE BOILING', the *Nebraska State Journal* reported on August 27, 1878, of 'An Alleged Attempt of the Mayor to Steal the Whole Town and Convey it to Senator Colby and his Friends.' The story described how a conspiracy was entered into between Mayor Hale, Senator Colby, and others, to transfer the title to certain public real estate intended as

Bounty Land for those who had served in the military service of the United States. The beneficiaries of the plot would be the Mayor, Senator Colby, his partner Alfred Hazlett, and several other local businessmen.

With the fraud discovered, 'the citizens turned out en masse, caught the parties to the scheme, and forced the cancellation of the deeds.' A crowd had formed, which the Journal described as having grown to the dimensions of a mob, with some calling for Colby to be taken down to the Market Street Bridge, where they would hang him. Cooler heads prevailed, fortunately. The crowd demanded that Hale and Colby join them at the Court House, where a Citizen's Meeting was quickly organized. A Chairman and a Secretary were appointed and the meeting proceeded, at which the Mayor was ordered to cancel all 76 deeds in question and to have them secured for safe-keeping. The Mayor's resignation was demanded and received, as was that of the Clerk of the Council. L. W. Colby was also requested to tender his resignation—to which he refused, 'greatly to the mortification of his constituents.' Leonard's chances of re-election were, from then on, improbable.

The firm of Colby & Hazlett continued to prosper and suffered no real consequences from the attempt at fraudulently taking city land. They thrived mainly from out-of-town clients and particularly the railroad companies, which benefited from public property.

Colby's reputation in the military was also entirely separate from the political arena, and in 1881 he was promoted to Colonel.[10] He took control of the Nebraska state troops and six companies of United States regulars during the labor strike in Omaha in March 1882. At this time, the city came under martial law.

The arrival of the troops brought an end to the violence and the strike, although one of the strike leaders was killed and a number were arrested for 'assault with intent to kill.' It was the first time that Omaha had drawn such national attention, with the *New York Times* reporting, 'The feverish excitement which has prevailed in this city for several days past, during the progress of the labor troubles, began to subside this morning upon the arrival here of eight companies of State Militia, under the command of Col. Colby.'[11]

Meanwhile, 1879 was not a good year for Clara Colby. On November 15, 1879, William wrote:

'Dear Darling Sister Clara, I just received Eby's note to say that you were down with the Diphtheria. We all feel very much alarmed by it.'

Diphtheria was the most common infectious cause of death in the nineteenth century, and earlier that year it had been common in Wisconsin, but in William's letter, he says it was decreasing in their region. Fortunately, there was no further mention of it, so Clara must have fully recovered.

CHAPTER 8

THE SUFFRAGE MOVEMENT

LIFE WOULD HAVE BEEN quiet and lonely for Clara following the death of her grandmother, particularly with her husband traveling around the district courts and doing his activities with the National Guard, but she had the additional role
of looking after Sadie and Eva. Her frequent letters to Leonard
at the time show how much she missed her husband, yet his
brief responses and the uncertainty of his return times would
not have been reassuring.

But she did not allow herself to get depressed, and she held
her emotions very quietly to herself. She always found some
other project to get involved in and take her mind away from
whatever might depress her. For example, she accepted the
invitation to be the Orator for the Fourth of July celebrations
of 1881 in the town of Hebron. The *Hebron Journal* reported:

Mrs. Clara B. Colby of Beatrice, handsome, vivacious and sparkling, will deliver the oration at Hebron on the Fourth. This lady is clear, logical and eloquent, and all who hear her oration on that occasion will hear something 'to fire the truly loyal heart.' We take much pleasure in commending Mrs. Colby to the people, for, as a speaker, she has few equals. Come out and hear her.[1]

Mary, meanwhile, completed her medical training in 1881 and returned to Beatrice. An announcement in the *Beatrice Express* 'tallies one for Dr. Mary Bridges and woman's rights. The board of county commissioners accepts her bid to perform the duties of county physician, and she has the contract for one year.'[2]

Shortly after that, on December 21, 1881, Mary married Charles Everett White, a real estate agent. They subsequently had two daughters, Charlotte and Dorothy.

Clara involved herself actively with the women's suffrage movement, which had gone through several incarnations in Nebraska. And so started many years of travel throughout America and later in Europe, striving for equal rights for all. In April 1879, Elizabeth Cady Stanton, the co-leader of the National Woman Suffrage Association, came to Nebraska to speak at several towns across the state. Susan B. Anthony would undoubtedly have informed Stanton of the leading players in the Nebraska association, and Clara Colby was one of them. It was during this visit to Nebraska that Mrs. Stanton organized the first working suffrage society at Hebron. This was the start of a campaign to get a resolution through the State Senate to put a vote to the people of Nebraska in November 1882.

Following the success of this campaign, at a conference in Lincoln in January 1881, a State Suffrage Association was formed. Clara Bewick Colby was elected as the first Vice-President and would later go on to serve as President.

In October of 1880, she spoke at the eighth congress of the Association for the Advancement of Women in Boston. The *New York Times* listed five of the most notable representative women, including Mrs. Clara B. Colby of Nebraska.[3] She was starting to develop a reputation as a very accomplished public speaker.

In 1881, Elizabeth Cady Stanton wrote to Clara expressing her friendship with Clara as one of 'confidence and sympathy' About the same time, Stanton wrote to Clara with the following request.

> *NWSA*
> *Dec 15, 1881*
>
> *My Dear Mrs. Colby*
> *I write to appoint you to serve in the special committee that is to work up matters in Congress with the intent of bringing a government action on a 16th Amendment while our convention is in progress in Washington.*[4]

Clara was ahead of the game. She had already written to Alvin Saunders, Senator for Nebraska, to gain his support. On December 8, she received his reply, which said, 'I have committed myself to the advance of woman's suffrage.... whenever the subject comes before Congress I shall vote for the formation of a permanent committee to take cognizance and direction of this important subject. Very respectfully, Alvin Saunders.'[5]

The campaign for Nebraska support of woman's suffrage took place throughout 1881 and 1882. At that time, there were two national organizations focused on achieving woman suffrage, the American Woman Suffrage Association (AWSA) and the National Woman Suffrage Association (NWSA). Stanton and Anthony were already with the NWSA. Both organizations converged in Nebraska for their 1882 annual conventions, holding them in Omaha on adjacent weeks in October. The AWSA was then under the presidency of Erasmus Correll, the founder of the Hebron Journal. Susan B. Anthony presided over the NWSA convention.

Acceptance of the campaign for woman's suffrage was not always positive. One Nebraska newspaper article made it very clear as to where their opinion towards the subject stood, when it reported on a lecture given by Mrs. Clara B. Colby.

It is not our province to abuse women lecturers, or women's 'righters' but it is our private opinion, publicly expressed, that when a wife and mother leaves her home, her husband and her children to travel over the country lecturing on women's rights or any other subject, she has departed from that sphere for which God and nature designed her, and has left vacant the place that no other can fill – the home.[6]

Not all newspapers wrote such negative comment about the suffrage movement's speakers, however. In the July 16, 1881 issue of *The Inter Ocean* in Chicago, the reporter wrote of Clara's lecture as follows:

The oration was one of the finest that it has ever been the good fortune of the Hebron public to hear. ... The natural

ability of Mrs. Colby, combined with her ease, grace and
happy address made her a great favorite. We may truly say
it was a brilliant success.

Outside of those who had been campaigning for the suffrage movement, there was a lack of interest by much of the population. Neither the Republican nor the Democrat parties took a stand on the issue. As well, the liquor and brewing industries were strongly opposed to giving women the vote, believing that the result might mean prohibition and reasoning that many of the women were members of temperance societies.

This disinterest didn't stop them though; Nebraska suffragists continued campaigning, right up to the moment voters cast ballots. Accounts from Election Day portray cheering women gathering at polling places, serving sandwiches and beverages, riding buggies emblazoned with suffrage slogans, and generally hopeful of a good outcome.

Ms. Anthony and other suffrage leaders had reserved Boyd's Opera House for the day after the election. By evening, it was clear that Nebraska would not support the campaign; the amendment was defeated 50,693 to 25,756 in what the *State Journal* headlined, 'Female Suffrage Buried under an Avalanche.' Among the supporters who filled Boyd's Opera House, the disappointment was sharp, but they listened eagerly to the words of Anthony, Clara, and others.

Clara, as the local voice, congratulated the campaigners who worked so hard, noting the vote was the largest cast for woman suffrage in a single state. Anthony announced that the National Woman Suffrage Association had spent over $5,000 on the campaign and was 'now $500 in the red.' The campaign had convinced her that it was 'impossible to canvass every town' and she vowed never to attempt it again, telling Nebraskans they should never 'submit the question...to a popular vote again.' Anthony reiterated her determination to focus NWSA efforts on passing a federal amendment.[7]

In the press, there was much discussion that voter fraud had taken place, in spite of the warnings printed in the Omaha Daily Republican on the morning of the election. Thus:

Read your tickets! It was never so important today that every voter read his tickets through, and see that he is not cheated out of his suffrage rights by the men who are trying to ruin the Republican Party by fraud and forgery. The main stock in trade of the Rosewater democrats is bogus tickets.

According to a 1967 dissertation,[8] Mrs. Colby insisted after the event that many tickets were fraudulently printed; such ballots contained no mention of the suffrage amendment at all. A further strength is added to Clara's charge by a perusal of the detailed voting instruction relative to the amendment issue offered by the Republican. These instructions warned the pro-suffrage voter to be certain that his ballot read: 'For a proposed amendment to the constitution relating to the rights of suffrage', this being the official form acceptable to the authorities.

Further, the editor warned the voter to take careful note as to whether a separate box for suffrage ballots was in evidence at his polling place. If such a box had been provided, the ballot relating to the amendment should be placed therein. It was clear that some fraud had taken place in the vote, but it cannot be determined if that was enough to affect the result.

With a couple like Leonard and Clara, it is sometimes hard to imagine how they stayed together, with both of them busily taking frequent trips away from home. They must have made the most of the times that they were together, expressing their love and looking for ways to improve their lives together.

It was on a day such as this in 1883 that an 'orphan train' pulled into Beatrice from New York with a carload of or-phaned, abandoned, abused, or homeless children. Charitable institutions like the Children's Aid Society had initiated this program as a solution to New York's homeless children, in-volving tens of thousands of kids. Each carload was sent out west to be fostered or adopted throughout the country. Some of the children were orphaned when their parents died in epi-demics of typhoid, yellow fever or the flu.

Finding a new home in the west was not always a success-ful outcome for the children as some were forced to work on farms or abused by their new carers, but many of them found beautiful homes with pioneer families. According to the re-port of the Children's Aid Society the following year, 3,459 children were placed out by the society, mainly in western homes.[9]

Leonard and Clara decided to go to the courthouse, where the children were to be inspected by the farmers and the townspeople. When they arrived, they found that all the chil-dren had been chosen and taken to new homes, with one ex-ception. Only one boy of about three years of age sat on the courthouse steps. It seemed that no one wanted him. Clara's tender-heartedness proved far stronger than any logical thought, and she had to take this poor boy home. They named him Clarence. Although he was always a likable child, he was developmentally slow. His birthday and his background were unknown, though they estimated that he was born in 1880.

It was fortunate Leonard and Clara could afford to have a housemaid to assist them at home because they were both extremely busy people and would need to rely on help in the raising of Clarence. For additional assistance, Clara could always call upon her sister Mary, for by this time she was living in Beatrice with her new husband, now joined by a third daughter, Charlotte.

To get an idea of how busy the two of them were, here is a partial calendar of their activities for 1883. In January, Clara became an executive committee member of the State Historical Society, based in Lincoln, and was appointed to the position of corresponding secretary. Also held in Lincoln at that time was the annual meeting of the Nebraska Woman Suffrage Association, with Clara elected to be the Chair of the Executive Committee. In February, Clara attended a birthday celebration for Susan B. Anthony, held at Dr. Painter's Infirmary in Lincoln. The function was reported by an admiring journalist in the *State Journal*.

A cup of pure Mocha coffee, some fruit cake and complimentary remarks of Mrs. Colby fully repaid the JOURNAL man for his tramp through the mud and slush last night to attend the sixty-third anniversary of Miss Susan B. Anthony, held at the Lincoln Infirmary. Mrs. Colby is a warm adherent of the lady who has devoted a lifetime to bettering the condition of her sex, and she cannot bear to hear her name mentioned in levity.[10]

On February 17, Clara made an unprecedented address to the State Senate on the subject of the woman suffrage bill, advocating for an amendment to the state constitution. Her speech was the first time a woman had addressed the Senate. She introduced her remarks by assuring the senators that she was not speaking as an advocate of a lost cause and they were not discouraged by the loss of the vote the previous year. She viewed the ballot as a victory for the suffrage movement because, while it was not a complete success, it was a gain.

Unfortunately, this was not to be a complete success either, since a motion to postpone the bill indefinitely was passed on a vote of 18 votes to 7. The *Lincoln Journal Star* seemed to put a positive spin on her efforts, however, and they reported that 'Mrs. A. J. Sawyer sent Mrs. Colby a box of beautiful cut flowers, including the choicest and most rare blooms, in appreciation of the eloquent speech delivered by Mrs. Colby on Friday night before the honorable Senate.'[11]

CHAPTER 9

THE WOMAN'S TRIBUNE

DURING MARCH AND APRIL, Clara was preparing to publish her own newspaper, targeted at women but not wholly
focussed on the suffrage campaign. At the Nebraska WSA
convention, held in Grand Island on May 9 and 10, 1883, it
was decided that the suffragists of the State must have their
own newspaper. Clara Colby was elected to head a committee
to investigate the issue of a paper, with a print run of 5,000
copies. Susan B. Anthony had declared Clara to be the best
writer in the women's movement, so she was a natural choice.

The committee canvassed the existing publishers throughout the state for interest in working with them, but the reac-
tion was not altogether positive. The following article, originally printed in the Gage County Independent, was reprinted
in many other newspapers, including the *Lincoln News*.

Mrs. Colby is considering the scheme of starting a newspaper for the advancement of woman's suffrage in this state. We will say here that almost anyone can sit down, put his feet on the stove and read a newspaper, but next to the management of a railroad company nothing requires such unlimited capital, shrewd judgement and good rustling qualities as getting up a thoroughbred country journal.... Our parental advice to all about to enter the ranks of journalism is, 'Don't monkey with the buzz-saw, and give it lots of room.'[1]

The article may have been taken as a challenge by Clara Colby because she did successfully publish her first issue of the *Woman's Tribune* in August of that year, and she continued editing and publishing the paper for the next 26 years. Clara Colby used her own money and donations from friends in order to get the first three issues published. It was not until January 1884 that the Nebraska WSA passed a resolution to incorporate a joint stock company under the name of the Nebraska Woman's Suffrage Publishing company, through which to finance the *Woman's Tribune*.[2]

Her husband was also incurring some media tributes. In August 1883, the annual camp of the Nebraska National Guard was held at Crete, Nebraska, during which Colonel Colby scored a favorable article in the *State Journal*.

Col. Colby, who is in command of the regiment, is an ideal officer. Straight and strongly built, with a clear cut face on which energy and decision are marked in every line, with a strong sonorous voice, and withal a strict disciplinarian, he presents a distinguished appearance.... He rides a mag-

nificent Arabian stallion, pure white, without a dark hair
from the top of his nose to the end of his handsome tail.[3]

Based on a complete report of the NNG Camp, published in
the issue of 26 August under the heading of 'The Grand Review,' it was almost as if the Colbys were the aristocracy of
Nebraska. 'Mrs. Colby also rode with the reviewing officers,
mounted on her handsome white pony.... The regiment presented a very fine appearance as it marched in review, the
colors flying, the bands playing, the horses prancing and the
bayonets gleaming in the sun.'

Leonard Colby was an aficionado of thoroughbred Arabian
horses, and over the years he invested a lot of money in the
hobby. In 1888, he purchased the Arabian stallion, Linden
Tree, from the son of President Ulysses Grant for $10,000.[4]
This horse had been presented to the President by the Sultan
of Turkey in Constantinople. Looking after the Arabians at
the stables was a personal responsibility of young Clarence.

In September 1883, Leonard was endorsed by Gage County Republicans for election again, this time as a judge in the
First district of Nebraska. Perhaps he thought that the voters
might have forgotten his involvement in the attempted land
swindle in Beatrice.

Acceptance of his candidature seemed to go smoothly at
first, with many of his colleagues at the bar supporting his
stand. The newspapers, however, looked forward to writing
up any scandal they could find, and the negative articles did
not take long to appear.

Omaha Daily Bee, dated Thursday, September 27, 1883, contains reports in which Leonard is starting to be known as the husband of Mrs. Colby, rather than by his own name.

Mr. Colby by this time probably wishes that he had declined to run for Judge of the 1st District of Nebraska. The revolt against his nomination, which began among the Republicans of Gage and Pawnee counties before the convention met, which placed him in the field, has spread like wildfire through the district. The leading paper in Gage county and one of the staunchest and most ably edited Republican weekly journals in the State is supporting with great vigor Hon. John Broady, and pouring hot shot and shell into Mr. Colby's camp....

Mr. Colby has a fragrant record and one from which his neighbors do not propose that he shall escape. As a member of the Legislature from Gage county, he was up to his eyes in every job and voted through thick and thin with Church Howe, and in the interest of the railroads. In August 1878, he was engaged in a swindle by which through the assistance of Mayor Hale he endeavored to becloud the title of a large portion of the town site of Beatrice and to transfer several blocks to himself....

In the *Lincoln Journal Star*, dated October 11, 1883, they refrained from criticizing Leonard directly, choosing to reprint a negative report from another newspaper.

L.W. Colby is being stirred up by the Beatrice Express with more political bombastic thunder than all the noise made by the attempt to disturb Shakespeare's bones. Editor Brown holds up the remains as a monument of dishonesty and immorality and protests against manufacturing the republican nominee into a judge.

Neither of these newspapers went as far the *Johnson County Journal*, which on October 6, 1883, printed the following:

No man living is inclined to dive deeper or can hold his breath longer in the dirty pool of politics than Mrs. Colby's husband.... Mr. Colby, a married man, now a candidate, visited the Arlington Hotel in Lincoln in company with a prostitute, and there took lodging for the night. The land-lord... ordered Colby and the woman to leave. Mr. Colby got down on his knees and begged pitifully to be allowed to remain overnight.[5]

Fortunate for Leonard Colby, his wife was away in Chicago at the time, attending the 'Congress of Women,' the annual convention of the Association for the Advancement of Women. She was returning with another role, the Vice President, representing Nebraska. He was also fortunate that he had a very loving and forgiving wife, who put these stories down to a political attack from a desperate opponent. Even so, she must have been aggrieved by the stories, evidently using all her powers of positivity to live through them and move on. Leonard could be charming and very persuasive when he chose to be, and this was an occasion when he turned on his best performance.

No sooner had Clara returned from Chicago than she had to attend the Nebraska WSA Conference in Hastings. The good news she received there was the fact that the Nebraska WSA would continue to support the *Woman's Tribune* as a weekly newspaper, based on the favorable response to the August issue.

The negative articles appearing in the Nebraska newspapers had done their work and turned people away from voting for Leonard Colby for Judge in the first district. He did have other factors working against him, however, as the *Lincoln Journal Star* reported. 'He was generally known to be antagonistic to temperance, and the temperance people gave an expression of their disapproval of such a man at the ballot box by a majority for the Democratic candidate, who is known as a temperance man. Mr. Colby did not carry one county in the district.'

The subject of temperance would have been a hot topic at home, since many of Clara's colleagues in the suffrage movement would have carried sympathies with the temperance cause. Elizabeth Cady Stanton had warned suffragists of the dangers threatened by a close relationship with the Woman's Christian Temperance Union, even though Stanton herself had served in the early 1850s as the president of the Women's New York State Temperance Society. At that time, the WCTU was the largest women's organization in the country.

Clara was busy throughout 1883 and even on 30 December, the *State Journal* reported that Clara passed through Lincoln on her way to Omaha, probably to prepare for the Mass Convention of the NWSA, which was coming up in York, Nebraska on January 17 and 18, 1884.

Throughout the following years, it was as if Clara was destined to repeat a very similar itinerary as she had done in 1883. Each year, she attended the NWSA convention in Washington plus several WSA state conventions, and she went on speaking tours with Susan B. Anthony, Elizabeth Cady Stanton, and other suffragist leaders.

Travel was not as convenient as it is today. The journey from home to the railroad depot would be by horse and buggy, hopefully to arrive just before a train came, if it was on time. Train connections would be many, sometimes involving long waits in cold, wintry conditions. Travel to the east coast took two days and at least one night sleeping upright in an uncomfortable seat, unless she could persuade someone to pay for a sleeper seat in a Pullman car. She generally tried to break her trips with a stop in Chicago or somewhere else along the way, where she could find an activity to advance the cause. It was a tough assignment in the late nineteenth century, but as we learned earlier, Clara loved 'riding the cars.'

In 1885, there was a conflict between the date of the state convention and the national event to which Clara was a delegate. It was also the year she was elected president of the Nebraska Association; a position she would hold for thirteen years. The secretary of the association was instructed to telegraph Mrs. Colby at her hotel in Washington to let her know that she was the unanimous choice for president. For five years she had covered the country from her home base in Beatrice, but after this period, she was persuaded to spend the first six months of each year in Washington. This included the dates of the NWSA conference (Nebraska) and the dates when Congress was in session.

In 1888, an International Council of Women was set to meet for an eight-day conference in March. By this time, the *Woman's Tribune* was the official organ of the NWSA, so it was decided to publish a sixteen-page daily paper for use at the ICW conference. Susan B. Anthony and Elizabeth Cady Stanton initiated this idea. The International Congress was not confined to the NWSA alone but would be composed of delegates from organizations of all descriptions that are made up exclusively of women.

The 1888 meeting was the foundation of the ICW, an organization which continues to this day and has its headquarters in Paris.

By 1888, the *Woman's Tribune* was used by many of the leadership to distribute their message. During the International Council of Women, the *Woman's Tribune* reached a peak circulation of 12,500 copies. Elizabeth Cady Stanton, who by now was a close friend of Clara, wrote the following letter praising the publication in the issue of January 21, 1888.

> *Dear Mrs. Colby*
> *A Merry Christmas and Happy New Year to you and the readers of the Tribune. The best wishes of the season for the success of the journal, in its new satin dress, good clear type, and its promise of weekly ministrations.*
> *I have just read it through, every word from the beginning to end, and have thoroughly enjoyed its courageous tone, its radical thought and its evident determination to go to the root of the evils that block woman's path to freedom.*
> *I was especially pleased with the articles by Mrs. Chandler, May Rogers and 'The Plan of Work for Suffrage Clubs,' all showing that women, having proved their right to vote, at least to their own satisfaction, are now beginning to think in what manner that right shall be exercised.*
> *Sincerely yours,*
> *Elizabeth Cady Stanton[6]*

has a very fine library, I doubt if there is a better collection of books in the State. She is a graduate of Wisconsin
State University and a member of a dozen different associations. Among them are the Nebraska State Historical
Society, of which she is the President; the Woman's Congress, Woman's National Press Association, etc. In person
she is a medium height; she has beautiful dark blue eyes
and heavy dark hair, which she wears plainly combed back
from her intellectual forehead. In conversation she is most
interesting, displaying an unusual degree of learning and
reading. She has all the Western push and vigor, as at least
one person is aware. That person is a would-be thief who
attempted to go through the house one night. Mrs. Colby
heard the noise and, hastening below stairs, she came upon
the fellow in a closet, into which, through a window, he had
just effected an entrance. Before he could say 'boo' Mrs.
Colby had grasped him by the collar and was engaged in
the delightful occupation of pounding his head against the
books and calling for help. There is one book missing in
that row and the suffering thief can testify that its absence
was caused by coming in frequent contact with his head.
Mrs. Colby wears her honors with becoming humility. Her
home life is very happy. Colonel L. W. Colby, her handsome and brilliantly intellectual husband, is one of the
leading lawyers of the State. His law practice takes him
from Washington City to Oregon. He has been a member
of the State Senate, is colonel of the State militia, and will
sometime gain high political honors in the Nation. He is a
faithful and able second to his gifted wife....

The women who do not want to vote will have to go else-
where than to Clara B. Colby's delightful home to find the
pictures they paint of woman-suffrage households.[10]

From 1888 onwards, Clara would pack up her office and together with her key staff she would move to Washington DC for the first half of each year, or at least during the time that the Senate and the House of Representatives were in session. The experience of printing a daily sixteen-page newspaper during the ICW had proven that she had the resources and the capability to continue publishing the *Woman's Tribune*, even if it meant alternating between Beatrice and Washington.

On October 1, 1888, Clara was in the Territory of Washington and finally became a citizen of the United States.

At a joint convention in February 1890, the National Woman Suffrage Association and the rival American Association merged to form the National American Woman Suffrage Association, and Elizabeth Cady Stanton was elected its first President.

The great disappointment for Clara from this merger was that the delegates voted to accept the rival *Woman's Journal* as the official suffrage organ of the new group. The rejection of the *Woman's Tribune* was a massive blow to Clara, yet for now, she had to find innovative ways of funding the *Woman's Tribune*, something she did for another twenty years. Unable to pay for printing, she learned to set type, and often was at once editor and compositor, sometimes even running the press.[11]

CHAPTER 10

ZINTKA LANUNI

DURING THE WINTER OF 1890-1891, General Colby and his command were called into active service on the occasion of the uprising of the Sioux Indians of Pine Ridge, but also to monitor other agencies in South Dakota and Nebraska. With the government fearful of a Lakota Indian uprising, the US Cavalry's 7th Regiment was ordered to take and disarm Chief Big Foot and his warriors, who were camped with their wives and children at Wounded Knee Creek, about eight miles from the Pine Ridge Agency.

On December 29, 1890, beneath a white flag of truce, the Army rounded up about 350 Lakota Indians at the creek in South Dakota and commenced to confiscate their firearms. According to reports at the time, a deaf warrior became engaged in an argument with a soldier, and in the process, his weapon discharged.

Hearing the gunfire, other soldiers opened fire upon the Indian concerned. A few other Indians may have fired back; panic broke out among the troops and they opened fire, including with Hotchkiss machine guns. Within a matter of minutes, about 300 men, women, and children were killed, and many were wounded, including troops of the 7th Cavalry, who almost certainly became casualties from friendly fire.

The two regiments of the Nebraska National Guard, under the command of General Colby, were not involved in the massacre itself, but they were ordered to proceed to the site. There they assisted in preventing the surviving Indians from burning the Pine Ridge Agency building and Mission School, and provided support in the clean-up of the massacre site.

The newspapers of the day reported the event as the Battle of Wounded Knee, but today it is known as the Massacre of Wounded Knee, and it ranks as the deadliest shooting in US history. At that time, people were angry at the American Indians for wiping out General Custer at the Battle of Little Bighorn. The following report from the *New York Herald* summed up the feelings of Americans of the time.

It is inconsistent with our civilization and with common sense to allow the Indian to roam over a country as fine as that around the Black Hills, preventing its development in order that he may shoot game and scalp his neighbors. That can never be. This region must be taken from the Indian.

In the days following, a terrible blizzard prevented the hospital and burial details from finishing their duties on the field of the massacre. The fourth day after the battle, on Thursday,

January 1, 1891, the miserable work was resumed and there was found, by the side of a dead woman, partly covered with snow, a dusky baby girl, alive and well. The child was about seven months old, with slight frostbite upon her head and feet. She had been snugly held in a papoose beside the lifeless mother's body, during all those days of darkness, carnage, and storm, and the snow had kindly covered her with its blanket. [1]

When told of the discovery of a child on the battlefield, General Colby immediately became obsessed with the idea of obtaining a 'living relic' of the battle, much like his hero Andrew Jackson. Andrew had adopted a full-blood Creek orphan during the Creek Wars and became a hero who saved the Child of the Battlefield. Colby, who was said to have some Indian blood in his veins, was touched by the pathos of the story of the little waif, and decided that he must find a way to obtain her.

There were two other people at Pine Ridge at that time who also had eyes on the little survivor, and who had already taken steps to secure her future. Buffalo Bill and his manager, Major John Burke, were at Pine Ridge, from where they recruited Indian performers for Buffalo Bill's Wild West Show. Burke had seen the opportunity to have the child adopted by a friend, with the possibility of using her in a future show. By the time that General Colby became involved, Burke had already sent a telegram to Washington to set up his arrangement. This was reported in the *National Tribune*.

Mrs. Alison Nailor of Washington, has adopted the Indian infant found on the battlefield of Wounded Knee. Maj. Burke who has been manager of Buffalo Bill's Wild West Show during the tour of Europe... was an intimate friend of the Nailors, and at the time of the battle was on his way to the reservation with the Indians who had appeared in his show.... Maj. Burke took the baby to Pine Ridge Agency, and had it christened in the name of Maggie L. Nailor, the major acting as godfather to the young savage.[2]

Burke must have been jumping the gun when he issued press releases because a reporter for the *Washington Evening Star* decided to check the story with the Nailors and the following was his report.

FIRST HE HAD HEARD OF IT.
What Mr. Al Nailor Says About the Indian Pappoose.
A Star reporter called Mr. Allison Nailor's attention yesterday to a telegram from the Pine Ridge agency received at the Star office to the effect that a small Indian papoose had been picked up on the battle ground at Wounded Knee and that it had been adopted by Mrs. Allison Nailor of Washington, Maj. Burke standing sponsor for it. 'Well,' said Mr. Nailor, 'that's the first time I have heard anything about it. I suppose Burke has picked up the papoose for me as a sort of Christmas present, but Johnny Burke wants to be mighty careful how he shoves off any Indian kids on me. But never mind, let the telegram go. It's about as straight as such things usually are.'[3]

In reality, Burke's arrangements with the Nailors were not confirmed, and his plan to have the child adopted with a friend was not going to work. The arrival of Colby gave Burke another opportunity to make a deal and secure a potential future attraction for the show. The bargaining took place around the woodstove at the home of Yellow Bird and his wife Annie, who were looking after the baby. A deal was done, and Colby departed for his tent with his newly acquired baby, along with Annie, who agreed to take care of the baby until Colby could make other arrangements. But that was not the conclusion of the matter. Annie was against having the orphan leave with the white general. She waited until the camp became quiet and crept out of the tent, slipping past the guards to return to her home. There she mounted a pony and rode away to the hostile camp, carrying the infant survivor.

The commanding officer, General Miles, had issued strict orders forbidding any troops to approach the hostile camp while negotiations were taking place for a surrender. This prevented Colby from pursuing Annie and the child. Several days passed during this embargo on their approach; meanwhile Colby discussed ways in which he might retrieve the child with the assistance of Yellow Bird and the wives of the Asay brothers, store-keepers at the Agency. They dressed him as a half-breed and took him to the camp, where, with an interpreter, he made the following plea for the child.

I am Seneca Indian – my grandmother was a full blood Seneca. I have brought food on behalf of my tribe for your children. I rescued the child who survived the massacre at Wounded Knee. Take pity on me and my wife. We have no children of our own. I want to give this child to my wife. We will take good care of her.[4]

After some consideration and discussion by the crowd of Indians that surrounded Colby, they took a decision to allow this man to take the child which they called Zintka Lanuni

– the Lost Bird. After this, the group boarded the wagon and returned to Yellow Bird's store. Colby retained the services of a mixed-race nurse and boarded a train to return to Beatrice. The next day, the *State Journal* reported on his arrival in Lincoln.

GENERAL COLBY'S CAPTURE
He Has Christened It Mary Elizabeth
A bright Eyed Indian Baby Girl Who Lay Four Days on
the Wounded Knee Battle Ground.
Brigadier-General Colby and staff arrived in the city last evening from his campaign in command of the state militia in the vicinity of the now happily terminated Indian troubles......

While most of the soldiers brought back with them a variety of mementoes of their trip, General Colby has brought one that is destined to far exceed in public interest any of the other keepsakes chosen. It is a bright little Indian baby girl aged about eleven months. This child lay four days upon the field of the Wounded Knee fight after the battle ere it was picked up. Its mother was doubtless among the slain.....General Colby secured possession of it, but ere he could get away it was stolen from his tent. He engaged two brothers known as the Asa brothers, who live at the agency, to recover it for him, and they finally found the child in possession of a squaw, who objected to the little one being taken to live among the hated white people. The General has named the child Mary Elizabeth, after the wives of the Asa brothers, and on Monday will endow it with the name of Colby by formal adoption in the probate court at Beatrice.[5]

Passing through Lincoln for Beatrice, Colby stayed overnight at The Capital Hotel, along with the child, the mixed-race nurse named Mrs. Going, and some of his staff. This we believe was to maximize the publicity he was receiving from the situation. No doubt, the hotel costs—like those of Burke's bargaining fee, the bribes, the provisions for the Indians and all other costs of obtaining Zintka Lanuni—Colby would charge to the Nebraska state government.

After returning home to Beatrice, Colby opened the doors of his house to introduce the baby to the surrounding citizens. After which, the *Beatrice Express* reported, 'no less than 500 persons called at the house to see it.' A reception held at the Beatrice Auditorium on January 19 honored General Colby and the troops of Company C. Here is the newspaper report from the *Omaha Daily Bee*.

Reception to Company C
The Auditorium was thronged tonight with citizens of Beatrice intent upon participating in the reception to Company C, First Regiment, Nebraska National Guards, in honor of their return from the Indian war. .....

An interesting feature of the reception was the presence of General Colby's adopted Indian baby and her half breed nurse. The little waif was formally and legally adopted by General Colby today, and is given the name of Margaret Elizabeth Colby.[6]

Massive changes were underway for little Zintka Lanuni. Her provision of care meant an introduction to a completely different environment to that which she had been living. The immediate effect of being stared at, breathed upon and handed round by hundreds of people was that she developed pneumonia. Leonard called upon the assistance of Clara's sister, Dr. Mary White, to treat her and then to help with the care of the new baby. Mary promoted Clara's kitchen maid, Marie 'Maud' Miller (formerly Moeller), a 15-year-old, German girl to be Zintka's governess and gave her training in how to care for the child.

They all meant well, but placing the child alone in her crib in a nursery and feeding on schedule, not on demand, forced an entirely new experience on the child. Indian children spent most of their early years closely bound to parents or other family members. They never experienced the silence which Victorian mothers supposed their babies needed, being more used to the sounds of drumming and singing going on in the background. Mary White's four daughters loved to play with little Zintka, and this may have offered the only activity presumably close to experiences from her previous life.

During the time that Leonard was enjoying his new celebrity status as *the General who brought home an orphan baby from the battlefield*, twelve hundred miles away in Washington DC, Clara had no idea that she was about to become the mother of the little girl. On January 23, 1891, she was lobbying members of the Congress. When she returned home, she found a letter from Leonard, instructing her to come back to Nebraska as she was now the adopted mother of his 'living relic', a full-blood Lakota baby girl taken from the Pine Ridge reservation after the Massacre at Wounded Knee. Imagine the shock that she would have felt from hearing this news after the adoption was already completed and done in her name. It is hard for us to place ourselves in her position without reacting strongly to what her husband had put her through.

Clara consulted Susan B. Anthony on the situation, who was appalled at the position that Leonard Colby had placed her in. 'You cannot accept this,' she said. Anthony had never had children, and so her natural response was one of despair at the thought of Clara being dragged away from the outstanding job she was doing in the suffrage movement.

Clara, forever trying to be positive about any situation, decided that she must identify how she could make the most of the circumstances. She was always reluctant to express how she felt, and the closest she came on this issue was to publish the following in the January 31 issue of the *Woman's Tribune*.

'In answer to many enquiries, the editor of *The Tribune* publishes the quotation from the Republic, and will state that, for herself, she rejoices in this opportunity, by the care and education of this child, to join in expiating, so far at least, the wrongs of our race against hers.'

THE INDIAN BABY

It seems it is not Mrs. Allison Nailor who has the Indian baby, but Mrs. Clara Bewick Colby, the editor of The Woman's Tribune, who is in Washington for the winter. Her husband, General L. W. Colby, who in charge of the Nebraska State militia has been engaged at the scene of the late Indian hostilities, has now returned, and writes Mrs. Colby that he has taken to their home in Beatrice, Neb., an orphan Indian girl, nine months old, who was found on the battlefield of Wounded Knee Creek four days after the battle. Her toes and the top of her head are a little frostbitten, but nothing serious. The battle was on Monday and the baby was found on Thursday, with two others, who were then alive but have since died. General Colby writes: 'She is my relic of the Sioux War of 1891 and the massacre of Wounded Knee, where Big Foot and his braves were slaughtered.' The baby has attained newspaper notoriety as Margaret Elizabeth, but is named Leonarda after its adopted father, and is now being cared for by Mrs. Colby's sister, Dr. Mary B. White, until Mrs. Colby's return. – The Republic, Washington D.C.[7]

On February 6, Clara was invited to speak to the Woman's National Press Association meeting held at The Willard Hotel in Washington. She published her talk in the February 21 issue of the *Tribune*, which is partly reproduced below.

Leonard may have registered her name as Margaret Elizabeth, possibly calling her Leonarda, but Clara was always going to call her by the name given to her by the tribe to which she belonged, the musical and soft-sounding Indian name of Zintka Lanuni, which means 'Lost Bird.' Zintka was how she was known for the rest of her life.

From her talk at the Press Association meeting, it is easy to see that Clara did not approve of Leonard taking the child home as a prized trophy from the Indian war.

ZINTKA LANUNI
The Waif of Wounded Knee.
Indian trinkets, elk teeth, necklaces, bows and arrows, war-clubs, tomahawks, and hundreds of articles of various kinds and character, are disposed of in the cities and towns of the United States, as valued relics of the late great Indian uprising in South Dakota.

*The long fasting of the Brules, Ogallalas, (sic) and
other Sioux tribes the wild and weird ghost dances, continued for weeks; the persistent work of Red Cloud, Young-
Man-Afraid-Of-His-Horses, Rocky Bear, No Neck, and
other friendly chiefs, in the interest of peace, the massing
of about eight thousand troops of the Regular Army, under
command of Gen. Nelson A. Miles, and of two regiments of
the Nebraska National Guard, under the command of Gen.
L. W. Colby, upon and near the great Sioux Reservation in
Dakota and Nebraska, are familiar facts to the American
reading public. Also the subsequent developments, including many of the incidents of the slaughter of Big Foot and
his band, the attempt to fire the Agency buildings and the
Mission School, and the withdrawal of the four thousand
hostile Indians to the Red Lands are equally well known.*

*There are many Prized trophies obtained by Army of-
ficers and citizens, of the leading scenes and characters in
this great Indian uprising; but the relics most valuable are
associated in the public mind with the terrible incidents of
the massacre on Wounded Knee Creek. The war-bonnets,
Indian Clubs, ghost shirts and bloody garments, all have
their historic interest and significance, but one of the most
pathetic mementoes of the annihilation of Big Foot and his
one hundred and twenty warriors and their families, is the
bright, seven-months-old Indian baby, found among the
dead upon the field, four days after the battle and obtained
by General Colby of Nebraska.[8]*

The article continued with the story of how the confrontation developed between the Army and the Indians, the gun
battle, and the terrible blizzard which prevented the medical

and burial teams from finishing their duties on the field of the massacre. Then came the discovery of a dusky baby girl, alive and well, protected by the lifeless mother's body. She omits the details of how her husband negotiated for the baby, and merely says that he went to the hostile camp, and after considerable difficulty, obtained the child.

Leonard wrote to Clara and said he thought she should return immediately to Nebraska to take up her new duties as a mother, but that was unrealistic for either of them as they were both fully committed over the next few months. Besides having her weekly newspaper to publish, she was the Nebraska delegate at the NAWSA Convention, which was scheduled to run from February 26–29 at Albaugh's Grand Opera House in Washington. On March 19, she was invited to a reception in her honor by the New York Woman Suffrage League to be held at the Park Avenue Hotel. The event commenced with entertainment by a pianist, a violinist, and a cellist, before another leading suffragist, Mrs. Lillie Devereux Blake, gave a complimentary welcome to the guest of the League. Mrs. Colby responded in a few well-chosen words, expressive of her confidence in the ultimate success of the woman suffrage movement.[9]

CHAPTER 11

NETWORKS OF WASHINGTON

Clara was rapidly making a mark within the Washington social scene, in much the same way as she had done in Wisconsin and Nebraska. The only difference was, that the friends she was making here in Washington were the most influential people at the top of the political world. One of her special friends was Caroline Scott Harrison, a talented painter and pianist, and also the wife of President Benjamin Harrison, making her the First Lady of the United States. Through her, she met the wife of William H. Miller, who was the US Attorney General.

During a meeting in February 1891, Mrs. Miller expressed enthusiasm to hear the story of Clara's adopted Indian daughter, which provided an opportunity for Clara to raise another subject. Clara promoted the idea that her husband was available for any Washington appointment; she made sure that these ladies and the wives of other government leaders got to know of his interest. Clara kept Leonard updated on her lobbying in Washington, while he made sure that his contacts in the Nebraska state government took every opportunity to recommend himself for any appropriate appointment in Washington.

Leonard was also busy in the months following. He left for Florida in February, where he was involved with the purchase of 15,000 acres of land for the Dunnellon Phosphate Company. Existing records do not describe the nature of Leonard's role in this business transaction, but we can be sure that it would be one centered around profit for the Colby family. Leonard showed his feelings in a letter he wrote to Clara, enclosing flowers that he had collected along the shore of Lake Dora. Whether his expressions were as sincere as Clara believed, or whether he was using his charm to encourage her very effective efforts at lobbying on his behalf, we will never know for sure.

Tavares, Florida
February 12, 1891

My Dear Wife
I arrived here this morning at 6.30 to find everybody still asleep. Left Jacksonville at 9.30 last night. Have just taken a walk in the sand and found some of the wild, yellow, sweet-scented jasmine. Lake Dora about 5 miles in length joins the little town...

I send you some jasmine and other posies including a little blue orchid.
Yours ... L.W. Colby

Leonard returned from Florida in March, traveling via Washington so that he and Clara could have a few days together before he returned to Beatrice. He brought back from Florida what looked like the fossilized skull of a large animal, which had been dredged up by the mining company with whom he had been working. He left the relic with the Smithsonian Institute to have it correctly identified.

Clara arrived back in Beatrice early in May 1891, just in time to see her husband leave for Denver. He was on an assignment from Governor Thayer as a special escort to President Harrison, who was traveling through Nebraska from Denver.[1]

The escort duty turned out to be a job interview. The President was especially curious to hear Colby's first-hand experience in the Indian wars. He also recognized his extensive legal and political background and showed a keen interest in the story of Colby's adopted daughter, the survivor of Wounded Knee.

The party left Denver at 6 pm on May 12 and made an evening stop at Akron, Colorado before heading overnight into Nebraska, arriving in Hastings at 6.12 am. Even at that early hour, 10,000 people were there to welcome the President, to hear him speak from the rear end platform of the train.[2] Following short stops in Fairmont and Crete, the President spent an hour in Lincoln before traveling on to Omaha.

As we have seen, Leonard was a superb communicator and was a master at making a good sales pitch. Spending two days escorting President Harrison would have been a golden opportunity for Leonard to cement home a good impression and one which would add to the message that Clara was passing through the First Lady.

The lobbying proved effective. On June 19 the *State Journal* reported that the president had appointed General L. W. Colby, of Beatrice, to be Assistant Attorney-General to represent the government in cases for Indian depredation claims. Leonard lost no time in getting to Washington, as we see in the following newspaper article.

SETTLED DOWN TO WORK

Washington, July 1 – General L.W. Colby, assistant attorney-general in charge of Indian depredation claims, has arrived and assumed the duties of his office. The two rooms in the department of justice building adjoining those of the attorney-general have been refurbished and are occupied by General Colby and his assistants in indexing and docketing the cases which have already been commenced and in systemizing the business. Over 3,000 cases have already been filed and it is estimated that the number of claims will aggregate from 15,000 to 20,000.

General Colby was in consultation with Indian Commissioner Morgan, Senator Pettigrew of South Dakota, and others in regard to the depredation matter and is considering the best methods to arrive at a speedy settlement of the claims, many of which are nearly a half century old.[3]

In 1796, the United States government established a system for dealing with depredation claims. Through this, both Indians and pioneers could apply for indemnity for losses incurred as a result of conflict between each other. The claims process was too slow to prevent violence, and it was ridden by fraud. The result did little more than obstruct the machinery of the federal government.[4]

By the time of Leonard Colby's involvement, most of the benefits for claims litigation went to claims agents, lawyers, or law firms, with very little going to the Indian and Pioneer claimants. Leonard was well qualified to understand this system, but whether he had the will and the means to make the changes required was unknown. What is known is that he was now in a position to control the distribution of a considerable amount of money, provided that he could remain in his new job, given that President Harrison was facing an election in less than 18 months.

This wasn't the only source of power forthcoming. An interesting report appeared in the newspapers at about the time that Leonard started his new position.

And now it appears from reports current that the Indian child recently adopted by General L. W. Colby of Beatrice, after it had survived four days of fearful exposure on the battle ground of Wounded Knee, is not likely to be a burden upon him for subsistence. It is claimed that she is likely some day to be heiress to millions. She belonged to the Unca-papa Teton Sioux, who were principal owners of the reservation. The tribe, it is claimed, was nearly exterminated in the battle of Wounded Knee, so she is one of the few remaining heirs. It is said that General Colby will take steps to see that her rights are preserved.[5]

It seems that Leonard was letting personal interest set his priorities in his new position. Although the depredation claims under the claims system had been accumulating over almost sixty years, his first priority was to settle a recent claim from Pine Ridge, drafted by the man who helped him in obtaining

Zintka Lanuni, James Asay. This suggested that this was a reward for his assistance.[6]

He also involved many of his contacts in the legal profession around the country, taking depositions to be used in the claims. One of these was Clara's friend, Belva Lockwood, who was soon acting for an Eastern band of Cherokees from North Carolina.[7] Leonard also recruited Mary's husband, Charles White, to come to Washington to assist him in his new role.

Clara's return to Beatrice at the beginning of May was the first time that she met her adopted daughter Zintka, and she wrote a short note about it in the *Woman's Tribune*.

So many correspondents have expressed an interest in Zintka Lanuni: the waif of Wounded Knee, that we are sure they will all expect a little mention of her at this time of home-coming. She has now but a slight cough and a fast fading scar on her cheek to show the result of her terrible four days exposure on the field of battle. As near as can be estimated she is now nine months old. She gets around in her propeller in a very lively way, and if there is any tendency in her to the gravity of her race it has been held in abeyance by being a pet and plaything of all in the sister's home which has been her friendly shelter until this date. She is quite as winning and lovable as babies of her age are apt to be and her awakening intelligence is watched with more than the usual interest. Her name is commonly shortened to 'Zintka' which is quite as musical as its English equivalent 'Bird.'[8]

Clara left Washington for Beatrice on Friday, May 8, which means that she did much of the writing and editing of the

Tribune on the two-day train journey. She had mastered the skills of being a newspaper publisher and editor, but now a new prowess was demanded of her: that of motherhood. It was a challenging, new experience for her, but with the help of Maud and by taking Zintka along to functions whenever she could, she managed. In fact, she continued to excel at her other tasks of writing, editing, public speaking, and lobbying.

It soon became clear that Clara's role included helping Maud, as well as Zintka and Clarence. Maud was only fifteen, having come to America as a child, and her command of English was fairly limited. Fortunately, Maud was a very willing student who held her new boss Clara in high regard.

It would appear that Clara managed to spend the months of June and July with her friends and family at home, although she continued to publish the *Woman's Tribune* without missing an issue. In August and September, she undertook local speaking engagements either side of a trip to Colorado.

The Chicago and Rock Island line had opened a new route, which went from Omaha through Beatrice and down to Denver and Colorado Springs. To celebrate and publicize its opening, the company invited twenty-six representatives of the leading newspapers to accompany its first train. She was thinking that she should decline the invitation but was strongly urged by the railway company to accept, and to bring along the rest of the *Tribune* staff, namely Clarence and Zintka Lanuni. Clara wrote up the travel experience in the August 29 issue, where she said that Zintka 'proved herself the lion of the party and was everywhere the object of much interest and admiration. She is already doing missionary work for her race, making people realize its possibilities and that there is a kinship in human nature deeper than race separation.'[9]

Clara, Clarence and Zintka had a delightful journey to Denver, where they were received by the Governor of the State and the Mayor of the city. They rode around Denver under the guidance of enthusiastic Denverites, including an old school friend of Clara's, Adele Overton Brown. In the afternoon, the party departed for Colorado Springs, where they secured excellent accommodation at The Antlers. After dinner, they went out by the electric railway to Broadmoor to visit a Casino owned by a German, Count Pourtales.

The following day, the party took a carriage ride to Manitou, along one of the finest macadamized roads in the world. Here, they took the 'cog-road' to the summit of Pike's Peak. Clara had previously remarked, 'that there was no romance in going to the top of Pike's Peak by steam.' Now, she claimed, 'But this foolish statement was taken back as we proceeded on the wonderful ascent. To all the sublime grandeur of this giant of the clouds is added the awful potency of the human will that had conquered even this.'

The summit is over 14,000 feet above sea level, and the first train of the cog railway had traveled to the summit only two months previously.

Leonard was back in Omaha, Nebraska in August and September, taking depositions in cases of Indian depredation claims before the court. Up until August 1, 'his office had documented 3,640 cases for Indian depredations, and under the law, five hundred of these are entitled to priority of consideration, under the provisions of the act. Most of the claims date back twenty or thirty years. The claims in Nebraska are confined mainly to between 1860 and 1870 and tribes of the great Sioux nation.'[10]

Further, on October 22, the *Daily Bee* reported, 'Upwards of $20,000,000 in claims had been filed and that if he can stay in office General Colby may just as well transfer his office to the District of Columbia.'

During this time, Leonard and Clara took every opportunity to get together, but even his annual reunion of the Nebraska National Guard was interrupted by the demands of his new role.

By the middle of October, he was back in Washington, and one of his first tasks was to find a new apartment that would better suit 'the Assistant Attorney General of the United States'. Clara's residence, at the corner of 11th and G Streets, suited her well, but it was understandably too small for Leonard and their added family members. A visitor had written in the *Tribune*, 'The sight of a courageous woman, under great hardships, and at the cost of many personal sacrifices, struggling by dint of economy, ingenuity, brains and hard work to publish a reform paper, and succeeding, was something to be remembered.'[11] Leonard found a three-story house at 1325 10th Street that would better suit their needs. Here, Clara would need to set up her printing works when she returned.

Clara planned an earlier return to Washington this year, but in the interim, she had engagements to fulfill in various states before she could get back to her winter home. In October she had to speak at the Congress for the Advancement of Women, in Grand Rapids, Michigan, followed by a speech at the Women's Congress in Saint Paul, Minnesota, before returning to Nebraska for the annual convention of the Nebraska WSA.

She made the journey from Beatrice to Washington late in October 1891, with Leonard already in residence there, and took Zintka, Clarence, and Maud with her, intending to create an environment where she and Leonard could settle into happy family life. Her hope was unrealistic and overly optimistic, as it did not take account of the commitments she had made to the suffrage cause. Added to that, she had a weekly newspaper to research, edit and publish. In fact, within a few days of arrival in Washington, she had to depart for a speaking engagement at the National Federation of Women's Press Clubs, in Boston. She traveled up with the Federation President, Mrs. Belva Lockwood, who lived in Washington. Mrs. Lockwood wrote, 'We will leave for Boston Tuesday A.M. 10 o'clock on the B.& O Bound Brook route.'[12]

The route would take them by rail to New Jersey and then by steamship to Boston, giving them a good night's sleep before going to the meeting. Clara had the assistance of Maud in the raising of the children, but Zintka was a demanding two-year-old and Clarence was an intellectually disabled eleven-year-old who needed extra care. So, very soon after arriving in Washington, it was decided to place Clarence in a nearby boarding school where he could receive special attention. Leonard was not the kind of husband who would provide any assistance with the raising of children and management of the home, plus he had his new high-powered role, which was very demanding of his time.

This period should have been the time when Clara and Leonard were at their peak. Living in Washington, with contacts in the pinnacle of American society and a regular stream of visitors to their social functions, they should have been at their happiest. For example, on February 9, 1892, Assistant Attorney General Colby and the ladies of his family were invited to a reception at the Executive Mansion, now known as the White House.[13]

Unfortunately, they had both taken on far more than they could handle, leaving them little time to enjoy life together. Clara had to establish her printing works after the move to the new house and no doubt little Zintka would have been eager to 'help' her with all the intriguing type fonts and ink supplies that were involved.

At the February 1892 convention of the National American WSA, Clara was made the chairman of the new Federal Suffrage Committee—with the power to secure a representative woman from each of the thirty-nine states. Yes, this would involve a lot more travel in the summer of 1892.

Just one month later, at a meeting in Chicago, another suffrage organization was formed, under the name of The Federal Suffrage Association. This one would concentrate on lobbying the federal government to gain equal rights under the constitution. Clara was present and invited to take a senior role, but she decided that she could accomplish the same goals through the NAWSA. She would probably come to regret that decision.

Quite apart from the workloads of Clara and Leonard, it is difficult to see how their relationship could ever be successful, given their differences of opinion regarding the institution of marriage. Clara gave a speech on 'Woman in Marriage' at the 1889 convention of the NWSA in Washington, subsequently reprinted in the *Woman's Tribune*, which outlined some of her views.

> *It is self-evident that marriage is a condition intimately concerning women, since they are drawn to it by an almost universal instinct either natural or acquired. .....*
>
> *It is customary to regard it as of even greater importance to woman than to man, since the maternal, social and household duties involved with it consume the greater portion of the time and thought of a large proportion of women. Love, it is commonly said, is an incident in a man's life, but makes or mars a woman's whole existence. ...... To one who believes in the divinely intended equality of the sexes it is impossible to consider that any mutual relation is an incident for the one and the sum total of existence for the other. ....*
>
> *Whether marriage is a purely business partnership for regulating the care and maintenance of children, or it be a sacrament to which the benediction of the church gives a peculiar sanctity and perpetuity and makes the parties 'no more twain but one flesh,' in either case it is an absurdity which we only tolerate because of custom for men alone to make all the regulations and stipulations concerning it.[14]*

True to her times, Clara's expectation of marriage was that of a union which would be permanent, at least 'until death us do part.' Her reference to perpetuity and one flesh indicates that she also thought their collective salvation into heaven might be dependent upon them both keeping their marriage vows. If we refer back to brother William's letter of concerns before they married, shows this to be a common view of the family. Indeed, Clara had fallen in love with an attractive and virile man, who was a high achiever in whatever he worked at, and one who would be incredibly charming when he wanted to be. She had overlooked the warnings of her grandmother, and she still disregarded any of the negative signals concerning the character and loyalty of her husband. She continued to be forever hopeful that he would settle down and become the faithful and steady partner that she longed for.

Leonard, by comparison, had expressed no belief in God and did not view marriage in anywhere near the same manner as Clara. He was an ambitious and charismatic person whose primary interest was in advancing his interests. He had initially fallen in love with Clara but then failed to mold her to the person that he desired, and she almost certainly did not satisfy him physically. His attraction to her during the time they were living in Washington may have had more to do with the introductions she was able to make than anything else. Leonard showed a great attraction to the social occasions that Clara would arrange at their home, including, in particular, their regular Saturday evening 'At Home.' As John Bewick's daughter Mary recalled:

My memory of Uncle Leonard is very dear. He never failed to bring in beautiful flowers for the Saturday evening 'At Homes.' He was a wonderful host and Aunt Clara's beautiful spirit always joined in with Uncle Len to make that a happy evening for the hundreds who dropped in.[15]

Leonard was not a person to miss an opportunity for self-promotion. Soon after taking up his position, he arranged to send a gift to the President, and, judging by the widespread press coverage achieved, he must have distributed a press release on the matter. Such a report follows. Perhaps, as an accomplished journalist and publisher, it was Clara who created and distributed the press releases.

A riding bridle and whip made of horse hair was sent to President Harrison by L. W. Colby, attorney general for the prosecution of Indian depredation claims, who explains, 'These were manufactured from hair taken from Linden Tree, the historic Arabian stallion presented to Gen. Grant by the Sultan of Turkey, and now owned by me. Please accept the gift as a sample of the skill and artistic taste of the cowboys of what was formerly known as the Great American Desert.'[16]

Following soon after this article appeared, another report, complete with an engraved picture of General Colby with Zintka Lanuni, appeared in newspapers around the country.

..... From time immemorial each war has had its particular hero or heroine, one, whose deeds, fate, or afterlife are always recalled in connection with the events of the first, greatest or last battle. On this page we give a correct likeness of the little heroine of America's last war in the arms of the brave and daring man who rescued her from a fate almost equal unto death, who has adopted her as his daughter and is as proud of her as though she were his own child.[17]

Among the interesting visitors to one of the Colby's 'At Home' evenings was a group of fourteen Indians, who were visiting Washington at that time. According to the *Woman's Tribune*, dated April 9, 1892, there were many ladies and gentlemen present, and therefore the Indians found themselves in a room full of company. This they appeared to enjoy. Several of them were well-educated and spoke English, assisted by an Episcopal clergyman, who spoke Chippewa. Zintka Lanuni recognized two of the Indians from a previous visit, but of the other Indians in their native dress, she seemed to be afraid. They also had with them a little Sioux boy about six years old, one of the orphans of Wounded Knee. He had great fun with Zintka, running in and out with a ball. Clara made a speech in which she asked them to take a cup of tea with her, as her way of smoking the pipe of peace.

Leonard always liked to remind people he met, especially Indian people, that his grandmother was a full-blood Seneca Indian. This turned out to be more of a romantic notion than anything else. Leonard's father, Rowell Colby, had written to Clara, indicating that he was unaware of having Indian ancestors.[18] With today's genealogy records available online through the Mormon Church and companies like Ancestry. com, it is quite clear that there were no Indian ancestors and that his family were all early colonists originating in England.

Clara's home in Washington was remembered, with pleasure, for the social gatherings she frequently held. It was her custom, whenever she made acquaintance with an engaging speaker from abroad, to arrange a lecture in her home. It could be anyone who had a message to give, on any subject, and she invited personal friends who were likely to be interested in the topic proposed. Among the fascinating visitors to the Colby's 'At Home' evenings in 1893 was Queen Lili'uokalani of Hawaii, who was visiting Washington. She was making an unsuccessful appeal against the annexation of her country by the United States. The 'At Home' evenings were also used to raise funds for causes that Clara derived interest in, as we see from the following letter from Leo Tolstoy.October 29, 1894

October 29, 1894
Dear Madam
I received your letter with the money order destined to be employed for needy Russian peasant women. I will try to make the best use of it in giving it to a family which is suffering from fire. I thank you and the givers of the money for their kindness.

I read your address on arbitration and was interested in it. ..... and I was glad to see that you are of the same opinion.... I heartily wish you success in your work.
Yours truly
Leo Tolstoy[19]

In the summer of 1892, Clara returned to Beatrice with Zintka, Clarence and Maud, but it was not a time for Clara to relax and enjoy time with her adopted children. Maud was going home to her parents, so Zintka and Clarence would be looked after by Clara's sister, Mary. Meanwhile, Clara was committed to traveling the country in her position as chair of the Federal Suffrage Committee, drumming up support for the 39 state organizations. She attended state conventions wherever possible, at which she was often a key speaker.

Her main lecture on 'The First Republic' involved her hearing before the United States Select Committee on Woman's Suffrage. She began by saying that the only true 'First Republic,' owing to the admission of women to use the ballot, 'was in Wyoming.' She said, 'On the western border of the state in which I live there is an invisible line across which, if a woman passes, instead of a subject she becomes a law-maker, a sovereign. The political nonentity becomes a person, a citizen, a part of the people, impossible thereafter to be ignored; one who makes legislators, governors, United States senators, and presidents, and who has in herself the possibility of filling any of these offices when in the judgment of her fellow citizens, she is the person best to do so.'[20]

Speaking engagements filled that summer, some of which were in Wisconsin, giving Clara an opportunity to visit with brother William and the other members of the Bewick family. Most of them were a conservative group who never really supported Clara's suffrage campaign. They would be polite, but Clara would see their eyes roll at her liberal views. William was an exception, however, and he consistently supported her success with the *Woman's Tribune*. Susan B. Anthony and Elizabeth Cady Stanton also joined Clara on some of her travels that summer with Mrs. Stanton referring to her as 'Beloved Saint Clara.'

Leonard and Clara would have had very little time together during the summer, sometimes passing like ships in the night. The *Beatrice Express* reported that General Colby had arrived home on May 23 but expected to remain only two weeks, during which time he was heading to Omaha and Lincoln. A further report on October 15 shows him returning home from Washington DC, five months later.

The summer of 1892 would turn out to be the last time they would be together in Beatrice. Clara, Zintka, Clarence, and Maud soon boarded the train to return to Washington. Another sad goodbye for little Zintka, who had so enjoyed the company of her cousins, the four daughters of Dr. Mary White.

No sooner had Clara returned in October to Washington, than the news came that her friend Caroline Harrison, the First Lady of the United States, had passed away. Clara recalled one of the meetings that she had with Mrs. Harrison in the next issue of the *Tribune*.

> On one occasion the writer called on Mrs. Harrison in company with Miss Anthony to explain to her the desire of the woman suffragists to have a representation of women in the management of the World's Fair. Mrs. Harrison received us with leisurely courtesy, of her own volition told us of her plans for the enlargement of the White House, spoke with enthusiasm of her discovery of household pieces belonging to its early occupants, and, as regarded the object of our visit, expressed the warmest sympathy with it. ... She promised to use her influence with Senators and Congressmen to provide for this future recognition of woman.[21]

The death of Caroline Harrison came just two weeks before her husband, President Benjamin Harrison, faced reelection. This was a contest that Leonard Colby predicted Harrison would win.

> General L. W. Colby returned home from Washington this afternoon. He goes to Chicago Monday to remain there until after the opening of the world's fair. He will return to Beatrice from Chicago to remain here until after the election. General Colby is enthusiastically sanguine of the success of the National republican ticket. ... The republican

cause is wonderfully increasing in strength in every quar-
ter, and the triumphant election of President Harrison is
as certain as certainty can be.[22]

The World's Columbian Exposition, or Chicago World's Fair, was set to open from May 1 to October 30, 1893, but the dedication ceremonies were to be held on October 21, 1892, and that is where Leonard was heading to in the above press report.

Unfortunately for Leonard, the Democratic candidate Grover Cleveland was the winner, which meant a change of administration and probably the end of Leonard's career as Assistant Attorney General. He had a few months to prepare for the likely termination of his position, but in March 1893 he was replaced by Charles Howry, a former officer of the Confederate Army and in recent years a member of the Democratic National Committee and an opponent of General Colby.

Howry's first task was to appoint Charles Corning as a special investigator. He was to go to the Pine Ridge reservation to seek evidence to show that General Colby had committed fraud. The investigation came to nothing, but only after the waste of thousands of dollars on the kind of politically inspired federal investigation that we still see today.

Leonard had covered his bases career-wise while working for the government, and as soon as he retired from the department of justice, he was out selling his services in Oklahoma.

General L. W. Colby, ex-assistant attorney-general of the
United States, visited Okmulgee last week, to try to induce
Creeks to think seriously of the Indian depredation claims
which the whites have against the Indians.... He said the

Indians have between 9000 and 10,000 claims against them aggregating about $37,000,000. The Creeks have 1003 cases, which amount to $1,472,000. Gen. Colby had studied the question thoroughly and advised the Creeks to employ a competent attorney at once to defend them against the claims.[23]

Leonard gained contracts with the Creeks, Cherokees, and Seminoles: three of the civilized tribes in Indian Territory, as their attorney in Washington. During this employment, he obtained a judgment against the government and in favor of the Cherokee nation for the sum of $6,742,000.[24]

CHAPTER 12

REVERSAL OF FORTUNES

BY DECEMBER OF 1892, Clara was fully involved once more with her lobbying activities on Capitol Hill. One day, upon her return home, Zintka came running to her arms, crying that Maud had left. Zintka had been left in the care of the laundry maid that morning, after which Maud had packed her things and driven away in a hackney. Clara had no idea what could have happened, and she had not noticed any unhappiness on the part of Maud or any other reason for leaving without discussion or even a note. Guilt overcame Clara at the thought that she had ignored some problem with the girl, realizing how likely this could be, considering her busy schedule.

She called a hackney carriage and immediately traveled back and forth through the streets of Washington, asking carriage drivers and street vendors if they had seen a girl matching Maud's description. One of the drivers remembered the girl and gave Clara the address of a run-down boarding house where he had taken her. Clara found Maud's room and knocked on the door, to which there was no answer, even though the owner of the place was sure she was there. After much pleading and persuading, during which Clara assured Maud that she loved her and was only interested in her welfare, the girl relented, and she decided to return home with Clara.

Eventually, Maud revealed the reason for her disappearance. She had become pregnant while in Beatrice, something for which she held great shame, and she had worn loose clothes in an attempt to conceal her condition. She was afraid that the Colbys would send her home in disgrace, so she had left with the thought that she could somehow make her way. Apparently, this was not possible, and Clara's kindhearted nature came to the fore, assuring Maud that she would not be sent away in disgrace, and they would devise a plan to accept the situation.

The baby was due around the beginning of April, so Maud needed somewhere safe to stay until she gave birth. Then the baby could be given up for adoption and Clara could find a job for Maud at the Chicago World's Fair, where Clara was planning to be in the summer of 1893. She had a friend in Philadelphia with a rooming house who would probably help her, and this would be a convenient location for Clara to visit occasionally. In the meantime, she would keep this secret from Leonard and her sister Mary, and she would ask her niece Mary Bewick to come to Washington and help look after Zintka.

The problems continued to mount up for Clara in early 1893. Clara had worked hard for the past year as the chair of the Federal Suffrage Committee, and she was ready to submit her report to the annual NAWSA conference. It had the enthusiastic support of all thirty-nine states. Strangely enough, the NAWSA passed a motion that year, discontinuing activity in the federal suffrage department, thus making Clara's position redundant. Olympia Brown said that Mrs. Colby had made a masterly report, showing an immense amount of work done.

At this same convention, the NAWSA voted over Susan B. Anthony's objection to alternate the site of its annual conferences between Washington and other parts of the country. Anthony's pre-merger NWSA had always held its conventions in Washington so as to help maintain focus on a national suffrage amendment. Anthony said she feared, accurately as it turned out, that the NAWSA would engage in suffrage work at the state level at the expense of national action. NAWSA routinely allocated no funding at all for congressional work, which at this stage consisted only of one day of testimony before Congress each year.

The abandonment of the Federal Suffrage Committee was a significant disappointment to Clara, having put so much work into the project, and as a result, somewhat neglected her home and family life. As a consolation, she was elected to attend the Chicago World's Fair, where she would run a booth that would still focus partly on federal suffrage. It seems like the merger of the NWSA and the AWSA to form the NAWSA had not been good for Clara. First, she had lost the acceptance of the *Woman's Tribune* as the official media publication, and now she had lost the chance to focus entirely on the federal government level, as she had been persuaded to by Susan B. Anthony. The old guard of Anthony and Stanton was slipping, and as one of their principal officers, Clara's influence had begun to wane.

The NAWSA's change of focus to campaigning for the vote on a state-by-state basis may also have slowed progress toward the success of women voting federally, for the eventual result was achieved by an amendment to the Constitution.

Clara spent the month of May in Chicago, where she attended the World's Congress of Representative Women, one of the most significant events of the exposition. There were 528 delegates attending, representing 126 organizations from 27 countries and 10,000 people visiting. Clara B. Colby, Vice-President of the Society, read the opening address to the Women of All Nationalities on behalf of Mrs. Warner Snoad of England.

During the Congress, she had met women from many parts of the world who inspired her to further work, and she received many invitations to travel and support various aspects of women's issues worldwide. At the Woman's Press Association, Clara's election as the delegate to the Chicago international press convention opened up more opportunities for her to meet similarly minded women from around the world.

At Congress, she also met Captain Richard H. Pratt, founder and superintendent of the US government's training school for Indian children. Captain Pratt advised Clara to educate Zintka in the East, entirely away from her kind, and to raise her a strict Christian.

May 5, 1893, marked the start of major financial problems for most Americans, when Wall Street stock prices plunged. For the Colbys, this was the start of a terrible period, for although Leonard had always found ways to make money, he

found it very easy to spend money and he had many invest-
ments which did not generate an income.

Indeed, the Nebraska newspapers of that year were full of
reports of court cases involving the Colbys, to do with debt
recovery and mortgage foreclosure. The *Omaha Daily Bee* reported on May 19 that General L. W. Colby had sold sixteen
of his young Arabian horses to a circus.

Clara returned temporarily to Washington and arranged
for Mary to take Zintka to Madison for the summer months.
She was expecting to have received a letter from Maud, but
there was none; all she found was her letters to Maud, returned and marked as 'not at this address.' She noticed an envelope from Baltimore, postmarked May 28, 1893.

> #5 E. Biddle St.
> Baltimore Md.

Mrs. Colby

*Will you kindly tell me what you know of the young woman
who formerly lived in your family calling herself M. C. Miller. She came to my house in the winter in a delicate condition, has since been confined – she says she was taken by
you when quite a child and lived with you until her marriage to John Miller, half brother of your husband – who is
acting as a salesman for a Chicago house. My suspicions
have been aroused as to her being married – the man treats
her in the most unkind way as far as attention and giving
her money goes. I have wanted to apply to Gen. Colby for
help but she says he does not care for her any more as they
parted in anger – for her sake and my own I would like to
know the truth.*

Mrs. Skinner[1]

A note on the envelope, in Clara's handwriting, states, 'The letter which broke the dreadful news to me.' Now it dawned on Clara who the father of Maud's baby could be. She was horrified at the implication. A scandal of this nature was enough to ruin Leonard's legal practice, and destroy Clara's own reputation as a leader of the movement to support women's rights. Her mind flashed back to her grandmother's warnings and the concerns expressed by her brother William. She also considered how the disgrace of this whole saga could reflect upon her mentor, Susan B. Anthony. The social circles within which she had freely moved would be closed, and everything which she had built would be razed to the ground.

Each copy of the *Woman's Tribune* had a poem on the front page, and these sometimes revealed Clara's feelings. The issue of June 10, 1893, displayed her hope for better days

> *Sometime, sometime.*
> *The clouds of ignorance shall part asunder,*
> *And we shall see the fair, blue sky of truth*
> *Spangled with stars, and look with joy and wonder*
> *Up to the happy dream-lands of our youth,*
> *where we may climb.*
>
> *Sometime, sometime.*
> *The passion of our heart we keep dissembling*
> *Shall free herself, and rise on silver wing,*
> *And all these broken chords of music, trembling*
> *Deep in the soul, our lips shall learn to sing,*
> *A strain sublime.*
>
> *Sometime, sometime.*

Love's broken links shall all be re-united,
But not upon the ashy forge of pain;
The full blown roses dead, the sweet buds blighted
Shall blossom beside life's garden walks again,
In fairer clime.

Sometime, sometime.
The prophet's unsealed lips shall straight deliver
The message of eternal life un-cursed;
Wind-swept, the poet's heaven-tuned soul shall quiver,
And from his trembling lyre at length shall burst
Immortal rhyme.
Arthur Wentworth Eaton.

Clara wrote to thank Mrs. Skinner for her letter and asked her if she would send a telegram if the man came to visit again. After a few days, Clara received the following note from Mrs. Skinner.

June 3rd 1893

Mrs. Colby
Your letter received. Mrs. Miller left here on Wednesday last and though stating that she was going to Annapolis she is I am sure still in Baltimore, I have just seen the man who got the carriage for her and he will send the driver to me and I can find out where he took her. She does need a friend some one to turn her from the path of sin she has entered.
Yours truly Annie Skinner.[2]

Mrs. Skinner had seen the man that arranged the carriage for Maud, but she said nothing which would suggest that this was the man referred to in her previous letter. Perhaps it was Leonard or maybe it was someone who was acting for Leonard. There was only one way for her to find out. She would go to the place where Maud was staying and confront whoever she met there to determine the truth.

So, Clara took the train from Washington to Baltimore. After talking with Mrs. Skinner, she found the place where Maud was staying, went to her room and knocked on the door.

Maud opened the door and immediately burst into tears, crying out how sorry she was and how she prayed to God for forgiveness. She was alone in the room, except for the baby, who was sleeping in a small cot in the corner. Clara placed her arm around Maud's shoulder and asked her to sit down and tell her everything that had happened.

Clara had known Maud since she was a young girl and here she was at seventeen, having had a child with her forty-seven-year-old boss, being left alone to figure out what she would do next. Clara's compassionate nature came to the fore, coupled with her talent for organizing solutions to problems. She quickly ascertained the situation and the level of involvement which Leonard still had. As she suspected, he had visited her since the baby was born and had given Maud enough money to secure the humble accommodation where she was staying. But, poor Maud had no idea what the future held. Having calmed her down, Clara assured her they would come up with a plan in the next few days, which would give her something positive to look forward to. She needed time to think, for Maud and herself.

Clara was still planning to return to Chicago for the rest of the World's Fair, and she wanted Maud to join her there. Perhaps this was where Maud could get some work and arrange support for the baby. Clara was thinking more of adoption for the baby, but she had not communicated this to Maud yet.

From the responses received from Maud, Clara must have been developing her ideas on the fly, revealing parts of her plans in two separate letters written on the same day. Maud's replies show how much she needed someone like Clara to help her, and how close Leonard had come to abandoning her.

407 East Lafayette Ave
Baltimore, Md.,
June 8, 1893

My Dear Mrs. Colby,
Your letter was received this morning and I am so thankful that you have thought of a plan that will do. The matter has been on my mind constantly, but I have been unable to come to any conclusion. But now, whatever you think best I am ready to do. I received $10 this morning and so paid my board till next Wednesday the 15th, but I am ready to leave any time. Write and tell me what your idea is.

You are a true and noble friend, and God only knows how I regret that I did not tell you how matters stood when I was still in Washington; had I known you then as I do now, I should have done so. I am still so young and have the future before me, and I am determined to make something of myself yet. I have prayed for help and strength as I have never prayed before, and my future will prove that I am sorry for my past.
Let me hear from you soon.
As ever, Maud.

407 East Lafayette Ave
Baltimore, Md.,
June 8, 1893

My Dear Mrs. Colby,
Since writing to you at noon, I have read your other letter in which you tell me what your plan is. I like the idea that you speak of; in carrying it out I would be independent, as well as have my child near me. But in that case, all the care and responsibility of the baby would be thrown on me, and that seems somewhat unjust, for I am not the only one that sinned, nor am I the greater sinner of the two. My youth and ignorance was taken advantage of. I was a pure minded girl as ever lived till that man got me in his power. But after all, that seems to be the best thing to do and I am willing, and not only willing, but thankful to do that, or anything else to redeem myself and make amends for the past as far as can be done. By earnestly praying for strength daily, I will yet, with God's help, lead a useful life, and my aim shall be to help those who are as weak as I have been. I knew only too well that I was sinking deeper in sin every day. I needed a true friend if ever a person did, and since you, above all other women, came to me to be that friend, I feel that God sent you. It must have been awful for you to find this out, and yet, it was the best thing that could have happened, and, dear Mrs. Colby, God will help you too.
Write to me whenever you can; your kind letters help me so much.

Yours, Maud.[3]

On June 12, 1893, Leonard wrote to Clara from Lincoln, Nebraska, and the letter was full of negative news concerning

mortgage foreclosures and judgments against them for un-
paid bills. It appeared that he had not yet heard about Clara's
discovery of Maud and the baby. On June 15, 1893, he wrote
again, this time from Beatrice.

Dear Wife,
Received your letter with the sealed package 'to be opened
on the train' also the Washington papers and Tribunes
sent: - thanks for the thoughts...... I have been taking de-
positions, trying cases and hustling to collect money or
sell something. This whole country is on the edge of bank-
ruptcy. Two banks went up in Omaha yesterday, and every-
thing is gloomy and at a standstill. Not a dollar of money
can be collected, or got at any bank. There will be failures
here and all over. I could not sell the best horse for $25
cash. You have no idea in what shape business is here. City
property cannot be sold for 1/3 its value. Financial ruin is
upon the nation. I do not think it possible to avoid it.
You should collect every dollar, make the paper a
monthly, get that place in Chicago at a salary, put Clar-
ence on the farm, Zintka with Mary, etc., etc. .... I write
this so that you can have an idea of things, they are the
worst I ever saw. I am writing this before breakfast at
Mary's.
Yours, L.W. Colby.

There is no explanation with regards to the sealed package 'to
be opened on the train.' It sounds as if Clara had asked Leonard to return to Washington and hoped that he would agree
to her request not to open the sealed package until he was on
the train. It probably updated him on what she had discovered
and outlined her conditions for continuing their marriage.

She still had an idealistic vision of what kind of relationship might be workable with Leonard Colby. More than likely, he opened the package as soon as he received it, realized what a mess his marriage was in, and decided to ignore things for the time being. His marriage, his girlfriend with an illegitimate child, and his two adopted children were just some of the many problems he was facing. Better to stay in the west, try to recoup some of the losses he was suffering in court, and see what money he could make from his new clients among the Indian tribes.

He was still pulling the wool over her eyes, especially as it pertained to his financial situation. He painted a picture of impending disaster, and although that was partially true, he hid the positive aspects of his position. For example, just four days before his letter outlining impending bankruptcy, the following article appeared in the *Omaha Daily Bee*.

> *General L. W. Colby has purchased of General Beall of Washington, D. C., the Arabian horse Leopard, once owned by General Grant. The animal is now quartered in this city, having arrived here the first of this week. He makes a valuable acquisition to General Colby's already valuable stables.*[4]

Not only did Colby purchase this valuable animal, but it showed that he had recently visited Washington to negotiate the deal. Reports in the newspapers, plus his letters to Clara, showed that Leonard spent most of the summer of 1893 in Nebraska, with some side trips to the East, during which he visited Maud—but not Clara.

In April and May, Leonard visited Washington as he was appointed to a federal role to investigate alleged corruption by a group of officials in the Weather Bureau. This appointment was perhaps the only time during his career that he was on the investigation side, rather than the one being investigated. By June 5, 1893, Leonard was back in Nebraska, seated in the front row of the Supreme Court in Lincoln when an impeachment decision was handed down. He attended a meeting of the military board in the adjutant general's office in Lincoln on June 17. At the end of June, he had a narrow escape from death in Fairbury, Nebraska, when he slipped in front of a moving freight train. The next week, as the commander of the Nebraska militia, General Colby was in Superior, Nebraska, at the annual camp of the National Guard, for five days.

Clara and Maud continued to correspond between Washington and Baltimore. Clara was now making it clear that Maud would have to find a foster home for her baby before she could make a move.

Clara returned to Chicago in July but continued to make quick trips from Chicago to undertake speaking engagements. Fortunately, the railroads serving Chicago offered free passes to journalists as an encouragement to cover the World's Fair. At the end of August, she also took a trip to Beatrice, where she could discuss with Leonard what they were going to do about their relationship.

Leonard was extremely apologetic, claiming that he made a massive mistake with Maud and that he wanted himself and Clara to stay together. Leonard's expression was precisely what Clara wanted to hear, and she returned to Chicago with a view that perhaps everything was going to work out.

By September, Maud had moved back to Washington. Whether this was as a result of a suggestion by Clara or Leonard, we don't know. It would undoubtedly have Clara thinking that the location was more convenient for Leonard to sneak away to if he was still involved with Maud.

> *Washington,*
> *512 8th Street, S.E.*
> *Sept. 11, 1893*
>
> *Dear Mrs. Colby,*
> *Your letters have been received, one last Monday morning, and one this morning. I would have written sooner but you said you were on your way to Beatrice, and I thought you would spend a few days there, and that it would be a week or two before you returned to Chicago....*
> *I would like to and want to go to Chicago, but I could not think of going without taking baby, for it is impossible for me to wean him before the early spring. He would never take a bottle, and of course he cannot eat food.... Baby's name has been decided on. His first name is Paul. .... But if I am to go, my baby must go too. I don't want to be an expense to you in any way, so if you don't think that I could make enough to pay my expenses I think I had better stay here.*
>
> *Yours truly, Maud.*

Clara wrote back, from her booth at the World's Fair, in an angry mood. She said, 'You have no right to think first of your selfish mother pain or pleasure; only of what is best for the child. You have sinned against the sweet confidence of trusting friendship. Used your maidenly grace and beauty to drag a man down instead of lifting him to nobler thoughts. Your sin is one that strikes back at every home in the land, and you have no right to consider yourself in the matter, only what is best for the baby. If you were going to reinstate yourself with your friends.... Give up the baby. I can give you a scholarship at Lincoln Business College ..... I cannot see how I can be of any material aid if you do not give up the baby nor will I consent to any deception on my part.'

One of Clara's last engagements in Chicago that year was the Congress of the Association for the Advancement of Women, which commenced on Wednesday, October 4. The World's Fair came to a close on October 30, 1893, which meant that after October, any further discussion about Maud going to Chicago would be pointless. Clara stayed until the end.

During the Congress, Zintka Lanuni had been brought from Madison to join Clara in Chicago. She entered the nursery at the Children's building, where she became the child who caused the greatest stir.

She is the adopted daughter of Mrs. Colby of Washington and is now between three and four years old. ... She evinces strong likes and dislikes, and although she was in the nursery daily for one month, there was only one nurse, Maggie, that she would go to, and to her she clung all the time. Her 'likes' included all men, and there was never any difficulty in getting her to go to them and stay with them, but if Maggie left her in one room to go into another she would raise a regular war-whoop and never desist until her favorite had returned.[5]

Clara returned home to Washington in November, and she was followed soon after by Leonard, who joined her in December. Both of them resolved to make a new start on their marriage.

Leonard had resigned his position with the previous administration, reluctantly leaving official life and a $5,000 a year salary. Since his departure, he had been traveling among the Indian tribes of the territories and reservations in the West. He planned to act as attorney in Washington for the various tribes of Indians, defending them in the court of claims against suits brought under the Indian depredation act. He had already entered into contracts with many tribes, and when Congress opened, he was full of enthusiasm and ready to present his agreements. His contract with the Creek nation was reported to be worth $4,000 per annum.

The tribes, in turn, honored him. General Colby had already received a title from the Cheyennes, by which he would be known hereafter among the tribes. It was, 'Hata-Sha-Wa-ha-Mah-Ta,' meaning 'The Man Who Smiles When You Sign.'

Leonard was busy in the next few months, arguing before the federal court on behalf of his Indian clients, the Cherokee Nation, in a case involving the sale of the Cherokee Outlet. Clara's friend, Belva Lockwood, as the attorney for the Eastern band of the Cherokee Indians, filed a petition that they are allowed to intervene and become parties to the case. They maintained that they were part of the Cherokee tribe and so were entitled to a pro-rata share of the $8,595,736 that the United States had agreed to pay the Cherokee Nation. The matter was resolved in April, when General Colby was successful in one particular suit. This resulted in turning over to the Indians $6,740,000the proceeds of the settlement of the Cherokee strip bond question.

The issue of Maud and her baby continued to plague the relationship between Clara and Leonard. Leonard swore that he was not seeing her, but evidence of them having contact was undeniable. Maud even admitted the same in her letter to Clara.

You ask me why I wrote to Mr. C. and how it was that I received money from him. My reason for writing was that baby was sick, and that I feel it my duty to tell him of it, for baby is his as well as mine, and I cannot see that it was a breach of confidence toward you for me to write to him under the circumstances. If baby had not recovered when he did I would have written again. When I wrote I told him how much money I had. He gave me some the day I left Washington, and naturally, he would want to know if I had any of it left, and how it was spent. So he sent me enough to pay my expenses for another week, and my board is now paid up..... To write to him as your husband may not be right, but to write to him as my child's father informing him of the child's illness is not an unpardonable wrong; it does not seem so to me.

You know I want your help and that I appreciate what you do for me. Don't have hard feelings toward me, but be my true friend as you have been always. My lot is so hard to bear and I need all the help I can. Write to me soon.

Yours sincerely, M.[6]

It seemed that both Clara and Leonard were sending Maud money and Clara wanted to restrict the contact so that only she would be in touch with Maud. On February 28, Clara wrote to Maud.

There is no money in our firm for family or other expenses save as I furnish it, and has not been for nearly two months: this condition must exist yet a while longer. I mention this that you may understand why I must figure down just the amount you need to have. .... I can give you no sympathy or friendship while you persist in writing to that party. I forgave the past and would stand by you as if you were my sister in any effort to make reparation or to live an honorable life in the future, but I have no tolerance or charity for such continuance of wrong-doing as is implied by your writing to him. You can take your choice. If you want my friendship, countenance or assistance you have to merit it, by showing a desire to break off all dishonorable relations and communications.

Hoping that you will receive this in a right spirit and respond to it as you were now standing before the bar of God where you must some day answer for all the sins not repented of here.[7]

Clara decided to move Maud to the boarding house in Philadelphia where she had stayed when she first became pregnant. This arrangement did not last long, as Clara received the following letter showing that the owner, Mrs. Watson, decided that Maud could not stay, most likely because Leonard was visiting her there.

1729 Vine St. Phila.
March 2, 1894

My dear Madam,
As I suppose you are interested in the welfare of Mrs. Miller, I will tell you a few things which may be of use to you. She was here only a short time before it was evident something was amiss. We thought she was the victim of misfortunes and she had our deepest sympathy. We have since had reason to believe that she was not blameless. We could not have allowed her to remain here as long except from consideration of her youth and interest in her dear little child to whom she seemed thoroughly attached.

She went from here to No. 3346 Lancaster Ave. saying she expected to stay there a few days waiting for some letter or letters, then go to Washington before going to her parents in the West. If she has a home and parents and you have any influence over her, I trust she may be persuaded to go there as soon as possible.

I must also add, in my own behalf, that you placed me in a very trying and questionable situation which even your interest in Mrs. Miller could not justify.

Believe me very truly yours, Mary H. Watson.[8]

On the same day, Clara received a letter from Maud, written from a new address in Philadelphia. Maud outlined her expenses, and she complained that she could not be expected to wash diapers. Maud asked Clara for a pass to go back to Nebraska for two or three months. She said, 'I am living here with Mrs. Spencer, who was a superintendent of a children's home, so I feel perfectly safe in leaving Paul with her when I go west. She would charge $20.00 a month to look after him.' She went on to say, 'I received a letter from home yesterday and the folks are looking for me now, and unless they see me very soon, I know there will be trouble, my sister's letter says so. It is now just one year and a half since I was home and no satisfactory explanation.'

Her letter was written as blackmail, for Maud knew that Clara would pay up to avoid the scandal from going public, hurting her husband's position and her work in the suffrage movement. It appeared that Maud was more clever than she seemed and she continued to receive money from Clara and Leonard. The letters kept coming in the same manner with Clara trying hard to cut contact between Maud and Leonard, and Maud asking for money for her living expenses.

By the end of March, Maud had found someone to care for her baby, and she left for Nebraska, using a rail pass supplied by Clara. She wrote the following undated letter from Chicago.

Chicago,
Friday noon.

Dear Friend,

I am this far on my way home and expect to arrive there tomorrow at about three. I did not leave Paul at that home, as I told you I would, but with a nice kind woman, who I know will be good to him. I gave her your address in case anything happens to him or me. I felt sure you would think it all right, and that you were willing to help Paul and me that much. God only knows what a struggle it was for me to give him up at the last moment, but I knew it would not be long before I saw him again. I feel so lost without him in my arms.

You must not be hard and cold toward me, and please don't be so. It would make life almost too hard to bear if you should turn against me too, for then I would have no one to go to in my troubles. My heart is almost broken as it is; baby and I seem to be so utterly alone in the world.

Please write to me, and write just Beatrice, do not give the house number, - I will call for the letters myself. I will write you as soon as I get home.

Dear Mrs. Colby, don't make things any harder by turning against me now.

Sincerely, Maud[9]

Leonard told Clara that he was not making much money from what he initially thought was going to be a lucrative contract with the Indian tribes, even though his deal with the Creek nation alone paid him $4,000 per annum. So, he chose to spend much of 1894 back in Nebraska, taking court-appointed cases and fighting off his creditors. Perhaps the opportunity to continue his affair with Maud might have had something to do with it.

Susan B. Anthony was losing faith in Clara Colby during this time. She believed that Clara had taken on too many commitments outside of the cause for woman suffrage, and she was opposed to the idea of Clara taking Zintka with her on official suffrage business. On May 26, 1894, she wrote:

As to your proposition to take the Indian baby to meetings with you, I say No, most emphatically. ... You would distract the thought from the one point of woman's enfranchisement, and turn to adoption of Indian babies, the amalgamation of the races, and all sorts of side thoughts.... My dear, it is a crazy thought, you had better not go into another state campaign than to exhibit that untutored Indian girl of yours – so don't think of it.

Lovingly yours, Susan B. Anthony.[10]

Clara was planning to stay in Washington during June, but she did have some time planned with Susan in New York State in September, followed by a month in Kansas in October, so she would have to make sure she had someone to take care of Zintka during those trips.

In previous years Clara had spent the summer months in Nebraska, but in 1894 she stayed in Washington, where one would think she would not have a busy schedule. But, being Clara, she would find things to fill her time. In June, she attended the Washington Peace Society, which was run by her friend, Belva Lockwood. Here, she proposed a motion to send the President a protest against military force in settlement of disputes, along with protesting the large expenditure on useless armaments. She was also involved in discussing questions to be placed at the next Universal Congress, to be held in Antwerp. Her involvement would subsequently lead to Clara being selected as a delegate at a future international congress.

If there was any campaign against injustice going on, you could be sure that Clara would be involved. That year, the Industrial Army movement was actively campaigning for unemployed industrial workers, and they had set up Coxey's Camp in Washington as part of their campaign to lobby congress. As the Editor of the *Woman's Tribune*, Clara was invited to join a group taking a tally-ho, to ride out to Coxey's Camp for the evening.

Her article appeared in the next issue of the *Tribune*, giving the Industrial Army the publicity they wanted directly to the women of America. Ever the critic, Miss Anthony did not approve of the *Tribune* covering other causes than suffrage.

June in Washington is usually hot and humid, but that year the heat was very intense, compounding Clara's feeling of exhaustion and mental anguish, which had been building after the affair of Leonard and Maud. Zintka was also not well, and so reluctantly, Clara did something she rarely did: she consulted a doctor. The doctor diagnosed whooping cough in Zintka and administered medicine that may well have saved her life. Taking one look at Clara, he prescribed a vacation for the two of them, suggesting a rest at the seashore, where the air would be bracing.

This vacation would result in the *Woman's Tribune* missing the edition of July 7, resulting in Miss Anthony writing to Mrs. Stanton that Mrs. Colby had given up her paper for the summer.

Not one to miss an opportunity to network and learn from her professional colleagues, Clara remembered that the upcoming National Editorial Association's annual conference was at Asbury Park, New Jersey, a beautiful place to relax by the sea. She found a three-room cabin close to the beach, within walking distance of the conference at Asbury Park Auditorium, and she was able to trade the accommodation for free advertising in the *Tribune*. Clara and Zintka spent their days walking the beach and out on the jetty; they built sandcastles and collected shells. Leonard's rejection of Clara and his fading interest in his adopted daughter brought them closer together, and they relished their time at the seaside resort.

True to her driven nature, this vacation resulted in an article for the next issue of the *Tribune*, covering the events of the editors and journalists of the National Editorial Association.

The sea air cleared Clara's mind. She decided that she and Zintka should travel back to Beatrice in August to catch up with Leonard and spend time with her sister Mary, the one person with whom she could discuss her marital problems. She knew that Leonard would be at the annual camp of the Nebraska National Guard until August 21st, so she would arrive in Beatrice before him. She had to leave Beatrice for her tour of upstate New York with Susan Anthony at the latest by September 4th.

Poor Clarence had to be left at boarding school while Clara and Zintka traveled back to Beatrice. Zintka was excited to be going to stay with her cousins, Charlotte, Dorothy, Sadie, and Eva, who ranged in ages from 9 to 19. Mary took one look at Clara and knew something was wrong.

Clara confided in Mary the whole sad story: how Maud had run away, only to disclose that she had become pregnant last year in Beatrice; how Clara helped her find a solution to the unwanted pregnancy, finding her a place to stay until after the baby was born. Then the letter received from the lady with whom Maud was staying, revealing Maud's lie about the baby's father, and Clara's realization that the father was Leonard. She reflected on the confrontation with Leonard and the promise from him that she longed to believe: that he was sorry and wanted to stand by Clara.

Mary was not surprised at Leonard's behavior, but she was sure that he would have no interest in a permanent relationship with this servant girl, thirty years his junior. The scandal of divorce was bad enough, but Mary could hardly believe that he would do so for a relationship with such a young and low-bred woman. Leonard loved moving in influential circles; he so enjoyed Clara's social events, rubbing shoulders with influential people, all the way up to the President. That life would be closed to him forever if he was to get divorced and marry his servant girl. She reassured Clara that there was hope for the future of the marital relationship.

A few days later, General Colby returned to Beatrice and a reunion of sorts took place. Both parties were cautious in their comments and body language, and Leonard continued to express his regret and his undertaking to change. Clara tried to be as warm and welcoming as she could. A revival of their love affair would take time, yet that was something they did not have. Clara would be in Beatrice for a week at the most, and during that time, Leonard had a court case in Lincoln, which meant that he would be away one or two nights. Leonard had his law practice and the National Guard, while Clara had her suffrage activities and the *Tribune*, so each of them was responsible for stealing time that could be spent together.

Clara still loved Leonard and wanted nothing more than to have him back as the partner she remembered from years past. She could not help feeling suspicious, however, especially being in the bedroom which Maud had shared. She wondered whether she had been here in recent days. She read into comments from neighbors and local service people that they knew about Leonard's cheating behavior but were too polite to say anything. Nothing felt right about the situation, and the old house no longer felt like the family home. She had to get out and get back into her other life, or she would break down in depression.

Clara was going to be on the road for the next two weeks before she returned to Washington, and then she would be in Kansas for the whole month of October. So Zintka was left with Mary and the girls. She would collect her before returning to Washington from Kansas.

CHAPTER 13

ON WITH THE CAMPAIGN

CLARA SET OFF FOR her speaking tour of New York State, where she would meet up with Susan Anthony. In the summer of 1894, New York State was holding a convention to revise its Constitution. Unfortunately for the suffragists, the vote for women was defeated. But Susan Anthony took little time to mourn the loss and, as was her way, she encouraged her followers to yet again plead the cause of woman suffrage.

After an overnight train journey, Clara arrived at Salamanca, south of Buffalo, where she was the guest of Dr. and Mrs. Alice Hamilton. She then went over with friends to the Cattaraugus County Fair, where she was the speaker on the Thursday. The record of her visit appeared in the *Woman's Tribune*:

In connection with this pleasant visit I must not neglect to mention a lovely ride with Mrs. Gibson along the Allegheny River, and among the Onondagas, who have their school, church and council house where they manage their affairs and live like white people. We chatted with an intelligent Indian, around whom was playing his pretty little daughter and a white boy about the same age who had been deserted by his parents when a baby and was being brought up by this Indian family as their own.[1]

By noon of April 8, Clara was eating dinner with Miss Anthony at her house in Rochester, where she remained in what she called a 'restful atmosphere of systematic work' for the next three days; she was preparing an address for the Religious Congress in nearby Erie. During this time, 'Aunt Susan' flitted in and out for speaking evenings at nearby points, and 'Sister Mary' (Anthony's sister) continued the package bundling and mailing, which had been ongoing since the NY campaign had begun. 'No one had done more for the campaign in New York than Sister Mary,' Clara wrote. 'To give up her quiet, orderly ways and be overrun with desks and workers filling up four rooms in the house is no small sacrifice for a woman in her 67th year, to say nothing of performing the very arduous labor of mailing petition books, bulletins, and literature of all kinds.'

They spent Sunday afternoon at the country home of Colonel and Mrs. Greenleaf, a rambling old farmhouse on the shore of Lake Ontario. It was among the rural delights of meadows slanting down to the lake; of woods full of knolls; of Jersey cows, blooded horses and all the accessories of a model farm. Mrs. Greenleaf had spent, at her own expense, every energy towards securing the freedom of the women of New York, from May until the vote in August at Albany.

Leaving Rochester for Erie, Clara stopped overnight at Buffalo as a guest of Dr. Sarah Morris. She described Dr. Morris as a most delightful physician and philanthropist, as well as President of the local Political Equality Club. The club held its monthly meeting that evening, at which Clara was invited to address the group.

The Religious Congress of the semi-centennial of the Universalist church was held in Erie on the next day. This Congress was modeled on the Parliament of Religions, which had been held in Chicago the previous year. It attracted an audience from a group of liberal denominations, and speakers across the country. Clara was presenting her paper on the 'Philosophy of Woman Suffrage,' which she had been preparing in Rochester. The next morning she gave a presentation on the subject of 'Dress,' a subject which she had often spoken and written about, comparing her desire for emancipation from the tyranny of fashion to that of her passion for political rights.

Her report in the *Tribune* described Erie as a favored spot, where almost all the working people own their dwellings. She particularly thanked her hosts, Dr. and Mrs. Hall, where she stayed for two nights.

The next day was a full day of travel, through central New York to Amsterdam on the Mohawk River, just north of Albany. Here, Clara was staying with the family of Mr. George VanDeveer, whose name would go down in history as the one man who stood with the women to champion their cause at the NY Constitutional Convention.

The VanDeveer's country home was set amidst a unique landscape, with a beautiful view of Amsterdam. A Granger picnic was being held in their yard the following day. The Granger movement was a fraternal order, established by farmers during the late 1860s to protest perceived victimization of the agricultural sector by railroads, banks, and other moneyed interest. Members of the Granger movement worked hard toward achieving significant economic and political goals, but they also took time to have fun, hence the picnic day.

Clara had the opportunity to speak about the suffrage movement, which many of the farmer's wives supported. This resulted in the formation of a local suffrage society and the election of a President, a Vice President, and a Secretary. Clara then went into the town, where she was scheduled to make another address that evening.

Amsterdam was the last stop on the speaking tour of New York State. Now Clara could return home to Washington in time to publish the next issue of the *Tribune* and make preparations for her upcoming tour of Kansas, which meant she had less than a week at home before she headed west.

The NAWSA had committed to sending speakers during October 1894 to work with the Populist party in Kansas. The Populists, also known as the People's Party, were an alternative party to the republicans and the democrats, who had gained leadership during the 1890s in the Midwest. Plus, they were a party which supported the women's vote. Clara had been assigned to speak at towns and villages across the north of the State, starting in Washington County on October 1st.

Usually, she would have started the trip from her home in Beatrice, but having no time to spare and not knowing what reception she might receive, she planned to travel straight through. On arrival in Hanover, she was intercepted with a telegram to inform her that she would be required to speak at Hollenberg that night. The change necessitated getting off the train and taking a twelve-mile horse-and-buggy ride across the country. It had been raining all day, and the water fell in torrents during the drive, soaking Clara to the skin. Although they made the trip in two hours, by the time she arrived in Hollenberg, the event had been canceled. The organization of the Populist Party was not looking good on the first day of this tour.

The next night, her event was at the Opera House in Washington, Kansas, followed by an evening at the village of Linn: an area with a significant German Lutheran element. No woman had ever spoken there before, nor had any woman suffrage speech been given. The event drew the largest audience ever seen in the village, with country people coming from as far as fifteen miles. Here she met Mr. James Pontius, a school teacher from twelve miles out, who was the author of a little pamphlet called 'Common Sense Thoughts About Equal Suffrage.'

Concordia was the next stop, where she was the guest of a long-time *Tribune* reader. First, she spoke at a day meeting, where the local congressman for the district took up most of the speaking time; so in response, the chairman urged Clara to return for the evening session and speak there too. As with many of the events which Clara spoke at, the speeches were followed by entertainment, which at Concordia was provided by a talented colored singer. Sometimes, there was a festive atmosphere designed to encourage people to attend and listen to the messages that candidates had to bear. In Vermillion, Clara was staying at a hotel, from which she and some of the candidates for election were escorted in the evening to the meeting place by a brass band and a procession of villagers, which included all the boys of the neighborhood. At the door of the school-house, the band made a double file for the speakers to pass through. They were also escorted back to the hotel and serenaded before dispersing.

Getting from one town to another was not easy, and the organizers had not taken account of the many connections required to make some of the cross-country journeys. Clara took many forms of transport, including 'riding the cars,' horse and buggy, riding a horse and even taking a freight train. At the town of Holton, she had a wait of ten hours for the train to Topeka. Here at least she was able to visit a friend who had provided articles for the *Tribune*. Mrs. Ella Brown was the city attorney of Holton and the author of a book on Parliamentary Law.

Topeka was her next stop, where she spent two days with the Woman's Progressive Political League. Many of the ladies showed great interest in Clara's views on dress reform. The next two towns were St. Mary's and St. Clere, alongside the reservation of the Potawatomi Indians. Here she visited the offices of the local newspaper, only to find that her next speaking events at Dunlap and Wreford had been double-booked. These towns were at least fifty miles apart, so the only choice was to telegraph Wreford to see if they would defer their event to the following evening, to which she received a favorable response.

The change of the Wreford booking to the Sunday night made the journey to the next town of Mankato a difficult one. An overland drive of four miles took her to Junction City for a short night's rest before she made the 4.45 am freight train for Concordia. Clara intended to telegraph from Concordia to say she would drive the forty miles across the country and be there in time. Unfortunately, the freight train was two hours late, so there was nothing to do but wait for the late afternoon train. She reached Mankato at a little after 6.00 pm, only to find she had missed a big meeting of over 6,000 people. It took Clara some time before she could get in touch with the committee. They felt that the enthusiasm of the afternoon had been so high they did not want to weaken the impression by an impromptu meeting. So this opportunity was lost, along with her long day's journey.

The organization skills of the Populists were now looking pretty thin, but Clara remained positive about the party. She considered what they had done for the amendment in Kansas, arranging meetings for advocacy and being willing to share the time of their regular speakers with the suffragists. Confirmation of her positive view came at her next experience, which was in Junction City. The chairman at a big Populist rally gave Clara half an hour at the close of both the afternoon and evening sessions to address the crowd that filled the courthouse yard.

So far, the campaign was blessed by beautiful weather, but this came to an end at a rally in Abilene. Six thousand people remained for two hours, mostly standing, virtually baptized with the suffrage colors in the falling leaves of the cottonwood and box elder... until the Kansas Zephyr became a dust tornado and the speakers were fairly choked off. Here, Clara was on the regular program, following the Governor in an evening address to a crowded opera house.

From Abilene, she spoke at Milford, north of Junction City, and then took the overnight train to Colby, followed by a twenty-mile drive to Oakley, for the first of three appointments in Logan County. She was caught in another dust storm during the trip to Oakley. This one was so furious that a commercial traveler at the hotel said he would not take the ride for a hundred dollars.

On arrival at Oakley, the appointments had changed, and it was actually two days later that she was to speak in Oakley, but she had to talk in Russell Springs that day, some thirty miles distant. She hired another livery rig and made the trip, only to discover that the appointment for that day would be in Winona, another thirteen miles away. She pushed on for Winona and eventually found a group that was expecting her. She returned overland to Russell Springs for a meeting and back to Winona in time to take the train to Oakley. By this time, she had ridden overland by horse and buggy for eighty-six miles and she had spoken at two points farther west than any suffrage speakers had gone before.

Most of Clara's travels in Kansas were written up in the *Tribune*, with the above taken from her last report before the fate of the amendment was announced. In this she seemed confident that the vote would be carried. 'Hurrah for the third star in our suffrage flag,' she wrote, meaning that Kansas would be the third state after Wyoming and Colorado gave women the vote. Sadly, that was not to be the case, as Kansas defeated the amendment in 1894, but went on to vote again in 1912, when they passed the vote. Kansas also ratified the Nineteenth Amendment on June 16, 1919.

Upon Clara's return home, the *Washington Times* gave her a favorable report.

> *The Suffrage Association was addressed by Mrs. Clara Colby of the Woman's Tribune, in a most eloquent manner, her subject being: 'The outlook in Kansas.' Mrs. Colby was one of the prominent speakers for the amendment, during the late campaign, she had information from headquarters and handled her subject, as she does every other, with master hand. Her language was logical, clear, concise, inspiring and carried with it the conviction she feels.*
>
> *She attributed the defeat of the woman's cause in Kansas, amongst others, to the opposition of the liquor interests; she thought that this was preliminary to the 'resubmission of prohibition of the liquor traffic.'*
>
> *Mrs. Colby is a clear-headed, educated brilliant woman; she is a fine logician, a companionable wife, and a gentle, tender, loving mother to her interesting, winsome, half-savage adopted Indian baby, little 'Lost Bird'.[2]*

Upon her return to Washington, Clara received a letter from Maud, updating her on the fact that she had enrolled in a college.

> *Western Normal College*
> *Lincoln, Nebraska*
> *November 21, 1894*
>
> *My Dear Friend,*
> *I want to let you know that I have started in school and that I will like it very much. My expenses are more than I*

thought they would be, but I think by careful management I will be able to get along all right; at any rate, I shall do my best. The studies I have taken are arithmetic, geography, chemistry, advanced German, besides drills in reading, debating and letter writing.

The only thing that may hinder me in my studies will be my eyes, for I find it simply impossible to study at night, and I can only read a few minutes at a time; they give me such pain in my head. I think my general health, which is not of the best, has a good deal to do with the poor condition of my eyes at present.

I do hope you will pass through Philadelphia soon, and that you can stop and see my little one. I am so anxious. I wish you would write me. I am lonely and sometime I feel I must unburden my heart to someone or I cannot stand it any longer. I will write you oftener than I have been and will let you know how I get along. Write me freely and always believe me.

Yours sincerely, Maud

In writing to me here put all mail in care of Western Normal College and address Marie, not Maud.

Good news came to Leonard Colby from Washington on December 15, as reported in the *Nebraska State Journal*.

CAN FIND NO FRAUD
Complete Vindication of General Colby of Nebraska
Corrupt Practices Charged Against Him Fail to
Materialize

There is a good chance that the Indian depredation claims allowed by the court of claims and were held up by the ap-

propriations committee in the last congress, will be fully allowed at the present session. ... The action was rendered necessary by the persistent fight made by Senator Chandler upon the office of Assistant Attorney-General Colby. The fight was caused by a disagreement between General Colby and a clerk named Corning, appointed at the request of Senator Chandler and who made numerous charges against the conduct of the office. ... The attorney-general's office at once proceeded to investigate the charges, and Mr. Corning, the clerk, was sent as a special agent to prove some of the allegations made. The attorney-general's office has utterly failed to discover any evidence of fraud in the claims so thoroughly sifted by the court of claims.[3]

Leonard Colby did sail close to the wind in many of his business and government dealings, and he may have gotten away with some corrupt behavior in this case, but this was not the only case in which he was involved. The chief of the Muskogee Indians, Chief Perryman, was charged with unlawfully paying $4,000 to General Colby on a contract that had been abrogated by the council. In 1893, General Colby secured the appointment as the Washington-based attorney for the Creeks for a term of three years at $12,000. He drew $4,000 for his first year's service, but the next council determined that General Colby's services were not required and repealed the contract. Colby came down to the Indian Territory at once to look after his claim. He quickly secured an opinion of the Supreme Court judges that it was unconstitutional for the council to repudiate a contract it had entered into, and on the basis of this, the chief released General Colby's second year's pay and the treasurer cashed it.[4]

Clara knew nothing about these payments, as the news was limited to little-read papers like the *Muskogee Phoenix*, from the Indian territory, and no information about the fees appeared in the city newspapers in the East. All this time, Leonard was crying poor and even borrowing money from Clara. Meanwhile, she was running the Washington home, supporting Clarence and Zintka, and sending cash to Maud. Since the NAWSA no longer endorsed the *Woman's Tribune*, Clara spent much of her time looking for financial support to maintain its regular publication; she did this successfully.

Contrasting with the reports of Colby's shady dealings with the Indians were positive reports of the excellent work that he put in on behalf of his indigenous clients—although it was his friends who published these positive reports at the *Nebraska State Journal*.

In January of 1895, General Colby passed through Lincoln on his way to Washington, where he expected to represent his clients—the Cherokee, Creeks, and Seminoles—for several weeks. He said he would vigorously oppose any partitioning of their lands or interference with treaties that already existed.

The General had spent five weeks in the Indian territory, during which time he rode 600 miles, visiting various prominent Indians. He denounced ex-Senator Dawes' report of the condition of affairs in the territory as false, and expressed a desire to be heard before the Senate committee on Indian affairs, before they recommended legislation suggested by the Dawes Commission.

After this, Leonard returned to Washington, expecting to stay for several weeks, which would mean a New Year reunion for himself and Clara. Clara was scheduled to leave for Atlanta at the end of January for the Annual Convention of the NAWSA, but at least she could spend almost four weeks with Leonard and, hopefully, reassure herself that they still had a future together. Unfortunately, this was not to be, because by January 15, he was reported to be back in Lincoln at a meeting of the State Historical Society.

Certainly, Leonard was a busy man, and by the end of January, he had formed a new law partnership with G. R. Chaney. Together they occupied Colby's handsome offices in the First National bank building. He had also expressed a desire to get back to running an active military campaign and had written to the President of Mexico offering to command a force in case of war with Guatemala.

According to the *Nebraska State Journal* of February 2, 1895, his desire was not a bluff.

'He wants to go and believes he would experience no difficulty in placing 20,000 fighting Americans at the disposal of President Diaz.' The next day's paper reported that 'General Colby is disconsolate over a report from Mexico that the war with Guatemala has been declared off.' How strange that Leonard was so keen to exercise his military skills in warfare, while his wife Clara was active in the Peace Congress.

The *Tribune* regularly published a section called Zintka Lanuni's Corner, in which Clara wrote articles about Zintka's progress, interests, and adventures. Occasionally, Clara wrote that little Zintka missed her Papa, but in reality, 'Papa' had lost interest in his living relic from the Indian war and the truth was that it was Clara that missed Leonard, not Zintka.

The little 'Lost Bird' is never so pleased as when running errands for the TRIBUNE, folding papers, carrying copy; and whether helping or hindering, having a finger in every pie. She delights to be called the TRIBUNE maid. So it is but fair to give her a little corner of it, all her own, where the poems and stories she is especially fond of may have place, and to which she can invite the little folks of other families to send also their favorites for publication.⁵

One evening, Zintka and her friend went out walking and came back home carrying a large grey cat. To which Clara said, 'Why Zintka, that is somebody's pet cat.'

'Oh, no,' she replied. 'It is nobody's kitty.'

Clara placed the cat back outside so that it could find its way home and soothed Zintka's feelings by reading one of her favorite poems.

Nobody's kitty was out in the snow,
Nobody's kitty had nowhere to go,
Nobody's kitty cried: 'Miew, miew, miew!'
Somebody pity me. Do, do, do!⁶

The next issue of Zintka's Corner introduced children to the custom of Egg-rolling Day on Easter Monday. There was no school in session, so for about five hours the White House grounds belonged to the children, who rolled their hard-boiled eggs down the grassy knolls around the house. The article explained, 'The White House is where the President lives, but which does not belong to him, but belongs to everybody in the nation. It is a very pretty sight to see the children going in every direction in the morning with their dainty baskets filled with colored eggs and some goodies for lunch besides.'

Two years previously, Zintka had enjoyed seeing the larger children play, and then go with her companion to shake hands with President Cleveland. This year, she was old enough to frolic with the rest.

Clara would take Zintka with her whenever she could. The stories of her trips often appeared in Zintka's Corner. When Clara was lecturing in Rhode Island, she and Zintka stayed for a week at the home of a friend who had two daughters, Helen and Aimee, of about Zintka's age. When they finally said goodbye to these friends, they took the train to visit Clarence at his school, where they spent the day climbing a high peak to take in the view.

The thing that most interested Zintka that day was a chicken-hawk that flew close to their heads and had a snake in its mouth. There was a battle in the air, as some smaller birds tried to get the snake from the hawk. While watching the scene, Zintka began repeating a little rhyme of which she is very fond:

> *Then stay at home my heart, and rest,*
> *The bird is safest in its nest,*
> *O'er all that flutter their wings and fly,*
> *A hawk is hovering in the sky.*[7]

In 1895, Atlanta was the site of the Cotton States and International Exposition. The expo featured the Woman's Building, designed by Pennsylvania's first woman architect, to display the accomplishments of women. The suffragists gathered in Atlanta at the end of January for the 27th annual convention of the National American Suffrage Association. Being located in the south, the conference was segregated; it seems that even within this socially progressive movement, racism persisted. Clara attended as the delegate representing both Nebraska and Washington.

It was here that Elizabeth Cady Stanton, sensing that Clara was in some financial difficulty, offered to assist in any way she could. The possibility that 'the best suffrage paper ever published' might fold brought Mrs. Stanton to the rescue. From 1895 until a year before her death in 1902, Stanton played a major role, as contributing editor of the *Woman's Tribune*. Stanton's involvement and her opinion pieces helped to keep the *Tribune* continuously in print. Clara urged Mrs. Stanton to write her memoirs for the *Tribune*. Often the two of them co-operated so closely together that it was difficult to determine who wrote which article. Stanton would send Clara a paragraph or two, adding, '... add something of your own and put your name on it.' Mrs. Stanton was unable to help Clara financially, but her involvement with the *Tribune* encouraged many of her followers to take up subscriptions and helped maintain its reputation as an official publication of the suffrage movement.

The *Tribune* did not have much financial support outside of its subscription base from that time on, and it certainly did not provide enough income to support Clara and her family. She augmented her income by lecturing on a range of subjects and by writing magazine articles. Her lectures often attracted a fee, but frequently she relied upon a share of the entrance fees of those who turned up, or a collection that was taken up for the speaker. Her requests for money from Leonard were generally unanswered. As for the conventions and speaking tours which she undertook as a delegate on behalf of various organizations, the organizer merely paid the travel and accommodation expenses.

In February, Leonard Colby returned to Washington, having been called there as a witness in several cases resulting from his Assistant Attorney-General days. Clara arrived back home from Atlanta at about the same time, so they could enjoy some time together which had eluded them in early January. The reunion was nothing like Clara had hoped for. Leonard displayed very little evidence of intending to move back to Washington on a more permanent basis. After he returned to Nebraska, she started to give up hope of ever attracting him back.

Back in Nebraska, her sister Mary heard the rumors about the brazen antics of her brother-in-law, and she watched on in anger as the new law office of Colby and Chaney hired Miss Maud Miller as their private secretary. Most of the wealthy families of Beatrice had nothing to do with Colby, while Clara's women friends of many years simply ignored Maud. Clara wrote to Mary, asking her to meet with Leonard to inquire about his feelings towards Clara and to see if there was any possibility of getting him to put the affair with Maud behind him and come home to Washington. Mary responded from Madison, where she had moved to, and her letter devastated Clara.

Dr. Mary B. White
Madison, Wis.
May 14, 1895

My Dear Sister

I must write you a few lines even if I do not write to the girls tonight. We had a good trip home, stopped nearly all day in Salt Lake and enjoyed it very much. At Beatrice I saw a great many old friends, and was invited out every day somewhere. I went to see Mr. Colby because you wished it, and I had promised it. I gave your desire (for him to come and make a home) as best I could. He ridiculed the idea, said 'when he wanted to become a nun or enter a convent he would as soon live with you as not' and talked at length along that line, then I asked him if he would not provide for you, he said he had offered to but you would not have it. I said you came from a family that did not believe in divorce. He said you were a dog in a manger, well we talked at length along those lines. He read me his letters where he had generously sent Zintka 10.00 and 5.00 dollars respectively, and I call that generous for three years support. I told him you had given him all your young days and that as a man he couldn't cut you off in your old age without any support. Well as I came through the hall I discovered that low creature had left the doors open just far enough to hear everything. I was so angry to think I had not noticed it before so that I might have banged them shut.

Well the next day after that I heard a story that makes your suffering seem light, but also shows you can never move that man to mercy, to say nothing of decency. He had a mistress long years ago by whom he had three children, he took a little child to this woman to care for and bring up, the son of another woman, he then deserted her, left her to take in washing or anything else she could find to do, and never provided her with so much as one dollar, the 4 children are living now – I know their names and address – there is no mistake about it, you know their mother – I did slightly – but a gentle, refined, educated, beautiful girl. She soon lost her beauty by that life – neglect and poverty. She died about a year ago and the children do not know who their father is, but her brother and her people do.

It was while she was toiling to support her family and this boy, that he had his children by Miss Frazier and then got her property – the old Col Sabin House away from her– then she had to go the same way Mary Davis did. I do not know how old Miss Miller's child is, but the youngest girl of the family I am telling you about is about 13 years. This with Miss Frazier's in between or about that time does not proclaim him very abstemious, neither does it argue much for your ever winning him back to a decent life.

I was used up; not with hearing this story but by the proof of it, and was still mad at the thought of that door being open – so I phoned down – 'Was he in? No! Was this his stenographer? Yes! Well you give him this message for me. This is Mrs. White, tell him that I know where his three children by one woman and the one by another one and I can tell him all about them. He has lost track of them for several years and I can give him any information about them he wishes, if he will phone or write.' She said with great impudence 'I think you'd better write.' I said, 'you give him my message and he'll decide which to do.'

In the pm, I was asked for – was not in and a message left to call up the office, which I did three times, but could get no response, and I left the next morning. Now if you believe this – which is not likely as you have never believed anything against him – if you wish to know the names, and where they are you must in your letter promise not to use the information to make the relatives any trouble, especially the brother who has devoted his life – since old enough to earn a living for them and he takes care of them now that *the mother is dead. The boy he took to her never knew he was not her son, and is now a worker in cut glass, and is a fine looking fellow they say.*

Darling sister I would not have written all this but I think you ought to know, and perhaps you will at last cease to try to get him back. Though I am less in favor of a divorce now than ever, as they say Miss M will move heaven and earth to give her boy a name, even tells he is going to get a divorce and marry her.

God bless and help you. Write soon.
Your loving sister
Mary[8]

As distressing as the contents of this letter were, Clara still tried to convince herself that she could contemplate a future with Leonard. She was scheduled to visit with her sister in Madison to attend the commencement at Wisconsin State University, where Sadie, Mary's oldest daughter, was graduating. Mary was able to reinforce her opinion that Clara was only causing herself great unhappiness by continually trying to get Leonard back, but she provided no further reports of Leonard's promiscuous behavior.

From Madison, Clara returned Nebraska to attend the 14th convention of the Nebraska WSA. Once more, Clara was elected as President of the association. She visited the house in Beatrice but did not see Leonard, nor the 'low creature', as Mary called Maud. It was an emotive time, recalling the happy years of planning and building the home, wandering through the rose garden which her hands had planted; all the time thinking of what treachery had transpired during her absence.

Even then, she believed that she could get Leonard back in a reunion, which would mean eternal salvation for him.

Clara continued to make speaking engagements during the next few months. In August, Clara was appointed as a committee member by the National Arbitration Association to lobby President Cleveland. They wanted to recommend to Congress the ratification of a permanent treaty of arbitration between the United States and France. Just another committee for another organization in which Clara could become involved. Susan Anthony's criticism that Clara had her fingers in too many pies was probably valid. In October, the Woman's National Press Association met in Atlanta at the Cotton States Exposition and Clara addressed the group on 'Woman's Debt to the Daily Press.'

Clara stayed in Atlanta into November to speak at the Woman's Suffrage meeting in Congress Hall on the subject of 'Woman's Suffrage in Wyoming.' Wyoming was admitted to the Union in 1890 as the first state that allowed women to vote, and in fact, it would not accept statehood without keeping women suffrage. Clara's presentation concentrated on the fact that no negative result had befallen Wyoming as a result, plus she added a few examples of positive results.

In November, it was the turn of the Association for the Advancement of Women, who held their conference at Newcomb Hall, New Orleans, starting on November 8th. At this conference, Clara chose to speak on 'The Philosophy of Women Suffrage.'

The speaker before Clara was Dr. Nellie Mark and her topic should have been of interest to Clara, for she was speaking on 'Divorce.'

November 12, 1895, was the 80th birthday of Elizabeth Cady Stanton, and the suffrage movement held celebrations from coast to coast. Clara and her colleagues sent a telegram from the AAW Conference in New Orleans to the event in New York.

'Fully 8,000 people', says Margherita Arlina Hamm, 'assembled in the Metropolitan Opera House in New York City to celebrate the 80th birthday anniversary of our honored leader, Elizabeth Cady Stanton. Every seat and box were sold and some re-sold at an enormous advance.'

The audience rose, cheering, and gave the Chautauqua Salute (the waving of a white handkerchief) upon the introduction of Mrs. Stanton. She thanked everyone for the tributes sent in telegrams and letters and expressed by this great audience. She apologized that she no longer could stand for long or speak loud enough for all to hear, and she invited Miss Helen Potter to read her paper on her behalf. She did prove that she was full of good health and vigor, however; after the lengthy ceremonies, she attended the reception given for her at the Hotel Savoy. Here she was presented with a silver 'loving cup,' bearing on one side the inscription, 'Presented to Elizabeth Cady Stanton 1815-1895,' and on the other side the motto: 'Defeated day by day, but unto victory born.' A motto which could equally apply to Clara Bewick Colby.

While this grand celebration—combined with local ones across the country—showed the enormous respect for this pioneer of the suffrage movement, another initiative of Mrs. Stanton and one which involved Clara and others was causing controversy, both within and without the suffrage movement. That event was the publication of Mrs. Stanton's *The Woman's*

Bible. The book consisted of comments on the Pentateuch (first five books of the Bible), as made by seven leading suffragists, including Clara Bewick Colby. It presented as a suggestion for a revised Bible version to better recognize women. The purpose of the revision was to refute the argument that the original book places a woman in an inferior position. Headlines such as the following in the *Boston Globe* resulted after excerpts of the book were published in the *Tribune.*

'Woman's Bible' a Bitter Attack Upon Christianity.
'It is a most bitter attack upon Christianity,' is the opinion expressed by one of the leading clergymen of the country, upon the much talked-about 'Woman's Bible,' part 1 of which is in print..... Clara Bewick Colby is quite orthodox when she exclaims at the end of the fourth chapter: 'Nothing can surpass in grandeur the account of the first chapter of Genesis of the creation of the race... ' She comments with a touch of sarcasm, however, when referring to Noah's Ark she remarks: 'the paucity of light and air in this ancient vessel shows that woman had no part in its architecture, or a series of portholes would have been deemed indispensable.'[9]

The criticisms were not limited to the Christian community, however, as Susan B. Anthony expressed serious disapproval. 'It seems to me that your espousal of the Woman's Bible and the publication of it in your paper, has cut off all possibility of your gathering around you the majority of suffrage women. The Woman's Bible is so flippant and superficial.'[10]

At the Next Convention of the NAWSA, held in Washington in January of 1896, the matter of the *Woman's Bible* became a big controversy. Clara decided that she should take a stand and defend the right of the *Tribune* to publish whatever it chose, and she made it very clear that she would not hesitate to give Mrs. Stanton's word on any given subject. Mrs. Stanton wrote to Clara stating that, '*The Woman's Bible* would have been a success if not for Susan and her cohorts,' meaning Susan B. Anthony, Reverend Anna Shaw, and Carrie Chapman Catt, the person who had taken over much of the engagements from Miss Anthony. Not for the first time, there was disagreement in the ranks of the senior members of the NAWSA.

In 1896, Clara was still living in the three-story house at 1325 10th Street, where Zintka would play in the small garden at the back of the house, but sometimes she ventured into the back alleys, where a different world existed. 'Zintka's Corner' in the *Tribune* reported on her experience of meeting with the neighbors behind the house.

Zintka has not failed to learn that there is prejudice against color, although she has never had to feel it on her own account. Washington is intersected with alleys, inhabited by negroes of the poorer class. The rule is that back of houses, tall, spacious and fair to see, there are small crowded tenements, whose tiny yards are usually filled with washing by which the women support their families. It does not need any color prejudice to necessitate very stringent rules that the child of the house shall not frequent the tenement of the alley. This restriction is made also by poor negro families who are so fortunate as to live on the streets. This latter class might feel their deprivation of playmates more were it not for their happy dispositions and their stolen snatches of pleasure with the white children who do not naturally object to their company because of color. It was one of these little neighbors that Zintka sought permission to play with in the hammock in the back yard. To head off any remonstrance, Zintka carefully stated her name and where she lived, adding: 'She is not very colored, only brown, about as dark as I am!' A little later she put her arm beside that of the little black girl and having made the discovery that there was not much difference in color, our little maid forthwith brought her friend to her mamma to show that she had stated the fact correctly.

Ex-consul Waller, of Madagascar called one evening with his wife at Zintka's home. This interesting and intelligent couple were quite the heroes of the occasion, but Zintka seemed to fear lest they might not feel quite at home. Laying her hand on Mrs. Waller's arm, she stood looking very sympathetically and earnestly into her face for some time, and then quietly said: 'I am not white neither!'[11]

Newspaper clippings for the years of 1896 and 1897 trace the trail of Clara Colby back and forth across America as she attended conferences and speaking engagements in support of woman suffrage and of the other associations of which she was a member. The year started with the 28th Convention of the National American Woman Suffrage Association in Washington DC on January 23rd to 28th, at which the controversy of *The Woman's Bible* made up a central part of the discussions.

By May, she was speaking in San Francisco at the Woman's Congress of the Pacific Coast, where she was supporting Miss Susan B. Anthony.

In July, she was in the mid-west, speaking at Chautauquas in South Dakota and Nebraska. The Chautauqua was an adult education movement which would set up large tents in a summer school format, in which they staged entertainment and educational events. In September, she traveled into Canada to speak at the Woman's Congress in Saint John, New Brunswick. She returned to Washington through Boston, before heading out to Abilene, Kansas for the Kansas Equal Suffrage Association.

In July, she was riding the cars again, this time up to Adams, Massachusetts, where she attended a reunion of the Anthony family. This time, she spoke in honor of Miss Anthony, paying tribute to her leadership of the suffrage movement. From August 12th to 14th she attended the Massachusetts Women's Congress at Onsett, where she made a presentation entitled 'From Eve to the New Woman.'

In September, Clara was back in Beatrice, staying with her sister Mary, before heading to Lincoln, Nebraska, for a two-day conference of the Nebraska Woman's Suffrage Association, of which she was still President. In October, she was back in Washington briefly, before heading back to Massachusetts to attend the 25th Annual Congress of the Association for the Advancement of Women in Springfield, Mass. Here, Clara's presentation was 'English Queens, their Influence on British Civilization.'

By December, she had been home long enough to attend the meeting of the 'Penwomen,' as the *Evening Star* referred to the Women's National Press Association.

Come January, the 1897 NAWSA Convention was held in Des Moines, Iowa, at which Clara made her report as Chair of the Plan of Work Committee. A discussion over her recommendation on the makeup of the management committee descended into a contest between the east and the west, and her proposition was defeated. Her proposal was opposed by Susan B. Anthony and Carrie Chapman-Catt of New York plus Anna Howard Shaw and Rachael Foster Avery, both of Pennsylvania. She did gain support for a proposal to retain a congressional committee, however, and informed a decision that the national executive would be left to elect the chairman.

After the NAWSA Convention, Clara returned to Washington through Lincoln, Nebraska, where she addressed both the State Senate and the House of Representatives. The NAWSA Convention decided to insist that the national organization should control State campaigns, where the national association gives aid. There seemed to be a difference developing between Clara– who wanted to concentrate on the Federal government–and the NAWSA, which wished to focus on the States, much as Olympia Brown had argued when forming the Federal Suffrage Association.

A month after the close of the Des Moines conference, the national executive of the NAWSA issued the following:

'Mrs. Clara B. Colby has been appointed the chairman of the congressional committee. In this capacity, she sends the *Women's Tribune* regularly free of charge, to every Senator and Member.'

No doubt she had gained some financial support from the association to cover her costs. Also, she had been looking ahead on the assumption that she would get that role, for she had already written to Chairman James Berry of the Senate Committee. His reply clarifies his stand on the issue, but he does leave the door open for her to present information for him and his colleagues.

> *Select Committee on Woman Suffrage*
> *United State Senate*
> *January 5, 1897*
>
> *Clara B. Colby*
> *Washington, D.C.*
> *Dear Madam,*
> *I have received your letter of the first of January in which you say that you will send to my Committee Room the Woman's Tribune, for which I thank you. You also say in your letter that you presume that one who is appointed Chairman of the Committee on Woman Suffrage is appointed by reason of his being familiar with the subject and because of his interest in furthering the same. You must not conclude from my appointment that I am in favor of woman suffrage. The appointment is not made for any such reason, and I have always been opposed to it. I will be very glad however to receive from you and lay before the Committee any papers or documents that you may see fit to send to me, and with the consent of the other members of the Committee will always be glad to give courteous hearing at all reasonable times to persons who are interested in the matter. Very respectfully*
> *James H Berry*
> *Chairman*[12]

In February of 1898, the National American Woman Suffrage Association held its annual convention at the Columbia Theatre in Washington DC. It would seem that Clara Colby was falling out of favor with this group. The association was probably led by her old mentor, Susan Anthony and her cohort, Carrie Chapman Catt. Clara ran for Vice-President, Treasurer, and Auditor, but was soundly defeated. She would still be involved as the Nebraska delegate and as Chair of the Congressional Committee.

11 Waterloo Place, Westminster, London.
The childhood home of Clara Bewick.
(Photograph courtesy of the London Metropolitan Archives.)

Clara in her student days
(Wisconsin Historical Society)

Stephen and Clara Chilton
(Wisconsin Historical Society)

The Colby residence in Beatrice, Nebraska.
(Wisconsin Historical Society)

Clara Bewick at about the time she graduated from Wisconsin University.
(Wisconsin Historical Society)

Elizabeth Cady Stanton
and
Susan B. Anthony

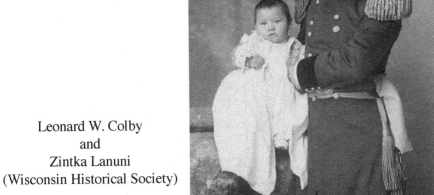

Leonard W. Colby
and
Zintka Lanuni
(Wisconsin Historical Society)

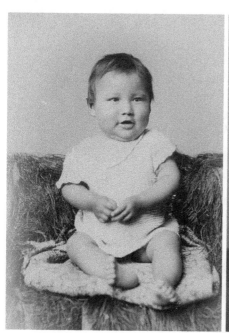

Zintka Lanuni Colby

Clara Bewick Colby

Suffragette demonstration in London in which Clara Colby marched with
the American delegates.
(New York Times, June 17, 1911.)

The Daily Mirror

THE MORNING JOURNAL WITH THE SECOND LARGEST NET SALE

No. 2,205. | Registered at the G.P.O. as a Newspaper. | SATURDAY, NOVEMBER 19, 1910 | One Halfpenny.

VIOLENT SCENES AT WESTMINSTER, WHERE MANY SUFFRAGETTES WERE ARRESTED WHILE TRYING TO FORCE THEIR WAY INTO THE HOUSE OF COMMONS.

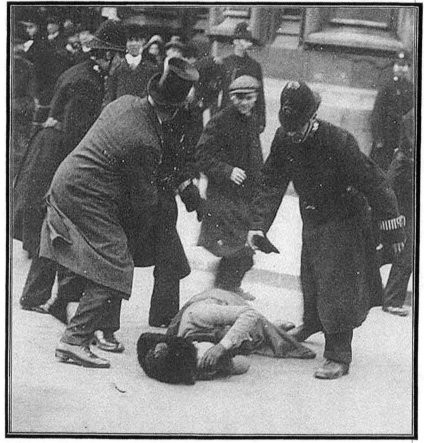

While forcibly endeavouring yesterday to enter the Houses of Parliament, great numbers of suffragettes used more frantic methods than ever before. Above is illustrated one of yesterday's incidents. A woman has fallen down while struggling, and she is in a fainting condition. The photograph shows how far women will go for the vote.

The front page of the London Daily Mirror. November 19, 1910
The man in the top hat was trying to protect the lady from the police.

Bessie Bewick, Dora Bewick, Clara Colby, Esther Bewick and Dr. Mary
White
(Wisconsin Historical Society)

Studio portrait of
Clara Bewick Colby
wearing a large hat.
(Wisconsin Historical Society)

The Court of Abundance at the Panama Pacific Exposition in San Francisco in 1915, the site where Clara Colby and Zintka Lanuni made their final appearance.

CHAPTER 14

CUBA

In 1895, Cuba and Puerto Rico were the last two of Spain's colonies in the Americas. Cuba was governed much as it had been since the Spanish arrived in 1511. Spain had experienced an economic decline following the loss of its other colonies and the war with Napoleon for control of the Iberian Peninsula. Meanwhile, Cuba's economy had become more closely linked with the United States, and sugar estates and mining interests passed from Spanish to American hands. In 1894, nearly 90 percent of Cuba's exports went to the United States, while 6 percent went to Spain.

The outcome was, the Cubans were starting to feel closer to the Americans than to the Spanish, and many believed that they should become a republic like the United States. A liberation movement developed and a leader by the name of José Marti, a middle-class poet and journalist, determined that the conditions were right for a bid for independence. Several uprisings broke out, to which Spain responded with the appointment of a ruthless commander in chief

General Weyler was put in command of 220,000 men sent from Spain. He decided to starve out the rebels and relocate peasants into garrison towns, but the lack of food and the poor sanitation resulted in the deaths of thousands; rebels and peasants alike

Most Americans were supportive of the Cuban rebels and their wish for an independent republic; opposed to the idea of a European monarchy ruling a country just 90 miles from Florida, and many looked for ways to help. One of the first people to be reported as having a plan to assist the rebels was General L. W. Colby, according to the *Nebraska State Journal.*

COLBY TO START FOR CUBA

General L. W. Colby's plans for his proposed Cuban expedition are maturing even more rapidly than he had hoped for at the outset, and in a few days he will go east in response to requests from prominent Chicagoans and New Yorkers, who have become interested in the cause and Colby's plans, with a view of lending him substantial aid. This trip will include a brief trip to Cuba.

General Colby, replying to the question of why the government should interfere and aid the Cubans at this present time, answered:

'Because the Cubans now demand liberty and self-government and ask all sister American republics for aid; because Spain's conduct of the war against Cuba has been characterized by barbarity, treachery and inhumanity, and is a violation of all recognized modes of civilized warfare.'

In July of 1897, Clara was reported to be on the platform of a mass meeting in aid of the American Red Cross, under the auspices of the National Relief Association for Cuba. It was held at the First Congregational Church in Washington. The purpose of the meeting was to put in place a plan to raise funds for aid to the people of Cuba.

Could this be a cause in which both Clara and Leonard were united? She relished the idea and seized the chance to assist Leonard in lobbying members of Congress to achieve some support for his efforts. Leonard played upon her enthusiasm, sending her flowers and promising to leave Maud and set up home together. The article about Leonard Colby adopting Zintka Lanuni began to appear in newspapers around the country, complete with their engraved picture, apparently the result of a promotional campaign.

Leonard was making sure that the Cuban campaign was a family affair, for he had managed to have Clarence enlisted in the United States Volunteer Cavalry as a bugler. His proud mother wrote of him in the *Tribune*, 'Many of the editor's friends will remember the curly-headed little fellow who used to accompany her on her lecture trips. And now, at the age of sixteen, nearly five foot ten, and a splendid horseman, he is a bugler in the United States Volunteer Cavalry.' The Volunteer Cavalry would go on to be known as the 'Rough Riders,' led by Theodore Roosevelt.

By April 1898, Leonard was in Washington to offer the government the services of his 25,000 members of the American-Cuban volunteer legion. After all, he had devoted nearly a whole year to organizing them. He hoped that he would be able to lead his men during the first invasion of Cuba, with about twenty or thirty thousand infantry, a troop of cavalry and a battery of artillery. It would not be his first visit to Cuba as he had been there twice during the past year, and hence he claimed to be familiar with Cuban affairs.

During this visit to Washington, he was staying at home with Clara, and he was, no doubt, being as charming and manipulative as he could.

In May, Clara received confirmation in the following letter that her lobbying might be paying off:

> *Committee on Indian Affairs*
> *United States Senate*
>
> *Clara B. Colby*
> *My Dear Friend*
> *I have been to see the President for Mr. Colby, and urged his appointment. It gave me great pleasure to do so, both on your account and on his, and also in the interest of the service, because I believe he would make a most excellent officer.*
>
> *Of course I am not a Republican, and not supporting the Administration very vigorously, and do not know that my recommendation did any good. However, I felt it was proper for me to urge the appointment, as it was from joint States, and Dakota troops were quite liable to be commanded by the officer from Nebraska. This was last week; since then our troops have been sent to Manila.*
>
> *I also saw the Secretary of War and told him about Mr. Colby's qualifications, and that South Dakota joined with Nebraska in urging the appointment. I very much hope he will secure it. I should be glad to do anything more I can if it will accomplish the desired result. – Believe me.*
> *Very truly yours, R. F. Pettigrew, Chairman*

The lobbying and Leonard's campaigning got results. On June 3, 1898, President McKinley sent the Senate three nominations for brigadier generals in the United States volunteers, including Leonard W. Colby of Nebraska. Just one month later, the War Department issued a War Correspondent's pass to Clara B. Colby of the *Woman's Tribune*, making her the first female war correspondent in the United States. Clara explained that it was her object to accompany her husband with a recognized status and in a capacity that would give her opportunities and protection to which she would not otherwise be entitled.[2] Newspapers around the world carried the story of Clara's appointment, and the *New Orleans Times-Democrat* added that she would have her Kodak with her and would have exceptional advantages for getting news

SHE IS WAR CORRESPONDENT
Mrs. Colby Will Accompany Her Husband to the Field of Battle.

Mrs. Clara Bewick Colby, the first woman in the United States to receive a war correspondent's pass, is founder, editor and proprietor of 'The Woman's Tribune,' published in Washington, and it is in the interest of her paper that she goes to the front, accompanying her husband, who is a brigadier-general.

Mrs. Colby has achieved distinction not only as an editor, but as a lecturer on civics, literature, dress and woman suffrage. She was professor at one time of Latin and history at the University of Wisconsin, and she studied law, and recently founded a public library at Beatrice, Nebraska. She is vice president for Nebraska of the National American Woman Suffrage Association.

> The Woman's Tribune was first published in Nebras-
> ka, but moved to Washington when General Colby became
> assistant attorney general....
> She has a son, now a bugler in Colonel Grigsby's regi-
> ment, and a little adopted daughter – an Indian girl named
> Zintka Lanuni. General Colby found the child in the arms
> of its dead mother, the latter having been shot on the bat-
> tlefield of Wounded Knee.[3]

General Colby took the oath of office before leaving Washington to return to Beatrice, where he was met at the depot
by a large crowd of enthusiastic admirers and led by a band in
procession to the opera house, to attend a reception, held in
his honor. The event was described in a letter to Zintka from
Mary's daughter Dorothy and published in the *Tribune*.
The letter is reproduced below.

Leonard only spent a few days in Beatrice, after which he
departed for the Chickamauga Military Park in Georgia. This
had been set up as a training center and a significant marshal-
ing point for the troops destined for Cuba. He left instructions
with Clara to follow him in a few weeks, and said he would
meet her there.

My Dear Little Zintka
I want to send you a letter to tell you about the great time
we had when your Papa came back from Washington.
Beatrice was very proud that Uncle Leonard was made
Brigadier-General. We all knew he was coming home be-
cause we got a telegram from Aunt Clara and the people
all turned out to meet him and cannons were fired when
the train got here. They took a carriage for him all covered

with roses and it was drawn by four white horses in a big parade to the opera house. Mamma and I stood by the side of Uncle and we were very sorry that you and your Mama could not be here too.

I want you to come and stay with Eva and Charlotte and me while our Mamas go to the war.

Your loving cousin, Dorothy.[4]

This letter was no doubt genuine, but Clara did publish letters supposedly written between Zintka and Clarence, even though Clarence could hardly read and write and Zintka was only eight years old. They documented how Clara had left Washington with Zintka and taken her to Beatrice to stay with Mary's daughters and how she had been given a wheel (bicycle) as compensation for her mother going away. The *Tribune* also published a letter which was said to have been sent from Papa to Zintka, although no original letters from Leonard to his daughter have ever been found.

On August 15, Clara reached Chattanooga, accompanied by her sister, Dr. Mary White, who was there on professional business. Her first Letter from the Editor in the *Tribune* explained, 'My husband met us and brought us to the beautiful Inn on this famous mountain (Lookout Mountain, Tennessee) until arrangements can be made for us in camp. We went over to camp on Saturday and took dinner at headquarters. As the officers pay for their mess themselves, they can have as good things as they wish, and on this occasion, Anthony, the black cook, had done his best. The table is set in a rectangular tent with board frame and mosquito netting walls so that we were not troubled with flies.'

The policy at the camp was to encourage sports and other activities to break the monotony of camp duties and alleviate disappointment felt by the soldiers when it was announced that peace had been declared. This took place on August 13th, after the regular United States army had defeated the Spanish in a mere three months. Now, it would seem, there would be no need for the volunteers to go; leaving them to return home without having distinguished themselves through some heroic deed of courage. It would also seem that there would be no need for a war correspondent or a lady doctor to visit the front, so Clara and Mary would likely be going home too. In the meantime, everyone would stay in camp until the position became clear.

Clara's next Letter from the Editor, on September 3rd, told how, since her last letter, her time had been mostly taken up with nursing the fever-stricken soldiers taken down with malaria. The soldiers had been brought up the mountain to assist with their recovery, and many of the locals had opened their homes to receive the sick and convalescents.

By now, the camp was in a state of confusion. Orders received one day were revoked the next; only one thing was certain, and that was that everybody was going away somewhere as fast as transportation could be obtained. About 40 percent of the men were sick, and fear of the dreaded malaria and typhoid fever that had disabled many was in the air. While thousands of women had volunteered to nurse the soldiers, in some cases there was only one nurse to twenty-five fever patients, making it more the shouts of the stronger ones or the ravings of the feverish to call for the help of a nurse.

By her next report, Clara said, 'The whole country is in arms about the tales of disease and death, suffering and neglect that comes from the various camps, and which now mostly refer to conditions that are past.' Before leaving Washington, Clara heard that Chickamauga Park, which had a reputation of being very healthy was, in reality, the worst of all for the prevalence of typhoid fever. She found, as far as she was able to investigate, that the percentage of troops on the sick list varied between 20 and 40 percent. In one regiment it was 75 percent. In addition, a large number of men called 'well' were weakened by the camp dysentery, arising from polluted water and badly-cooked food. She said that there was scarcely a regiment in the Park in months that was fit for military duty.

There had been between 4,500 and 5,000 cases of typhoid fever in various hospitals in the Park, and these were staffed only by male nurses who were inexperienced and inefficient. Usually, these were volunteers who were trying to avoid drills, and in two cases, it came to Clara's notice that regimental officers congratulated themselves for disposing of their least desirable men by this means.

From the ignorance of the attendants and the carelessness of the officers in charge, the hospitals became disease breeders. Kitchens and hospitals were located too closely together, where infection could quickly transfer, and nothing was done to keep mosquitoes off the fever patients, thus broadcasting the disease through the camp. Sick men were going home on leave from the hospital but were left without railroad transportation. After some hours of misery, the Station Master offered seats in one of the waiting rooms and the ladies of the Soldier's Rest brought cots, blankets, and pillows and made the men as comfortable as they could under the circumstances. The waiting time for transportation lasted for more than twenty-four hours.

The report about the Second Division hospital was the most startling, as it proved that medical supplies and attendance were inadequate. Men went for days without medical attention and most died of neglect, the tents being filthy, and sanitation wholly disregarded. The record of the revolting facts would send a shudder through the nation.

Another hospital was dependent on the water filter, which gave it pure water, after the charitable donation of a private citizen. The typhoid fever had so thoroughly infected the hospital that within three weeks of its opening, fifty patients died and five of the contract nurses were down with the dreaded disease, while others had gone home to recuperate. A Red Cross nurse from Canada, a volunteer, became the first woman to lose her life in the service of this war.

For a short period, Clara had found a new cause in which to employ her ideas and energies. Her newly-awarded status as a war correspondent and the added resource of having a medical doctor (her sister Mary) alongside gave her the ability to write confidently on this matter. She laid the blame on Russell Alger, The Secretary of War in the McKinley administration, who had rebuked medical authorities at one camp for disobeying orders because of some red tape regulation. She said that if only he had taken in hand the duties that belong to his office, those concerning the medical department of the service, how much suffering would have been spared. Her article was compelling, and it must have had a substantial effect on readers nationwide, particularly considering that a copy of every issue of the *Tribune* was now going to every Senator and Member in Congress.

Whether it was as a result of Clara's reporting or not, the next Letter from the Editor in the *Tribune* of October 1, 1898, reported that Secretary Alger and the Surgeon-General visited Chickamauga Park. Clara felt gratified that she had influenced his decision to visit the hospitals in the Park

Following up from the visit by the Secretary of War, Brigadier-General Sanger was asked to prepare a report regarding the situation. According to Clara, General Sanger showed that the system of centralization in Washington left commanders powerless to perform duties necessary for the wellbeing of the army. A commander, he believed, should be invested with supreme control of those things which make up the necessities of the military personnel under him. He also thought that the hospitals should have trained nurses and not have to rely upon untrained men detailed from the regiments. Dr. Charles Craig, Acting Assistant Surgeon, made an examination of the water in six localities in Chickamauga Park and found that in three places it was unfit for use, on account of the excessive amount of bacteria. He was not able to separate the typhoid germ or any other intestinal bacillus to which the fever might be attributed.

Leonard, by this time, had moved down to Camp Shipp, near Anniston, Alabama, where he and his brigade were still waiting to hear whether they would go to Cuba. He wrote to Clara and said, 'The troops are in good health and anxious to start for Cuba or at least to know what is to be done. Anniston is a fine, healthy place for a camp, the best I have seen.' He told her that he would come back to Chickamauga soon to take her down to Camp Shipp. He would have to be quick because she would soon have to leave.

Among the soldiers infected with the typhoid was Clarence. He had been sick for four weeks, with a high fever, and he was growing weaker every day. A southern gentleman told Clara that he had seen a lot of typhoid cases on his plantation and he said that the best diet would be boiled milk and bananas. This diet appealed to Clarence. His fever went down gradually, and eventually, the fever left him. He was still not fit to return to his unit, but his recovery looked good.

Clara had to leave Chattanooga in time to get to Omaha for the start of the National Council of Women, which was to run from October 24-27, 1898. This was to be followed by the Nebraska Woman Suffrage Association conference. Both of these conferences were being held in Omaha, mainly because this was the site of the Trans-Mississippi and International Exposition, which was the latest World's Fair held in the United States. In the absence of Mrs. Catt, Clara was required to attend the Executive meeting of the National Council of Women as a consequence of being the delegate of the National American WSA. She also had to preside over the Nebraska WSA, as it was her last year as President.

One of the milestones they had to celebrate was the news that South Dakota had adopted a woman suffrage amendment, becoming the fifth state to gain voting rights for women.

Susan B. Anthony was in attendance at both conferences in Omaha, and she took the opportunity to speak about the poor preparation of Chickamauga as a camping ground for the volunteer army. She said, 'If women had been selected to procure the clothing for the soldiers who rose as flowers from

an education program offered in Beatrice by the Chautauqua movement. This program would typically require a study period of several years, but since Clara had encouraged Maud to go to college five years earlier, then this graduation was probably the result. There was no mention of a Mr. Martinez in Nebraska at any time. In fact, in June of 1902, Marie filed for divorce from Thomas Martinez, on account of desertion. The final divorce was granted on December 5, 1902, and the report stated that Mr. Martinez was in Mexico.

Upon his return home to Nebraska, Leonard continued his fascination with Cuba. He announced that he had invited General Maximo Gomez, the late commander-in-chief of the Cuban army, to visit Nebraska in June or July. Leonard declared that he was intimately acquainted with the great Cuban patriot and was arranging for his presence with every assurance of success. Gomez did visit the United States in 1901, but he never made it up to Nebraska.

Leonard's obsession with visiting a town in Cuba—and Maud's sudden marriage to Thomas H. Martinez—remained a mystery until 1906, when the following article appeared in the *Beatrice Daily Sun*. It disclosed why Leonard had been so interested in Matanzas.

SECURES LARGE ESTATE
Beatrice Woman Awarded Half a Million in the
Cuban Court of Claims for Damages to Property.
A special dispatch from Havana announces the allowances
by General Cortes of Cuba of the claims of Mrs. Marie C.
Martinez for personal property injured and destroyed during the Cuban insurrection, and the establishment by final judgement of the highest court of her title to the real and

personal estate of her husband, Tomas Hernando Martinez, who went to Mexico and thence to South America at the close of the Spanish-American war, leaving valuable properties undisposed of in several of the provinces of Cuba.

The claims allowed by Cortes are to be paid from government appropriations and amount to $216,666, while the real and personal estate of Mr. Martinez settled by decree, consisting of 17,000 acres of land, sugar and tobacco plantations and other interests near Matanzas, is appraised at over $400,000.

Mrs. Marie C. Martinez, the fortunate litigant, is a resident of Nebraska, her girlhood home being at Beatrice, and she having resided at Lincoln during the past year. She was represented in Cuba by Freyre de Andrada, one of the ablest lawyers of the Cuban republic, and in this country by General L. W. Colby of this city.

Mrs. Martinez is certainly to be congratulated upon her good fortune, as are also her attorneys, whose fees will doubtless be commensurate with the amount obtained for the client upon the successful termination of litigation which has been pending for six years, finally resulting in the recovery of assets valued at over a half million dollars.[7]

According to the letter written by Maud Miller-Colby in 1933, the visit by General Colby to Matanzas in Cuba was a clandestine rendezvous for the purpose of bilking nearly half a million dollars from the United States government in war claims.[8]

CHAPTER 15

BACK TO ENGLAND

By 1899, ALL HOPE of Leonard moving back to Washington had gone, and that left Clara with a large house which she could ill-afford. So she downsized to take a smaller house at 2420 14th Street NW in Washington.

The changed location did not stop her from holding her regular 'at home' social evenings whenever she could. Mrs. Carrie Harrison, her friend at The Press Club, recalled in a letter to Olympia Brown that Clara's home on 14th Street in Washington was remembered with pleasure for the social gatherings she frequently held. Mrs. Harrison noted, 'When I lived in Mrs. Colby's house, I saw something of her capacity for work. No matter what she had done or how hard the work she had accomplished, she would always clear up the room for an informal party Saturday night. And where did all the people come from? They were judges, doctors, North American Indians, Hindu philosophers, and what not. If there were a crank in town, he would find his way to Clara B. Colby's Saturday evening. She was a mixer extraordinary. At about eleven o'clock she made coffee and, crowded around a long table, we talked on till midnight.'[1]

The International Council of Women was formed in Washington in 1888. The next meeting of the ICW was to be in London in 1899, to which 100 American delegates were invited, including Clara B. Colby. Clara had been in Grand Rapids for the NAWSA, after which she stayed as a guest with Susan B. Anthony at her home in Rochester NY, but when she returned to Washington, she found Zintka suffering from trachoma, a form of conjunctivitis. The one local doctor who Clara trusted suggested that Clara consider taking Zintka with her to Europe, as the sea voyage would be good for her. Clara had already thought about taking Zintka and had discussed the matter with Miss Anthony, who was utterly opposed to the idea. Mrs. Stanton also wrote to Clara, 'Above all things, do not take a child with you.... children are considered a nuisance... leave her at home.'

Always independent of mind, Clara booked herself and Zintka on the Anchor line, whose ships sailed from New York to Glasgow. She chose the slower of the two vessels, the *Anchoria*, which took nine days for the crossing but was slightly cheaper than the *City of Rome*. Or perhaps the Anchoria was the choice because Miss Anthony was traveling on the *City of Rome*. Using the last of the money that Leonard had given her, she departed on June 10, 1899, from Pier No 54, taking two days longer than expected to reach Glasgow.

The *Woman's Tribune* of July 15, 1899, reported on a pleasant trip, with neither she nor Zintka experiencing any seasickness. This, in spite of the ship, on one night, rolling from side to side to the sound of breaking glass and a din that banished any sleep. They were particularly fortunate to see an iceberg, a rather small and upside down one, but an unusual sight at this time of the year. She read the beautiful poems of Henry Wadsworth Longfellow, Evangeline and Hiawatha to Zintka, which she was sure Zintka would remember as part of the new and wonderful pleasures of the voyage.

They spent three days in Glasgow, during which Clara noted enough detail to later write an article entitled 'A Tale of a City, the Municipal Government of Glasgow,' subsequently published in *Arena* magazine. Glasgow was one of the most advanced cities for its time concerning municipal reforms. Clara got the assistance of city officials, who took her on a tour of many of its branches, covering sanitation, baths and wash-houses, lodgings and tenements, parks and playgrounds, tramways and schools. She was a prolific note taker and scribe, and how she managed to do all this while taking care of her nine-year-old daughter is hard to comprehend.

Since leaving New York, Clara had taken up company with Mrs. Fray, another delegate to the ICW. After three days in Glasgow, they took the train to London, with Clara note-taking and snapping her Kodak at any interesting stopping place. The delegates were gathering at St. Ermin's Hotel on Victoria Street, close to the Central Westminster Hall, the headquarters of the Council. But, Clara and Mrs. Fray found lower cost accommodation at 6 Smith Square, Westminster, located between the Houses of Parliament and Lambeth Bridge.

The International Council of Women was made up of delegates from each of the ten countries where national women's organizations existed. The Council itself only held one meeting, and all the other sessions were part of the Congress. There were 41 Congress meetings, at which there were 303 advertised speakers. These meetings were held in town halls and meeting places throughout the parishes of Westminster and St. Martin's. Clara was not there as a speaker, but more as the Editor of the *Woman's Tribune* and as a member of the NAWSA. She was, therefore, a free agent, able to pick and choose whichever event took her interest, while at the same time taking in the sights and experiences of London. During this time, and again before she left for America, she walked the length and breadth of London, usually with Zintka, taking copious notes for articles intended for the *Tribune*. The result was a series of 37 articles published over the next two years and eventually compiled into a book of at least 70,000 words, which she titled, 'London, Past and Present.' She tried several times to get it published, unfortunately without success.

The second article in the series covered the area around Clara's childhood home, which she described in the *Woman's Tribune*:

Waterloo Place was my childhood home when from the age of two and a half years until nearly nine I lived with my grand parents. The houses in Waterloo Place are distinguished by the large, dark red double story columns which make them look like palaces. Where, as a child, I remember a few professional doorplates now our American Ambassador lives at No. 1 and No. 3 is the office of the American Express Company. I was extended the courtesy of entering some of the rooms in No. 11, so hallowed to me by association with the sainted loved ones who had cherished my childhood with unremitting care and love, and who spent their last days with me in my far Western home. Although altered for business purposes I recognized the rooms and described to the courteous gentleman who showed me about, the color of the paper which had been on the walls. 'I have been here twenty years,' he said, 'and when I first came the paper was such as you describe.' It was heavy flock paper, as we called it, dark green in one room and red in another, and the same kind of red paper is now on the drawing room of the house occupied by Ambassador Choate.*

How well I remember the Duke of York's monument, a rear view of which could be had from our door and a front view of which cannot be had from anywhere, for it is so high that when you are down the steps and far enough away to get it in range the features are indistinguishable. My Kodak views of No. 11 are priceless to me and were the best I succeeded in taking in the murky atmosphere of London, sunny as it was almost the whole time I was there.[2]

Clara walked through St. James' Park, where her grandfather used to take her nearly every morning before breakfast to feed the ducks. The ducks were still there in great variety, the descendants of those introduced by Charles II when he enlarged and beautified the historic park. It seems that attitudes towards the protection of children were very different to those we hold today, as Clara often left Zintka in the Park during one of the sessions. As she wrote in the *Tribune*, 'It was quite safe to leave Zintka for hours in the Park as there were places near the water's edge where the ducks used to come and take bread from the children's hands, not at all disturbed by the near-by wading of little urchins in the shallow water. There were plenty of keepers to maintain order, of which, however, I never witnessed a violation. A portion of the Lake was reserved for these plays of children, a part for pleasure boating, and along other parts shaded seats invited the tired pedestrian; but woe betide him if he dropped into a chair instead of a public seat, for in a moment someone would be upon him asking for a halfpenny, as the chairs were private property.'[3]

One of the lasting memories of their visit to St. James' Park was the occasion of 'one of the most brilliant military reviews that have taken place in London,' the commemoration of the 40th anniversary of the formation of the Volunteers. It involved a total of 28,000 soldiers 'passing in review' on Horse Guards Parade. Clara, Mrs. Fray, and Zintka joined the crowd of 200,000 people that day who pressed into the Park. During several hours of waiting, without much chance of seeing anything, Clara amused herself by snapping groups of policemen with her Kodak and chatted with other members of the crowd.

Suddenly, they were transported out of the hustling crowd and led by a private path through the shrubbery. They then ascended a step-ladder, over a wall to a shady hill slope that overlooked the road where the reviewing and the reviewed had to pass. Here, they were near enough to see the Princess of Wales with her daughter and grandson and see the Prince of Wales lift his hand in salute as each regiment passed. They could hardly believe their good fortune and struggled to reason how it had happened. Then they remembered a lady they spoke with whose husband had been a military officer in India. Though keenly interested in each other, at the right time,

seem such a waste of your marvelous powers of expression for you to be forever trying to raise money to pay the current expenses of running a house, a newspaper office, and about a thousand other things.... In such a state of perfect physical and intellectual collapse as you must be in, it is worse than idle for you to think of doing yourself or your audiences justice. You cannot go before audiences with intellectual and magnetic power, nor can you put on paper the magnetic power of which you are capable, unless you religiously keep your mind and body in proper conditions, and that you cannot do while you have to walk the streets trying to collect old bills for the *Tribune*, nor in moving from house to house to save rent.[6]

In spite of her criticisms of Clara taking on too many tasks and too much work, it was generally Susan B. Anthony who engaged Clara for tasks whenever she could. As reported in the *Buffalo Times*, on March 11, 1900, 'Mrs. Clara B. Colby has lectured in the cause of suffrage throughout 30 states of the Union also in England and Canada. She was wisely chosen to accompany Susan B. Anthony to plead their cause before the United States Senate in Washington.' The letter above also reveals that Clara had been forced to move house again, moving into less desirable areas of Washington.

CHAPTER 16

COAST TO COAST AND BACK AGAIN

MOVING INTO THE NEW millennium, the old guard at the NAWSA was changing. Miss Susan B. Anthony retired as President and handed over to Mrs. Carrie Chapman-Catt at the 32nd annual convention of the NAWSA, held in Washington. On Miss Anthony's arrival in Washington, she was hosted at Clara's home, with a reception to honor her many years as their leader.

With cohort Miss Anthony stepping down, Clara's influence was declining, a process that started when the NWSA and the AWSA amalgamated in 1889 and the *Tribune* ceased to be a national suffrage organ. Before stepping down at the convention, Miss Anthony led her team of speakers to address the Senate select committee on woman suffrage, as she had done for several years.

Clara was the first speaker, who delivered an address on 'Our Work Before Congress,' outlining the work done before Congress took place, in the way of petitions presented and bills introduced. It was interesting to note that the anti-suffragists were also making a presentation before the committee, opposing the extension of suffrage to women. As in previous years, Clara Colby featured several times as a speaker and was also appointed the chairman of the committee on 'Industrial Problems Affecting Women and Children.'

Hard times had not cramped Clara's style on the social scene. *The Washington Times* of April 8, 1900, announced that 'Mrs. Clara Bewick Colby, 2420 Fourteenth Street, will receive her friends informally Saturdays from 4 to 7 o'clock during April.'

In May, Clara was required to attend the convention of the Woman's International Press Union, in Detroit. It seemed like a good idea to take Zintka with her and then continue to Wisconsin, where she hoped to leave Zintka with her family for the summer. Her second cousin, Thomas Pope, and his wife Anna had a dairy farm close to Madison, so she approached Anna to see if she would look after Zintka for the summer. Anna was very reluctant to take the child for the summer, but she did not want to refuse her entirely. The Pope family was not that different from the Bewick family, especially when it came to being of strict Christian belief, only Thomas Pope took a more literal interpretation of the Bible than Clara's father. It all seemed like Zintka would have a memorable time spending summer on the farm. Clara wrote in *Zintka's Corner*:

John Holliday

Zintka went to Wisconsin with her mamma in the Biennial days and has remained there for the summer. What a happy experience this is to the little girl from the city may be judged from this story of her doings as told in her letters, and done into jingle by her mamma, out in the backyard with the peach tree, the trumpet creeper, Zintka's three cats and two visitors.

A DAY ON THE FARM

Zintka Lanuni's up early and bright,
And hastens into her clothes.
For the boys milk the cows almost ere it is light
Then with Henry to the creamery she goes.

Ol rattlety-bang go the big milk cans,
As the big wagon jolts along.
But louder than noises of wheels and of pans,
Are the chatter and laugh and song.

For Aunt Anna's box I've piled the wood in,
So full that the lid will not down.
Now I can tell mamma how good I have been,
In the letter I'm sending to town.

I've written mamma how dearly I love her,
And told her to come for me soon.
But Oh, my dear Aunt, you must finish this letter,
For now it is nearly noon.

Now 'tis time for good night and kiss all round,
Then Zintka remembers her prayer.
God bless my own mamma and all the dear friends,
Who give me such loving care.[1]

225

The next issue of the *Tribune* had a letter from Zintka, no doubt slightly edited by the publisher.

> *Sun Prairie, Wisconsin.*
> *July 30, 1900.*
>
> *My Dear Mama,*
> *I have not written to you since last week. I hope you are well. You must come for my birthday. Aunt Anna is going to make me two kinds of birthday cake.*
>
> *Just last week I had some choke-cherries; they were black. And our apples are almost ripe.*
>
> *Uncle Thomas is now getting up his oats. Roy is watching his cows; Ruth is ironing and Aunt Anna is making apple pie for dinner and I am going to make one too.*
>
> *We have got such a great high swing in the barn, and we can swing so high in it. Ruthie and I jump up high. We stand up in it.*
>
> *I was glad to get your card when Ruth and I got the mail. Aunt Anna says the poem was very nice. Ruth said it must have taken you a long time to write it, but I said it took you but ten minutes.*
>
> *We have two pet lambs, and we keep them in the front yard, and Roy and I have lots of fun.*
>
> *I have learned the table clear up to the tens.*
>
> *I must close. Good-by. I love you.*

From these reports, one would think that everything was well and Zintka was a happy little girl. But it turns out that she had been having many problems from the time that Clara left. The children were embarrassed to have an Indian girl sitting with them in church, and she did not act like the white girls at all. She ran and climbed as fast as the boys and often challenged them at their games. Henry was the oldest boy, at eighteen, and he had a grudge against Zintka. He had previously been taunting Indian boys who lived in the area, and now he transferred his animosity to Zintka, chasing her with an angry, clawing tomcat to scare her.

Zintka started to feel desperately frightened at night and insisted on sleeping in Aunt Anna's room or with Ruth. She was particularly scared of thunderstorms, and Henry chose to use this fear to play a cruel trick on her. The boys asked Zintka if she would like to play in the cornfield and not wanting to be left behind, she jumped at the chance. They took a wagon and headed out to the fields just as the dark clouds gathered in the west. When the storm broke, the boys held Zintka down in the muddy field and then ran away in all directions, just as bolts of lightning lit up the sky and thunder cracked all around her. She screamed in panic, which was precisely what Henry and his mean brothers wanted to hear. Some time later Zintka found her way home but when she came into the farmhouse she was filthy, and Aunt Anna was furious.

Clara did not return to Wisconsin when she had promised because she could not afford the fare for herself and Zintka. So, Zintka waited week after week as she silently faced her tormentors. Depressed and alone, she refused to bathe, her hair became matted and her ears flamed with infection. Finally, in October, Clara arrived to take Zintka home and recoiled in horror at her disheveled state.

Zintka's experience on the farm initiated a severe depression in the child; although it was probably just another episode in the life of someone growing up in an alien culture, constantly reminded of how different she was. The depression descended into a full nervous breakdown and a physical illness which manifested in sores that spread to her face. She was naïve and did not seem to be able to recognize dangerous situations. For example, one time when Clara left her to go to the post office, she returned to find Zintka sitting on the lap of a traveling salesman. She was showing signs of having been sexually abused.

Clara had always been open and honest about Zintka's background, which now gave Zintka a reason to be a victim and blame her current unhappiness on her removal from her native culture. She asked Clara to take her to Wounded Knee to join her people, but Clara had neither the money nor the contacts to accomplish that. It was too late for Clara to change how open she had been with Zintka, who was completely aware of where she came from. Nine years ago, when Clara met Captain Richard H. Pratt, superintendent of the US government's training school for Indian children, he had advised Clara to educate Zintka in the East, entirely away from her kind, and to raise her a strict Christian. Too late now to go back and follow that advice. The solution, Clara thought, was to find a school where she could be educated among some of her people, and thus take her away from some of the bad influences found in the backstreets of their neighborhood. In the meantime, Clara would have to restrict her travels or only accept speaking engagements in places where she could take Zintka with her.

Clara was busy in the first three months of 1901 with the usual meetings and activities in Washington. This included the National Press Association, the National Legislative League, the District Woman's Suffrage Association, the International

Press Union, as well as volunteering to read for the blind at the Library of Congress. She was getting more active with the DC chapter of the WSA, believing that this organization could make a significant contribution to the national cause, on account of it being located in the nation's capital. Clara was scheduled to speak at the annual convention of the NAWSA in Minneapolis in June, but another opportunity arose which was hard to refuse.

When in London at the International Council of Women, she had met many interesting and wealthy people. One of these was Miss F. Henrietta Muller, a Chilean-British woman's rights activist and theosophist, then living in London. Expressing a desire to visit America, she had asked whether Clara would escort her across the country, introducing her to like-minded people along the way. She could take Zintka as far as Nebraska and leave her with Mary or possibly even with her father, and Clara's attendance in Minneapolis might still be possible.

Clara Colby and Henrietta Muller shared many common traits and experiences. Muller graduated from Cambridge University and had also started a woman's publication in England, known as *The Woman's Signal*, in which Clara's articles often appeared. The claim made at the time was that *The Woman's Signal* was the only paper in the world conducted, printed and published entirely by women, a claim which manifestly disregarded the *Tribune*.[2] Muller joined the Theosophical Society in 1891, and for some time she lived in India where, in 1895, she adopted a young Bengali man, marking another similarity with Clara.

Clara wrote a regular column in the *Tribune* called *Wandering Westward*, in which she documented their travels. Part of this relates to Henrietta Muller.

WANDERING WESTWARD

Quite suddenly a work has come to me which will be opened up to you later and now takes me to the Pacific Coast.

On Thursday of last week, Miss Herdman, Zintka and I, literally shook the dust of Washington off our feet in one rush to the train, for we had made a mistake in the time of departure of twenty five minutes, and only because the train was five minutes late did we succeed in getting on at all. Miss Herdman who has been a member of the Tribune family on and off for more than fifteen years, now returns to her other home in Highland, Kansas.

Reaching Omaha early Sunday morning I was soon in the home of my niece, Mrs. Davis, whose name Eva Bewick White, stood next to mine on the Tribune for sometime, and who now as wife of a Baptist minister, finds ample scope for the many gifts and graces which brightened the editor's sanctum......

In this early morning hour in Colorado Springs, with the street life of the pretty town waking up, and the glory of the sun shining on Cheyenne Mountain, I must give a little sketch of our doings before we leave this morning for our real Westward trip. Miss F. Henrietta Muller whom I am accompanying to the Coast to assist her in meeting women who may be interested in the deep spiritual significance of the 'woman movement,' was detained in Indianapolis a little longer than expected so that she could not speak as arranged before the Social Science Department of the Woman's Club which held its meeting for the season May

25. I had, however, the honor of addressing the Club and after speaking of Miss Muller's work by invitation, I told them about the wonderful meetings and delights of the International Council of Women in London, of which little had been known in Denver.[3]

Miss Muller joined Clara in Denver the following day, and during the next week, they were invited to speak at the Colorado State Woman Suffrage Society, the Clio Club, and the Denver Woman's Press Club, as well as receiving several private invitations to some of the most beautiful homes in Denver. From Denver, the ladies stayed with a family on the Glen Eyrie estate, bordering the Garden of the Gods. It was a perfectly appointed home amid the wild grandeur of an awe-inspiring region.

During a reception held by their hostess, they met Thomas Moran, the great American painter, famous for his landscapes of the Rocky Mountains. He had just completed his latest work, which was a picture of Shoshone Falls. From this home, they hiked up Queen's Canyon, a picturesque gorge, where a dashing little stream comes madly down in this season of snow melting on the summits. They ignored the fact that some of the rustic bridges that used to cross the creek looked close to being broken down, and were pleased to reach the other side, finding a path along the walls of rock.

Clara and Miss Muller left Colorado Springs, taking a local rail line to La Junta, Colorado, where they could pick up the California Limited, which went all the way to Los Angeles. Unfortunately, the timetables had changed, and it would be two more days before they could get a connection. The result was beneficial though, because they got to spend more daytime travel with stopovers, which meant they experienced scenes of more significant interest than on the Limited. Another advantage to the change in their travel plans was that they got to spend more time in New Mexico, which resulted in Clara writing an article that was picked up by several newspapers.

West of Albuquerque, they left the train to go to visit the Acoma Pueblo, a traditional township of the cliff-dwelling Pueblo Indians.

In the morning we set out to Acoma pueblo, passing on the way the Mesa Encantado, 'the Enchanted Table,' up which no Indian, it is said, will go because it is supposed to be the abode of spirits.

Of all the Pueblo Indians, the Acomas, it is said, are the least untouched by civilization and therefore for this reason, the most interesting to the student. The Acoma Pueblo, a thousand feet in length on the summit of a cliff apparently a hundred feet high. From all sides but one it is inaccessible and appears surrounded by a blank wall broken here and there with turrets. This is the back of adobe houses, some of which are three stories high. By the one way in which the cliff can be climbed, the walk is still very difficult for it is sand which carries the foot backward almost as fast as she can lift it forward.

By the time we had reached the summit a number of women had come out and they invited us very cordially into their homes. One must go up rickety ladders to enter most of these houses and sometimes up another ladder to reach the second or third story. All the homes were clean; so were the women and children, and there was everywhere an attempt at ornament. It is said that the women and children all understand a little Spanish and certainly it must be so for they are all Catholics and the Padre comes semi-occasionally to hold service in the large church on the hill, to marry, to baptize, and to instruct in the faith whose symbols are seen on every wall. One man, Pedro, spoke English very well and he took us to his house, one long, large room, even cleaner and fresher looking that the others.

Coronado and his followers were received as celestial visitors by these simple-hearted children of the hills, who like all other Indian tribes, perhaps had their prophecy concerning the white Savior who should come from the East. The Spaniard soon showed his purely human character by treacherous cruelty and bloodshed. After three days war, the Spaniards stood victorious on the hill of the Acomas. Then came priest and nun with their religion of mercy to efface the memory of the wrongs done to the Indians and bind their hearts with cords that have outlasted the mastery of the sword and the changes of centuries.[4]

Thus, they parted from these friendly, unspoiled children of nature, feeling privileged that they had been able to turn back the dial of time and take a peep at a people for whom it has practically stood still for centuries. Later in the day, they visited the Pueblo of the Lagunas, where the government school teacher gave them much more information and introduced them to the Indians, who all seemed very friendly. Clara was interested to know the effect of sending the girls away to school, no doubt thinking about Zintka and considering a plan to send her away to school. It is true that the Pueblo children return to their native customs when they graduate, but at least they are better equipped to adapt themselves to civilization.

That night, Clara and Miss Muller took the train into Arizona, reaching Flagstaff. From there, they hoped to make an overland route to the Grand Canyon, but the road was not open for the season. Not to be discouraged, they took the train on to Williams, where they could transfer to a narrow-gauge branch line which runs within twelve miles of the Grand Canyon. The train was met by a choice of stage coaches for the last leg. At the recommendation of Mr. Thomas Moran, they took the stage to Berry's, where they had accommodation right on the rim of the canyon.

It was sunset when they arrived at the hotel and so, without going to their rooms, 'we rushed to get the first glimpse of this spot which for grandeur and sublimity is conceded by all who see it, to surpass all that their memory or imagination has to offer. The view from this point has furnished some of the most notable pictures of the canyon. How inadequate are words to describe it; one is obliged to take refuge in the commonplace.'

They took long walks the next day on each side of the rim, and the day following went down the trail to the river, 1,000 feet below.

'This day so filled our souls with its mystery, its grandeur, its supreme ecstasy, and pain that there was nothing to do but leave the place as having had all that mortal life could endure.'[5]

Clara and Miss Muller then left Flagstaff and went direct to Los Angeles to attend several meetings and speaking engagements, under the auspices of the Woman Suffrage Association. A large and earnest audience was present to listen to

Miss Muller, followed by numerous questions and a gratifying appreciation.

The meetings in Los Angeles were followed by ten days in San Francisco, Oakland, and then they went across to San Rafael. In Santa Rosa, the three got close to nature in a camp in the forest of the mighty redwood trees. It was then time for Clara to say goodbye to her friend Henrietta Muller, since she was heading up to Vancouver. From here, she would sail for Japan, China, and India before returning to England towards the end of 1901. She promised to return to the United States, planning to make Washington the center for her work.

Clara returned from her travels to the Pacific Coast, promising to return the next year to Los Angeles, when that city would be hosting the Biennial of the General Federation of Women's Clubs. Upon returning through Beatrice to collect Zintka, Clara was brought back down to earth to face the problems of being a separated single mother of an adopted Indian girl. Zintka was staying with Clara's sister, Mary, who was also able to update Clara on the situation with her husband. It seems that Leonard was now living openly with his mistress as his private secretary.

Leonard had been having a successful year, due to securing as clients a group of settlers who had claims for compensation from the Indian Court of Claims. Governor Savage had recently appointed him as the Adjutant General of Nebraska. The most shocking newspaper report for Clara, however, would have been the following from the *Nebraska State Journal*.

CLAIM FOR HEAVY DAMAGES
MRS. MARTINEZ OF BEATRICE A WAR SUFFERER
LOST A SUGAR PLATATION
Wants Government to Reimburse Her for Cuban Property
Dispatches from Washington state that Maria Soler E. Martinez has filed a claim with the Spanish war claims commission in the sum of $216,666. This amount is stated as the value of personal and other property connected with a sugar plantation in Cuba which was destroyed during the late insurrection in the island. Mrs. Martinez makes the claim by virtue of the naturalization of her husband as a citizen of the United States.

*Mrs. Martinez has been in the employ of Gen L. W. Colby as stenographer for a number of years, and in this capacity she was with the general during the Spanish-American war, and while in the south she met and married Senor Tomasso Martinez. At the close of the war she returned to Beatrice and again assumed her former duties in the office of General Colby, where she is still employed. Senor Martinez has never visited this city. He is reported as having gone to South America where he is said to have large personal interests.*⁶

Reading this article was the first that Clara had heard of this story, and it must have shocked her that this denoted a conspiracy to steal money from the United States government, involving the man she married and the young German girl that she cared for all those years ago. The shame of a divorce seemed small compared to the scandal of a crime such as this.

News about Leonard Colby's care for Zintka was not much better. It seems that Zintka had visited her father's home at a time when Leonard's brother and his family were visiting.

Zintka was climbing on David Colby's wagon and bounced up and down on the black leather seat. David's two sons were sitting around, and one called out for Zintka to get down from the wagon. When she refused, the boys started chanting, 'Zintka's a dirty squaw!'

Zintka responded by jumping off the wagon and landing feet first on the younger of the boys. The boy's screams brought his parents out from the house, and they rushed the boy to the hospital to check for what they thought were severe injuries. When Leonard heard about the altercation, he dragged Zintka out of the stable and beat her with a riding whip, while her cousins watched. Then he threw the whip at her fallen body and stomped off in disgust, leaving Zintka huddled in the hay, her legs blistered. The cousins crowded around to see if she was crying, so she sprang up, grabbed the horsewhip, and chased the terrified children into the house.

By the time Clara heard the story, Zintka's legs had healed, but Mary told her they were quite badly bruised. Clara was strongly opposed to physical discipline, so she must have been very angry with Leonard. He was just too impatient to take care of Zintka. When he heard that Clara was scheduled to attend the conference in Los Angeles the next year, Leonard quickly offered to pay for Zintka to go with her.

Returning to Washington brought Clara back to her work for the suffrage cause, through the DCWSA, through the *Woman's Tribune*, and her lectures whenever she could secure them. But it was not going to be a good year on the Federal scene. The Select Committee of the Senate on Woman Suffrage was made up of Senators from the East and West coasts who did not believe in Woman Suffrage. They unfortunately excluded the great Midwest, with four States where women had the full ballot and whose Senators knew something about the matter from experience. As Clara wrote in the *Tribune*, 'To have persons on a woman suffrage committee who do not believe in woman suffrage or who are not actively interested in forwarding its interests, is analogous to what it would be to have the Committee on Railroads composed of men who thought we ought to travel entirely by stagecoach.'[7]

At a conference of the officers of the NAWSA, meeting in Baltimore before the national convention in Washington, Clara addressed the group, saying she agreed with 'the belief that it is the indifference of women themselves that have prevented the extension of suffrage to them.' The main conference started on February 12, and in the absence of one of their Honorary Presidents, Elizabeth Cady Stanton, Clara Colby was asked to read her paper of 'Educated Suffrage.'

Clara's presentation to the convention was an address on 'Industrial Problems,' in which she criticized the pending legislation in Congress. The legislation provided for the abolishment of sick leave for government clerks, on the grounds that women were continually absenting themselves. A statement such as this, she said, was a covert attack on womanhood. And in the interstate commerce commission, where no women were employed, the percentage for absences was greatest.

It was nearly time for the Sixth Biennial of the General Federation of Women's Clubs, held in Los Angeles on May 1-8, 1902. Clara was to attend as a delegate from the Women's National Press Association and as Editor of the *Woman's Tribune*. It was for this trip that Leonard had promised to pay for Zintka to travel with Clara, and now that he was Adjutant-

General of Nebraska, he could hardly say that he did not have the money. So it was, on the evening of April 21st, that Clara, Zintka, and a few of their friends left Washington. They traversed the Sunset Route via New Orleans, San Antonio, and El Paso, to the 'City of Angels.'

They were traveling in the Tourist Car, which she reported as having two advantages: one, the lack of upholstery, which gave a sense of cleanliness and coolness, much appreciated in going Southward; and two, the gas stove, available to passengers who travel with lunch baskets. In this first two nights to New Orleans and the next night to San Antonio they got a sleeper car, but the last two nights they had to make do with a makeshift bed in the Chair Car. With three stopovers in New Orleans, San Antonio and El Paso, they took a total of eight days to complete the journey to Los Angeles.

Their day spent in New Orleans was under the guidance of an excursion agent of the travel company, who was anxious to get some positive media in the *Tribune*. The day was a history lesson for Zintka, visiting the house that was the headquarters of General Andrew Jackson, followed by a taste of the different food found in the French Market. Clara made sure that she called upon old friends and anyone who might be known to readers of the *Tribune*, and she retraced the steps she had taken at the New Orleans Exposition back in 1885. Then, it was a ferry crossing of the Mississippi to the Algiers station to catch the train and another overnight journey to San Antonio.

Zintka's history lesson continued in San Antonio, where 200 years before Columbus discovered America, the Nasonites were driven out of Mexico by the Aztecs. When the Aztecs came over the highlands and looked down on the San

Antonio Valley, they cried out 'Texas,' which meant 'Paradise' in their tongue. Nearly 400 years later, the Spaniards arrived and interpreted the name 'Texas' as meaning 'welcome.' Five Spanish missions were founded to convert and civilize the Indians, one of which was named Alamo. Here Zintka's history lesson advanced to the year 1836, when the Battle of the Alamo was fought between 5,000 Spaniards (under Santa Ana) and 182 citizen soldiers... and inspired Texas to gain its independence. Always reverting to her classical education, Clara wrote that 'Thermopylae had its messenger of defeat; the Alamo had none.'[8]

They reached El Paso the next morning, where they took a room in the Hotel Orndorff. It was a hotel managed by a woman, Mrs. A. C. DeGroff, formerly Mrs. Orndorff. Clara always appreciated a successful woman story; the story of a hotel extended to become one of the finest hotels in the South, with 100 rooms with hot and cold running water, electric lights and all modern conveniences, particularly inspired. 'From the galleries which run around three sides, almost every room has access to a beautiful hillside view, the main part of the city and the pretty little park below where live alligators sun themselves beside their pool; carefully wired in of course; where musicians play in the season; where semi-tropical trees give beautiful shade the year around and where Mount Franklin shows up finely to the North.'[9]

Clara went across to the Mexican town of Juarez to visit the Cathedral, but she left Zintka behind in El Paso, for reasons we will discover later. She first went to admire the old cathedral, which she said was in an excellent state of preservation, considering that it had entered its fourth century. Sitting in the cool shade of the church was refreshing after the climb up the bright white street and steps. Clara watched a class of devout girls taking their instruction from the priest. Soon the churchgoers departed, and she went out into the hot streets, with their long rows of adobe houses, almost windowless, on one side.

It was as quiet as a city of the dead; everybody had gone to take a siesta. A Mexican lunch cost her little more than ten cents in United States money, and it filled the time until the people started returning to the streets. As they did, she noticed that all the people generally sauntered in one direction, which was towards the Plaza de Toros. Clara wrote up her experience in the *Tribune*.

One side of the wide street leading to the plaza was devoted to gambling tables where all sorts of games of chance were being played. The saloons were open on every hand and drinking was going on, but without the boisterousness that marks such places in our country. To the right was the rival attraction of the cock pit. The crowd grew into the thousands, a goodly number of them being Americans from El Paso, and some being my fellow travellers and fellow delegates to the Biennial.

At length the doors were opened and I can hardly bring myself to write it, but I went in too. All things are 'material' to a writer and this was an experience that would never be duplicated. Could a bullfight possibly be as bad as one's idea of it when these well dressed, well mannered people, many of whom I had seen at the cathedral that day, were hurrying in with merry laugh and careless grace as if going to a fiesta. I am sure I wore a very solemn face as I passed on and took my seat.

Eventually, the signal was given, the band played, the gates below were thrown open and a half-dazed bull was driven into the arena which was entered at the same time by several toreadors, the matador and two picadors on horseback. The former flourished their crimson cloths and did their best to excite the bull. The men on horseback chased the animal around and if the spectators might have thought the bull had no fight in him they were quickly un-deceived as one of the horses was soon gored horribly on his side while his rider kept urging him round and around after the bull with the blood dropping at every step upon the ground. The horsemen have but five minutes in which to do their part and drive so many of the barbs into the quivering flesh of the bull. At length by a sudden turn the animal tossed the other horse in the air, the rider was thrown and for a moment it seemed as if the bull, who had my sympathies at least, was to get the best of it. But the to-readors rushed up and waving their mantles attracted the attention of the bull and the dying horse and the man were taken from the gory field.

Now came the turn of the toreadors who were to have five minutes to see how many barbs they could plant in the body of the bull and to amuse the spectators by showing how near they could come to the infuriated animal without being gored. Five minutes are up and the matador must now relieve the victim from his sufferings in five minutes or lose the reward of his afternoon's work. All had been child's play before to the thrusting and parrying which this gaily-costumed performer now achieved. The spectators had broken into loud applause as each thrust had nearly *reached its mark and now they cheered on the matador as he prepared to finish his bloody work. Two or three times he plunged his poniard in lightly, wounding and weakening the animal who now reserved his last strength for one mad rush at his tormentor who met it with the thrust of the dagger to its hilt and the poor beast was dead. Immediately horses were brought in to drag out the quivering body, the gore was wiped up and the arena was ready for the next combat.*

The final scene was perhaps no more brutal than may be seen any minute at a slaughter house and at worst the torture of the animal may not last more than fifteen minutes. The men are almost never in danger that their skill cannot avert, and, it is said that the horses that are gored are of little money value. But I must confess that I cried like a child at the sight of their hurt and in my tears was mingled a pain for all the brute things that suffer from their human fellows, and for pleasure loving, polite and devout people that they had missed the training in love for all living creatures, which is true worship.[10]

Although four other victims were brought into the arena before the day was over, Clara felt that she could endure no more, so she left the Plaza de Toros and walked back across the bridge into El Paso. She wanted to tell Zintka about the beautiful cathedral that she had seen, and not much more.

The train for the last leg of the journey left El Paso the following morning; this section being without the comfort of a sleeper car. The train reached Tucson long after dark, so although they stopped for some time, they could see little of this interesting place. In the morning, they arrived in Yuma, and a stay there gave them the opportunity to enjoy a break-fast in the town, and for the Indians the chance to offer their wares for sale. Zintka purchased for a quarter, a pottery medi-cine man, with paint and feathers.

The first stop in the Los Angeles area was at Colton, where the ladies of the Woman's Club of Colton were at the station to welcome the delegates with gifts of large, splendid oranges.

The Biennial was a big event for Los Angeles, a city then of 175,000 inhabitants. The annual Fiesta de las Flores had been delayed to 1902 to coincide with the General Federation of Women's Clubs. This was so that the women could enjoy the spectacle of its floral parade.

Over the next four months, the *Tribune* published a travel-ogue of Los Angeles. LA was about to be the fastest growing city in America, and the first to have all of its streets lit by electricity. Clara wrote that it would be difficult to find a more impressive city view than that obtained from the hill just to the north, reached by a funicular railway called Angel's Flight. This had opened the previous year. 'As the sunset deepened into twilight, the myriad electric lights come out as gleaming dots in the gathering gray,' she wrote.

With her connections in the women's press clubs and her suffrage associations, Clara accepted invitations from recep-tions at private homes of some of the wealthiest residents of the City of Angels.

From the moment Clara arrived, what caught the attention of everyone she met was her traveling companion, little Zint-ka Lanuni. *The Los Angeles Times* published an article upon her arrival headed, 'MRS. COLBY'S LOST BIRD,' in which they described Zintka as 'a pretty little Sioux Indian girl, who was adopted into the Colby family a little more than eleven years ago. She shows great interest in the novel sights of the Fiesta season and is delighted particularly with the beautiful decorations of the city.'[11]

No doubt Zintka loved the three-hour sailing trip across to Santa Catalina Island, even though it was a rough crossing. Clara, in her usual way, documented the history of Santa Catalina in the *Tribune*, complete with tales of the Indians removed from the island by the Franciscans and one in particular who was left alone for twenty years. Clara and her friend, Laura Johns of Kansas, set up housekeeping apartments on Santa Catalina for nine days. Laura Johns and Clara Colby had both been fellow State presidents of their suffrage associations, plus a friend of Mrs. Johns had a daughter of Zintka's age.

Clara and Zintka started heading home but stopped along the way, in Madison, for the Wisconsin WSA conference. This was followed by the Ohio WSA conference in Cleveland, where Clara was also speaking. They returned home in time to receive the sad news that Elizabeth Cady Stanton had passed away, on October 26, 1902, at her home in New York City. Clara had lost a mentor and longtime friend, whom she now wrote about in the *Tribune*:

> *In making this number of the Woman's Tribune a memorial for Elizabeth Cady Stanton, the editor not only expresses a sense of Mrs. Stanton's service to women, but also a personal friendship which extended through the last twenty-five years. It began with admiration, when Mrs. Stanton came to lecture in Beatrice, Nebraska, in the seventies. It deepened into reverence as the writer came to the*

National WSA conventions and noted her never-failing ge-niality, her serene dignity, her love of justice and her splen-did courage. It grew into gratitude as Mrs. Stanton became a constant contributor to the Woman's Tribune, saying she would write for it while she could still hold a pen. It ripened into joy of fellowship as the full and deep significance of the woman movement opened up, its grand onward sweep coming to seem a chord in the majestic harmonies of the universe, the Hallelujah chorus of God's creation.[12]

Clara had lost her mentor... and in many ways one of her strongest supporters from among the pioneers of the women's movement. Susan B. Anthony was frequently critical of Clara Colby; especially of her marriage failure and the adoption of an Indian child, neither of which Clara had any control over. Mrs. Stanton, by comparison, never criticized Clara from a personal standpoint. She had more understanding that a woman does not carry the responsibility for everything her husband does. Mrs. Stanton led a separate life from her husband in the later years of her marriage, before her husband died, and that probably helped her to be more understanding than Miss Anthony, who had never married. The younger leaders of the movement tended to side with Miss Anthony and some even displayed racism in their opinions towards the adoption of Zintka. In the future, Clara would direct her energies in other directions than the National American Woman's Suffrage Association.

CHAPTER 17

BETRAYAL

IN DECEMBER 1902, CLARA received a letter from the Principal of the Salem Academy and College in Winston-Salem, North Carolina. Reading with pleasure, the letter said that they would have no objection to accepting an Indian girl in the school and they were prepared to receive her immediately. Clara took the train with Zintka down to the school in North Carolina. It was to be a very short stay.

On January 9, 1903, the Principal wrote that they had found that Zintka could not remain with them and must be returned to her mother's care. She had been thrown in contact with young people in the city schools, from whom she learned things which she should not have discovered. In a subsequent letter of January 19, the Principal said that they had sent her home not because of trivial matters, but because there were clear-cut indications of influences which they knew would bring grave evil to the school.

Clara tried other schools throughout 1903, and for a few months, she attended St Mary's Academy in Alexandria, Virginia. But, in a letter dated August 16th, they wrote: 'Dear Mrs. Colby, I regret very much we cannot take Zintka back. It is out of the question. She was too troublesome, and many of our children object to her. We regret it, but we have decided not to admit her.'

In September, Red Springs Seminary wrote that they were anxious to have Zintka because they believed that Americans owe everything possible to the Indians. Then came the 'but': there was a tribe of Indians located close to the school with a nasty reputation in the community, and they were afraid that local people might think that Zintka was from this tribe.

Leonard Colby's cries of having no money to support Clara and Zintka might finally have had some substance, for he lost his job as Adjutant-General in January of 1903—although he was still earning money as a successful defense attorney.

The loss of his position with the state government might well have been the first move by some of his enemies to destroy him, if the reports in December 1903 were right. On December 8, 1903, a grand jury began investigating the appropriation of money to reimburse the government for blankets supplied to the state penitentiary after a fire at that institution two years before. One of the main witnesses was the person who had replaced Gen. Colby, Adjutant General Culver. One of the difficulties faced by the grand jury was in finding a bookkeeper who had worked in the department during the period in question, and who may have signed a warrant as 'per M.' There was a stenographer named Meachan, but she had been replaced by Mrs. Martinez, who had previously been

employed by General Colby in his Beatrice law office.[1]   The
decision to charge Colby with embezzlement was reported as
follows:

> ### COLBY IS INDICTED
> *Before the adjournment of the grand jury, a bill was found
> against Colby for the embezzlement of amounts aggregat-
> ing $3,000 of government funds, paid to him in trust by
> the state of Nebraska and others for equipment, belonging
> to the United States army. The bill charges that while ad-
> jutant general of Nebraska, General Colby turned over to
> the state penitentiary during January, 1901, 700 United
> States army blankets to be used in an emergency caused
> by a fire in that institution: that the state legislature ap-
> propriated $2,280 to reimburse the government for these
> blankets, the amount was never paid into the United States
> treasury when Colby's term as adjutant general expired.*
> *There are thirty seven counts in the bill, mostly for
> small sums, charging Colby with selling small arms and
> other equipment to members of the national guard and ap-
> propriating the money to his own use.[2]*

It would be more than a year before the matter would come to
a head and in the meantime, Leonard would have been incurring costs and losing business as a result. Mrs. Marie Martinez
(Maud) continued to work for the government in Lincoln, and
she continued to press Leonard Colby to divorce his wife and
marry her. No doubt she had plenty of information that she
could use to put pressure upon Colby if she chose to.

   In August, Leonard sat down and wrote a letter to Clara,
documenting his request for a divorce, the first time the de-

mand was put in writing. Finally, the reality that her marriage was over dawned on Clara. She wrote a letter to herself, which described her feelings at the time.

The second fateful day in my life. How cruelly kind is destiny that holds one to the ordinary round of duties and conventionalities when one would give anything to get away from everybody just to think. I want to think and yet I dare not think. I must have time to get accustomed to the idea presented, so that when I think I may be just to all. Just now I seemed absolutely stunned into a strange unnatural calm. Why is it that I can laugh and tell and plan when I am actually dead. Only on August 5, my birthday, I was trying to think what I had to be thankful for, being determined to find something. And this seemed the greatest boon that life had to give: that my love had lost the power to grieve me. That out of ten years of suffering had come peace – not loss of love. I have not thought to call it that, but surely it is terrible when one's happiness is in the power of any human being. I can see that one should depend only on God for happiness. It was something of the feeling that I was finding my freedom in the rest of trust in the Infinite wisdom that gave me the calm which seemed to tell of victory. I must express myself and am putting down my thoughts the better to analyze them. For I am to have the most momentous question to decide that can ever come to me: and I must look at it for others as well as myself. Can I for love's sake tear love out of my heart? What do I owe to myself in the matter? I ought to have stood for my dignity as a wife ten years ago, but I was so much in the bondage of my love and conventionality that I could not. I made myself believe and have given up the illusion, that by my forbear-

ance I should win him back. How different my life would have been, how much more honourable and sincere if with one great wrench I had settled the matter then. And others would have been happy all this time too. It is impossible to conceive a state of affairs farther removed from what I hoped, and from what I had a right to expect my magnanimity would have brought about the what exits now. God help me to do the right thing now, whatever it may be shown to me to be.[3]

Clara wrote to her sister, and Mary responded with strong animosity towards 'that creature.' She strongly urged Clara not to let him get a divorce. Given the encouragement from her sister, Clara wrote back to Leonard to let him know that if he had become involved again with that woman, Maud's own marriage freed him from all obligations to her. 'Free yourself from degrading associations and return to fidelity to your marriage vows and hold yourself to the same moral standards which you demand, as a lawyer, as a man, and as a good citizen.'

She still failed to see that Leonard did not share the same moral standards as she held herself.

Leonard responded with a different tactic. His letter laid out how they should start the divorce proceedings, and he laid out the benefits that would accrue to Clara as a settlement

...It would probably be advisable for you to bring the suit there in Washington and have summons sent me to accept service of. I will bear all of the expenses, and furnish the required proofs. I will also agree on the amount of alimony to be paid you, and sell everything I have to pay it.

You should have enough to purchase a home, if you wish, and two or three thousand dollars beside, say six or seven thousand dollars in the aggregate. If you wish I will take care and provide for Zintka in addition.

... I have no charges or faults that I wish to have brought against you. I want to be as just and honorable as my nature will allow. I am willing to assume all blame in such proceedings, the many excellent qualities and virtues which you possess....

Please write me your views and what you are willing to do, taking matters as they are and not as you might hope or wish them to be.

Yours respectfully
L. W. Colby.[4]

With Clara having among her Washington friends some of the most successful lawyers in the country, she could well have turned this offer into a successful conclusion to her marriage. But she still fought back on principle, coupled with a feeling of concern for Leonard, which she expressed in her reply.

I must add to this letter a statement concerning the new divorce law of the District, of which you may be unaware. Divorce is now only granted for adultery, and the co-respondent must be named. Could you bear to be the accuser? Could you endure to be disgraced here where you have been so honored?[5]

Clara's diary notes for August showed how she tried to continue life, but her mind kept returning to the problem of the divorce. She visited the Indian office and met with A. O.

Clara continued to struggle to meet her living expenses and those of publishing the *Tribune*, and she continued to write to Leonard, requesting that he fulfill his responsibilities for supporting her and his daughter. In July 1904, she received the following:

TELEGRAM

Mrs. C. B. Colby,   2420 14th Street, Washington DC.
No money before Aug first. Make your own arrangements.
L. W. Colby

By the beginning of August, Clara was getting desperate and was about to get evicted because of non-payment of rent. On top of this, she had planned to move to Portland, Oregon in May, from where she would publish the *Tribune*. This was in support of a major campaign for the suffrage amendment, currently underway in Oregon. She thought that this would be a much better environment for Zintka, rather than bringing her back to Washington. There was also the problem of paying the outstanding tuition fees for Zintka at All Saints, without which she would not be allowed to return after the summer vacation.

Zintka had gone to stay with friends in Maine for the summer vacation, and Clara was supposed to go to Boston to bring her back to Washington, but unfortunately, she did not have enough money for the fare. Before she could resolve how she was going to get Zintka, her hosts, Mr. and Mrs. Mauger, caught Zintka sneaking out to see boys. Mrs. Mauger offered to return Zintka as soon as possible. Afterward, Mrs. Mauger discovered that a ring and some sheet music she had loaned to

Zintka had gone missing. Truly worried, Clara was still looking for a way out of this financial mess with the help of some
assistance from her husband.

2420 14th Street, Washington DC.
August 11, 1904

My dear Husband,

*I have been anxiously awaiting a reply to the letter I wrote
eight days ago. Remember there is now probably only two
weeks to arrange everything. I must remind you that if you
could not send the rent money by August 1st you certainly
ought to have sent it by this time. I have been able to meet
the June rent but this crippled me so that I have not been
able to do anything else, even to buy the boxes for packing.*

*The climax of my troubles you may gather from the
imperative call in Mrs. Mauger's letter, I cannot go to Boston for lack of money. The situation must be dealt with
at once and you must send me the money to get her down
here and to Chicago.*

*This is a good time to settle what is to be done with
her. The Sioux Falls school opens some time in Sept. and
I will keep her until that time and see she gets safely there
if you will agree to pay the old bill by the time the school
opens and guarantee the future payments so that Miss
Peabody will look to you instead of to me. If you will not do
this I shall send her right on to you to place in the Atchison
convent as you proposed before. This attraction to boys is
the all dominating influence of her life at this time. When
she is older and her judgement developed let us hope she
will be different. But safety is now the thing to be thought
of. I cannot give it to her, for when she was here that three
weeks although I devoted myself to her I could not keep her*

CHAPTER 18

CLARA COLBY IS FREE

LIVING IN PORTLAND DID not mean that Clara would not frequently travel to the East. She accepted an invitation from the Wisconsin Suffrage Association to speak at their 1904 convention, held in Janesville in November, and she took opportunities to fill lecture engagements while in that State. Her friend, the Rev. Olympia Brown, had already set some dates for her to speak, so Clara used the *Tribune* to promote to local clubs and associations that might be interested in her lectures. Subjects which she offered to talk on included 'Old Louisiana,' 'Municipal Ownership in Glasgow,' 'Margaret Fuller' and several other topics, and she would give these lectures for a moderate fee or on a partnership plan. Payment for some of her speeches was by a voluntary collection from the audience.

Just as she wrote about her London Walks during her 1899 trip, and her Wanderings Westward about her 1901 and 1902 travels to the Pacific coast, Clara wrote an Editor's Letter for the next three issues of the *Tribune*. These articles covered her travels on the Northern Pacific Railroad to Wisconsin and her travels back to Washington for the Congressional hearing of the Federal Suffrage Bill.

There were several reasons for Clara to be visiting Wisconsin, the first being the annual meeting of the Wisconsin Woman's Suffrage Association in Janesville, presided over by the Rev. Olympia Brown. At the end of 1902, Olympia Brown had asked Clara to join her in a reincarnation of the Federal Suffrage Association, the one which had initially been formed in Chicago in 1892. The revamped organization would be known as 'the Federal Woman's Equality Association', and its primary objective would be to seek the enfranchisement of women through an act of Congress. Rev. Olympia Brown was elected the President and Clara Bewick Colby as the corresponding secretary, a position she would hold for the rest of her life.

The Editor's Letters printed in the *Tribune* provide a beautiful travelogue of the journey through the Cascades, across the Rockies and the northern prairie states into Minneapolis. The large advertisements displayed in the *Tribune* indicate the method by which Clara paid for her seat and her bed in the sleeper. She reached Madison in the early morning of November 15th and spent a few hours with her sister Mary, before moving on to Janesville. As a continuing member of the Wisconsin Association, Clara always felt that she was returning home when she joined their meetings.

'Gentlemen of the jury, if this poison kills me you can convict my client, but if I live, as I shall, you will have to bring in a verdict in her favor.'

With a parting bow to the judge and the twelve men in the jury box he walked rapidly out of the courtroom to his office, where he locked himself in. In twenty minutes he was back in the court room, smiling and confident. It took the jury about three minutes to bring in a verdict of acquittal.

A few days afterward it leaked out that General Colby had a doctor in his office and that the physician removed the poison with a stomach pump. Of course, there was an uproar, but the law says a prisoner's life cannot be twice placed in jeopardy. And then, as a wise old lawyer suggested, Colby had destroyed the only evidence upon which conviction could be secured in the event of another trial.[3]

Whether this story was true or whether it was just part of the self-promotion that Leonard Colby loved to engage in we do not know, but it certainly helped his notoriety throughout the United States. One thing was sure; his acquittal in the court in Omaha would have been a great relief and allowed him to concentrate on other legal matters, including getting divorced from Clara.

At about the same time as Leonard was celebrating his acquittal, Clara involved herself in numerous activities connected with her reasons for moving to Oregon. Portland was the site of the Lewis and Clark Centennial Exposition, running from June until October 1905; not officially a world's fair but close to it. As well, the National American Woman Suffrage Association was holding its national conference there from

June 28th to July 5th, at which Clara would be the Wisconsin delegate. The Oregon state government had scheduled a vote for an amendment to its constitution for June of 1906, and the suffrage movement was planning a big campaign to support this.

There had previously been a woman suffrage newspaper published in Oregon by Abigail Duniway, but that folded some seventeen years prior, so the *Woman's Tribune* became the only newspaper of its kind west of the Rockies. Before the Lewis and Clark Exposition started, Clara rented a house where she could sublet rooms to visitors to the show, and she advertised these rooms in the *Tribune*.

The other reason for Clara's move to Oregon was to try to find a home where Zintka would be free of the negative influences she had fallen under in Washington. In April, Clara received a letter from the superintendent at the Indian school in South Dakota. Zintka's eyes had been sore for about six weeks and were examined by a specialist in March, who said there was a white speck on one eye that would get better, but it would take some time. This news was significant anxiety for Clara, and she asked whether Zintka could come home to Portland before the summer vacation. The superintendent wrote that Zintka had been a very good girl and 'that if you wish to return Zintka after vacation, that is next September, I will be pleased to take her.'[4]

On May 3, 1905, Zintka boarded the train for St Paul. Here she was met by a friend of Clara's, who saw to it that she caught the Northern Pacific train for Portland.

Clara was eager to spend time with Zintka, but she was frequently away on speaking tours. This meant that she was *city.... General Colby and wife have not lived together for the past twelve years or more. When Mrs. Colby departed from Beatrice she located in Washington, D.C. where she edited the Woman's Tribune for a number of years. She later went to Portland, Oregon, where she continued the publication of the journal and where she was living at last reports.[7]*

The *Nebraska State Journal* reported that the divorce hearing had been held back until the end of the day, just before adjournment, when all others (except parties to the suit) had left the court. Leonard Colby probably arranged this to keep the proceedings from the public.

Reactions from leading suffragists was adverse. The President of the NAWSA, Rev. Anna H. Shaw wrote to Ida Husted Harper, 'I wish she had waited until the campaign was over,' believing that having a divorced woman among their members would lead to a loss of votes. She revealed her ignorance of the circumstances of Clara's situation by her assumption that Clara had control over the timing of the divorce.

From this time on, Clara never got to speak at any of the national conferences of the NAWSA, and as a consequence, she concentrated her efforts more towards the Federal Woman's Equality Association.

On April 18, 1906, an earthquake with an estimated magnitude of 7.9 on the Richter scale hit San Francisco. Up to 3,000 people died, and it destroyed 80% of the city. The people of the whole west coast of America reacted with shock. News of the earthquake disrupted classes at the Chemawa Indian school, so Zintka saw her opportunity to run away and head home for Portland. The staff at Chemawa called the police, who found Zintka at home with Clara. The superintendent of the school came to collect her and take her back to school. Clara persuaded Zintka to give Chemawa another chance. The superintendent wrote to Clara once Zintka was back in school.

Department of the Interior
United States Indian Service
Chemawa, Oregon
April 20, 1906

Mrs. Clara Bewick Colby
65 Union Block
Portland, Oregon

Dear Mrs. Colby
I have just received your letter of yesterday relative to Zintka's visit with you at Portland. I regret very much the unfortunate conduct on her part and hope that we may be able to prevent such in the future.

I think, as you express yourself in your letter, that Mrs. Little did wisely in having the Police take care of her. In talking with the matron at the Police Court, I found that she had been there once before, which was a surprise to me.

Taking the case as it now stands, I would suggest that if you desire us to keep her, that you place her in our hands permanently without giving her any hope of leaving the school until such time as we are satisfied there is a radical change in her. ....

The first step, of course, would be the necessity of having her change her manner of dress. She said to me as we were leaving Portland, that it seemed to her that the Police and everybody watched her when she was on the streets. I informed her that the reason was apparent to any one who observed her flashy way of dressing. ... the time has come, it seems to me, to insist that she dress in a more modest manner. ...

We would be pleased to have you visit Zintka whenever you can make it convenient. With kind regards, I remain, Yours very respectfully,

E. L. Chalecraft, Superintendent.[8]

Having tasted freedom from Chemawa, Zintka tried again, this time with another girl, and she stayed away for several months. Although only sixteen years old, she was smart enough to look after herself and find people from whom she could solicit support. It was not until September that she returned home to Portland, as revealed in a letter from Mrs. Theisz at Chemawa in response to Clara's letter. Zintka had traveled to South Dakota to try and determine whether the rumor that she was Sitting Bull's daughter was correct. There, she had met up with 'Indian Pete' Cuthbertson, who hired her as a cowgirl for his 'Wild West' show.

During Zintka's absence, Clara was traveling throughout Oregon in the lead-up to the Equal Suffrage Amendment on June 4, 1906. Much of her travels were in the more remote and mountainous areas, where she traveled by traditional stagecoach; all documented carefully for her articles for the *Tribune*. Towards the end of the campaign, many of the events the suffragists attended were annual country fairs. These fairs attracted large crowds from neighboring towns. In spite of the continuous rain of those last days, the crowds turned out to hear what the suffragists had to say. In Junction City, Clara reported that twice as many people gathered as could come within the range of her voice.

Sadly for the suffragists, on June 4th, they lost the vote once more, but with her 'never say die' attitude, Clara managed to announce the result with the headline, 'VICTORY DEFERRED.'

The news was coming through to her from Nebraska, although it was to have little effect on Clara. The headline in the *Lincoln Star* of June 9 was, 'LINCOLN WOMAN GETS A FORTUNE.'

The claims made by her lawyer, General L. W. Colby had resulted in Mrs. Marie Martinez being awarded $216,666, plus 17,000 acres of land, sugar, and tobacco plantations and other interests near Matanzas, Cuba, appraised at over $400,000.

The following week, the *Beatrice Daily Sun* announced the marriage of General L. W. Colby and Mrs. Marie C. Martinez.

Colby-Martinez
General L. W. Colby and Mrs. Marie C. Martinez of this city were married at the M. E. parsonage yesterday, Rev. N. A. Martin officiating. Both have resided in Beatrice for many years, and have many friends who will wish them a pleasant voyage over the matrimonial seas.

General and Mrs. Colby left for a trip to the mountains yesterday, and will return to Beatrice, their future home, in a short time.[9]

The news from the Colbys of Nebraska continued to feed the newspapers across the United States; the following article appeared in a Lincoln newspaper in June.

AN INDIAN BRAVE WANTS HIS DAUGHTER

Beatrice, Neb., Chief Little Cloud, head of the tribe of Sioux traveling with the John Robinson circus which showed here yesterday, claims to have documents to show that the adopted daughter of General Colby, 'Lost Bird,' is his own daughter. On alighting from the train here yesterday morning, the chief and his braves started at a brisk trot searching the city for General Colby with tomahawks raised. They searched house after house, finally locating the Colby home on Fifth street. Entering without ceremony, they demanded the little girl, and incidentally asked for the general.

The braves were informed that the child was not there, as the 'Lost Bird' is living in Portland, Oregon. Little Cloud was also informed that the general and his new bride had left but the day before on a wedding trip.

It was at Horton, Kas., that the chief learned who the soldier was who picked up his little daughter at the battle of Wounded Knee. He learned that it was Colby of Beatrice, and so pleased was the chief and his tribesmen that they took to the woods and danced the dance of Good News. At Beatrice, they danced the 'Dance of Good Cheer,' but on finding themselves baffled in their search, went away with dark frowns.[10]

Chief Little Cloud and his tribe of Sioux braves came to Beatrice with John Robinson's circus, in which they, in conjunction with a company of United States cavalry, put on 'the battle of Wounded Knee.' This particular Indian uprising was just a very creative promotion for the circus.

CHAPTER 19

THE FINAL
INJUSTICE

BY THE END OF 1906, Clara was getting desperate for money. She had been trying to sell shares in the land around she thought she owned. During the early 1890s, some of her titles had been deeded to others, while other properties had taxes owing that took up most of the value. Her attorney, Nellie Richardson, wrote several letters concerning the difficulties of raising money from these properties, but she did offer to assist Clara in collecting cash from delinquent subscribers to the *Tribune*. Nellie closed her letter with a note to say, 'A Merry Christmas and a happy, contented year to come is my cordial wish. May you prosper as never before.'

Unable to control Zintka anymore, and unable to help her financially, Clara sent the girl back to Beatrice to live with her father. The Colbys were rich and could well enroll her in a

281

private school, with music lessons she would love. On January 1, 1907, Clara wrote to Leonard.

> *I love and pity Zintka but I have tried all my resources. ... as your adopted daughter you ought to know her and plan for her; I send her to you.... You must assume the responsibility for her future. There is much prejudice against the Indian here and I could never get her in a store even in the holiday rush.*
>
> *While she is unemployed and uncontrolled she will not be happy. She would resort to any expedition to get money to go to the theatres, the dime vaudeville, the most demoralizing thing on earth. Then, there is the Oaks, where it is most dangerous for girls to go. Without her being willing to mind me I simply could not protect her; and was in terror for fear she would get into serious trouble.*[1]

The Colbys were not happy to have Zintka come and live with them, especially Maud, whose newfound position as the wealthy wife of General Colby was the high social position that she had always dreamed about for herself. Now, Maud had an Indian girl living with them. She was horrified. She also quickly became jealous of the attention that Leonard was paying to the seventeen-year-old. According to interviews conducted by the author of *Lost Bird of Wounded Knee*, Leonard Colby had a reputation as one who could not be trusted with young girls. One Beatrice woman recalled that her mother told her never to speak to Leonard Colby on the street and to cross the street whenever he approached. Clara also became concerned by something that Zintka had written about her father, and she wrote to Leonard:

CHAPTER 20

VOTES FOR WOMEN

CLARA LEFT PORTLAND ON May 23, 1908, with her friend
Florence Sullenberg. This trip took them to England, Holland,
France, and Ireland, with stops in Wisconsin, Washington,
and Buffalo along the way, returning to Portland at the end of
October. She left the management of the *Tribune* in the capable care of mother-and-daughter friends from Nebraska, who
produced six issues during her absence. While away, Clara
wrote a regular column under the title, 'A-Foot With My Vision,' a phrase originally penned by her favorite author, Walt
Whitman.

Clara sailed on the White Star liner *'Celtic'* for Liverpool
and then by train to London. They arrived in London on a Friday evening and Saturday morning, quick smart, they walked
over to the offices of the publication *'Votes for Women,'* run by
Miss Christobel Pankhurst. This group were the militant suffragettes, whereas the march that Clara was planning to join

on this day was organized by the more conservative National Union of Suffrage Societies.

By 2 p.m. they joined the other delegates from overseas on the Victoria Embankment, ready for the procession destined for the Royal Albert Hall. More than 10,000 demonstrators made up the cavalcade, interspersed with fifteen bands and vehicles of all kinds. Clara had the honor of carrying the Susan B. Anthony banner all the way to the Royal Albert Hall. The newspapers reported the Hall was filled to its capacity of 13,000 people.

The next event that Clara was required to attend was the International Women's Congress in Amsterdam in the week after the Albert Hall marches, with Carrie Chapman Catt being one of the featured speakers. Traveling via Harwich and the Hook of Holland, the delegates were able to take in visits to Rotterdam, Delft, and Amsterdam, but then hurried back for another big rally by the suffragists in London.

The rally was 'Women's Sunday,' held on June 21st and comprising 30,000 women marching in seven different processions. It culminated in a gathering of up to half a million people in Hyde Park. This event was being organized by Emmeline Pankhurst's Women's Social and Political Union. Emmeline Pankhurst, her daughters and many other leaders of her movement had received repeated prison sentences, where they staged hunger strikes to secure better conditions, and as a result, were sometimes force-fed. Among the attendees were George Bernard Shaw, H. G. Wells, and Thomas Hardy.

The 'Women's Sunday' suffragette march and rally was reputedly the largest demonstration seen in London up until that time. According to the *Daily Express*, 'Hyde Park records dom League at Caxton Hall on Tuesday was reported in *The Times* under the headline 'The Lady from Oregon.' The article covered the meeting in general but also included several quotations from Clara's address. They summed up with the final paragraph, 'When women get the vote they will, one fancies, think somewhat regretfully of such stirring nights as that on which they welcomed the delegates home from Amsterdam and listened breathlessly to the eloquent lady from Oregon.'

Following the suffrage demonstrations and meetings in London, Clara traveled down to Cheltenham to visit once again with Mrs. Frances Swiney, whom she had stayed with on her previous visit to England.

SUFFRAGIST GARDEN PARTY
Favoured by such beautiful weather as to give rise to the suggestion that the Autocrat of the Weather Office has become a suffragist, or had for the day delegated his duties to his wife, the garden party given to members and friends of the Cheltenham Women's Suffrage Society on Saturday was an altogether successful and enjoyable function. ..... supported by Mrs. Clara Bewick Colby (editor of 'The Woman's Tribune,' and USA delegate to the recent International Women's Suffrage Congress at Amsterdam), ...

Mrs. Clara Bewick Colby proceeded to remark that of the countries represented at the congress, seven had gained increased electoral rights during the preceding year.[2]

Clara spoke about the suffrage movement in America and emphatically denied that the anti-suffrage organization was killing the suffrage movement in the United States: a statement made by one of the other ladies attending. In conclusion, she reminded those she was addressing that endurance was the supreme quality. Would the women of Great Britain hold out? The women of all nations of the world were looking to them, and if they gave out, it would be a blow from which the cause would not recover for half a century.

When Clara returned to London, she took up some of the invitations she had received earlier from the three suffrage organizations. She was to speak at events around London before the opening of the International Peace Congress in July.

The largest of these events occurred when the Woman's Social and Political Union sent a delegation to the House of Commons, asking the Prime Minister to give a more satisfactory answer to the resolution made in Hyde Park. After announcing their intention to march to the House of Commons, a police warning was issued, advising the public of the danger of gathering in Parliament Square and obstructing access to Parliament. Clara marched with the WSPU members to the demonstration site, at which several of the leaders were arrested and subsequently jailed.

Many of these leaders were women of independent means, for the employed could not afford to risk position and wages, and they were treated as ordinary criminals, not as political offenders. Upon arrival at Holloway prison, they were called on to give up all their belongings and select clothing from the heaps on the floor. The cells were small; the beds of stuffed grass were hard. Suffragists were given one, two, or three month sentences, depending upon the decision of the judge. When they protested against their conditions by going on hunger strike, they were force fed. It was much tougher campaigning in England compared to Clara's experiences in America.

On July 27, Clara was joined by her friend Belva Lockwood at the Seventeenth Universal Peace Congress. Mrs. Lockwood, a prominent representative of the peace movement in America, was able to introduce Clara to many people of note. The great social event of the Congress was the formal dinner at the Hotel Cecil on the Friday night, at which the Prime Minister was the guest speaker. The Hotel Cecil was a grand hotel located between the Strand and the Embankment in London, which was demolished in 1930.

Another event that Clara wrote about was an afternoon when the delegates all went to Windsor Castle by invitation of the King, at which they had access to many rooms not generally shown to members of the public.

The Peace Congresses were held every year to find ways in which to avoid wars. It is sad to think how little success they had when you consider that this was only eight years before 'the war to end all wars' broke out.

Clara's friend, Florence Sullenberg, had been her traveling companion during the visit to Holland and had marched with her in the two grand processions and the demonstrations at Parliament Square. Miss Sullenberg was now planning to go to Paris and other locations, so Clara decided that she would accompany her to Paris, before returning to take up further speaking and lobbying engagements around Britain.

They took the ferry from Folkestone, UK to Boulogne and spent a week touring the sites of Paris. Clara was so impressed on her first evening to find herself walking through the Place de la Concorde: the place she associated with the most brilliant, thrilling and tragic events of French history. They toured Versailles, Notre Dame, the Louvre, the Musee Luxembourg, and the place where the Bastille once stood.

All the while she kept the suffrage flag flying. She made attempts to meet the editors of *La Suffragiste* and *Le Journal des Femmes*, one being away from Paris and the other who made contact during the evening. She wore her 'Votes for Women' badge while she was in Paris, which gained her friendly comments from two Frenchmen, neither of whom who knew the local suffrage papers or the movement there. She concluded that there was much stronger sentiment for women's suffrage than the leaders knew.

Upon her return from Paris, Clara toured England and Ireland to speak at the suffrage functions and events to which she had been invited. Remuneration was usually a contribution to her expenses or sometimes a fee charged to those attending. The Women's Freedom League paid Clara £3-3s to produce a pamphlet that compared the campaign in America with that in England. The Irish Suffrage League invited her to speak in Dublin but advised her that she might not be able to cover expenses outside of Dublin, even in Belfast. Her most significant support seemed to come from the Cheltenham branch of the Women's Freedom League, home to her friend Mrs. Swiney in the County of Gloucestershire, where Clara was born.

On September 16th, Clara was back in London for a historic breakfast at Queens Hall. It was put on to welcome the release of those suffragette prisoners jailed after the demonstration at Parliament Square in which Clara had participated. Upon the release of the suffragettes from prison, it had become the custom to take the horses away from the carriage, to be replaced by fellow suffragettes, who would then draw them away from Holloway. On this day, three prisoners were met with cheers and embraces by a large group of suffragettes as they came out of the prison yard. Ten young women dressed in white had long, tri-color sashes, with which they fastened themselves to the heavy wagon and drew it the long distance to Queen's Hall. Clara described the scene in the *Tribune* as follows:

I had the opportunity to ride on the first wagon next to the carriage in which the ex-prisoners were and thus had a good chance to see the pretty sight of young girls in white with sashes and streamers of the colors of the W.S.P.U. drawing the carriage. There was a goodly showing of women walking behind with banners and self-sacrificing young ladies who tripped along beside the procession selling copies of the suffrage paper, 'Votes for Women.' People thronged the streets and waved handkerchiefs from windows all the way along the route to St. Clement's Inn, the office of the W.S.P.U., where the long march ended.[3]

The final commitment of Clara's 1908 European travels was to attend the International Congress on Moral Education, to which she had been appointed a delegate by Governor Chamberlain of Oregon. She returned to the United States at the end of September on the '*Lusitania*,' reported as a glorious voyage, as far as the weather was concerned.

She returned first to Washington, where she stayed with her friend Dr. Clara MacNaughton. The doctor hosted a reception at her home for members of the Woman's National Press

Association to welcome Clara home. The Washington papers described the event:

Mrs. Colby entertained the many guests with an interesting description of her trip abroad, describing the scenes and incidents of the great suffragette demonstration at Hyde Park and in Caxton. Mrs. Colby, who is visiting only a few days in Washington, goes from here to the National Woman Suffrage Association, which opens in Buffalo, N.Y., tomorrow, after which she will return to her home in Oregon, having travelled nearly 10,000 miles.[4]

After leaving Washington, Clara stopped in Buffalo for the annual NAWSA conference, although she was no longer invited to be a speaker.

By November of 1908, Clara was back in Portland, where she worked in getting the local suffragists to support the program of the National Petition, as promoted by the NAWSA. The National Petition was an initiative to get women nationwide to sign a petition to show the level of support held for woman suffrage across the United States. It was to be sent to Congress on February 15, 1909, Susan B. Anthony's birthday.

The Oregon State President of WSA, Abigail Duniway, had shown no interest in getting her members to sign the petition, and Clara had found her a difficult person to deal with since moving to Oregon. The most likely cause of this would have been the fact that Mrs. Duniway also published a woman suffrage newspaper, called *The New Northwest*, and she resented the competition from the *Woman's Tribune*, when Clara moved it to Portland. It seems others shared the difficulties of dealing with Mrs. Duniway; the problems with the National

Petition program led to the NAWSA reaching out for Clara's support.

The Chairman of the NAWSA at the time was Carrie Chapman Catt, who Clara knew well, although their relationship had not been close ever since Clara had published Elizabeth Cady Stanton's *Woman's Bible* back in 1896. On November 28, 1908, Carrie Catt wrote to Clara, enclosing a supply of petitions and leaflets, asking her to help her get the program moving in Oregon. She warned, 'I beg you to take no steps until you have seen Mrs. Duniway and Mrs. Evans and there is agreement among you as to how the work shall be done.'[5] It looked like Clara was being set up to mediate between the warring suffragists, but she replied to say that she would try.

The next letter from Carrie Catt was more revealing of her feelings about Abigail Duniway.

Your letter came this morning. The result of the conference with Mrs. Duniway is exactly what we should expect, of course. Now the question is how to go at it without her. I am sure the state could be organized if she were only out of the way. If the board do not take up the work I hope you will let me know what can be done.

The kind of militant suffrage which is needed most in Oregon, I should think, would be the kind which would knock out those who stand in the way of better organization and of a higher type of work. I sometimes thought, and I say this confidentially, that many suffragists who think they are making great sacrifices for the cause, fail to make the one which would be most effectual, and that is, to stop working. It is a pity that it is so, but we all know of cases where people hang on, and like the dog in the man-

*ger, keep anybody else from doing the work which cries out
to be done.*

*I shall await with interest your further report to learn
what we are to expect of Oregon.[6]*

A further letter from Carrie Catt reveals that Mrs. Duniway
had decided that another petition must not be circulated in
Oregon. In her letter to Clara, Mrs. Catt asks, 'Now the question is, what shall we do?' She says that Oregon will be the
only state in the Union not represented on the petition. Mrs.
Duniway has the support of the WCTU, and without the Oregon WSA, they have no up-to-date list of individuals.

She closes with, 'I shall await your reply with interest.'
With this, she passes the problem to Clara, but with only
three months to go before the petition was to be handed to
Congress, it was an almost impossible task.

CHAPTER 21

INDIAN MAID WEDS

AMONG THE PILE OF mail waiting for Clara when she returned home to Portland was a letter postmarked 'Milford, Nebraska' and dated August 8, 1908, from Zintka. Clara's letters addressed to Haskell had been forwarded on to her, and she sounded so happy to hear her mother writing about London, recalling their times in Hyde Park and at the Tower of London. The next part of the letter came as a bolt from the blue.

> *... No. I am not at Haskell any more. I don't know where I'm at. I'm in the United States somewhere. The weather here is awfully hot. Worse than South Africa, or down in Mexico, I think.*
>
> *With lots of love to you, hoping you will write soon, I am as ever,*
>
> > *Your loving daughter, Zintka L. Colby*
>
> *PS. Be sure and bring me something from the old country.[1]*

Clara had heard of Milford, it was not far from Lincoln. In the course of her campaigning to change the legislation to increase the age of sexual consent, she had become aware of the place, but she had no idea why Zintka was there. Her ex-husband was not forthcoming with information, but Clara soon discovered that Zintka was committed to being held there for twelve months, ending in February 1909. She feared that her husband had something to do with the reason for Zintka's incarceration, but she dare not bring such an awful thought to mind.

Clara wrote to Leonard in an attempt to have him visit with her at Milford—but without success. Knowing that the Colby couple were now among the wealthiest people in Beatrice, owning the Paddock Hotel and Opera House, Clara asked Leonard to consider financing the tuition for Zintka to become a nurse at a training college in Lincoln. Clara had already determined that enrolling Zintka in the course would result in an immediate release from Milford. Clara also mentioned the fact that Zintka needed a pair of glasses, which would cost no more than ten dollars. Unwilling to pay for the nursing school, Leonard left Zintka at Milford for the whole year. On December 28th, Zintka wrote to her mother, a letter which would have to be approved by the matron.

My dear Mama,
I am going to write you a letter t-day, telling you what a nice Christmas I had. The presents you sent me were very nice....
Christmas night we had a very lovely entertainment, the program of which I will send you later. Another girl and myself sang a duet called The Bethlehem Star, and at

possible date. The marriage license was taken out in the name of Margareta Elizabeth Colby, the adopted name of the Indian girl, and her age given as 19. Chalivat is 25 years old.

Zintka dressed in buckskin for the photographer and later for the ceremony..... Chalivat dressed up in the clothes he will travel in – the typical garb of the American lumberman. With his wife he will be sure of traveling in comfort on his two-year journey to Hudson (sic) Bay. ... Zintka said she felt he could lead the roving life they were going to undertake. 'I feel the call of the wild,' she said. 'I want to get into the open. I will care for him always. We are in for a hard time but we will care for each other, and we shall be very happy indeed.'

Mrs. Colby said she was pleased with the match. Chalivat had a happy, care-free idea of things, but he would make just the right husband for the little caged-up, lost bird – lost bird being the translation of Zintka's Indian name. Chalivat and his bride intend to settle in Canada but this will be after Chalivat has appealed to his father for funds to set up a ranch. Chalivat says his father is well able to supply him with money for this purpose.[3]

The next day, the happy couple went across the border into Washington to repeat the ceremony and then returned to Portland. Not having any money, the trip to Hudsons Bay was postponed while they found a way to cover the cost. Clara wrote to Leonard requesting that he send his daughter some money for the wedding, which of course, he ignored. Clara arranged to let them have some privacy for the first few days, while she stayed with friends.

Within two weeks of the marriage, Zintka became sick and had to visit a doctor, only to find that her husband's wedding gift was syphilis. In 1909 this was nigh on a death sentence, although victims of the disease could live for years with the ailment. Zintka erupted in a frenzy of anger.

SPURNED BY BRIDE

Married but a few weeks to the lady of his choice, who is a full-blooded Indian girl, Albert Chalivat, a young French trapper, has found that his romance is not the smooth joyous life he had imagined, and Sunday night was turned out of the happy home of his mother-in-law, Mrs. Clara B. Colby, although she staked him to 25 cents that he might not have to sleep in the rain.

Worse even than being turned out was the declaration of his bride that she does not like him any more, and will no longer live with him.

Chalivat is the young fellow who gained notoriety some weeks ago by his plan of crossing the continent from the Columbia River to Hudson's Bay in a canoe.

Shortly afterward he gained more notoriety by his whirlwind courtship and marriage to Miss Zintka Lanuni, an Indian girl who is the ward of Mrs. Clara B. Colby. The couple went to housekeeping in a little home at Mount Scott, but the bark didn't sail smoothly. There have been rumors of more than verbal encounters between the two, and it is even hinted that the young woman on one occasion was more than a match for her husband.

Last night Chalivat made a scene at the home of his mother-in-law in the Selling-Hirsch building on Washington Street. It is said he had been drinking and had attacked Mrs. Colby when she interfered with his attempt to do harm to his wife. He made a great deal of noise about it all, and a crowd gathered, hearing screams and loud talking.

Sergeant Kienlen quieted the man after he had been appealed to, to protect the women, and took him to the police station. Mrs. Colby asked that he be released, which was done on his promise to return to his Mount Stott home. He went back to his wife however, and pleaded for admission, saying he had no place to sleep. Then his mother-in-law gave him the 25 cents, but both women were firm in their refusal to let him come in.

Mrs. Chalivat says her husband had threatened to take her life, and she left him to go back to her foster-mother. Chalivat followed, and made the scene last night. She will be sent away where she will not have to live with him.[4]

Clara again wrote to Leonard to inform him that Zintka was suffering from syphilis. He replied on May 11:

I regret to learn of Zintka's serious ailment, but hope that she may obtain such medical service as will produce permanent recovery. When she came to me over two years ago she was a sight to behold, but by patient work and the administration of remedies she was cured. ...

Her fare, Pullman and expenses of trip cost me $36.00. I also paid out $25.00 for room rent and board before she obtained work after her return here from Milford school.

Under the circumstances, in my present financial condition, you can not depend on my making any more advances, and I can see no more reason why you should call on me to pay for her buckskin suit, etc. which she did not need, than I should call on you to pay for the clothing, food, etc. furnished by me.[5]

Clara was once more left to pick up the pieces of the life of the daughter whose adoption was thrust upon her by the same man who now wanted nothing to do with his trophy from Wounded Knee. For the rest of that year and into 1910, Zintka was unable to find work and was totally dependent on her mother. Zintka suffered a relapse of her condition in December of that year, and her Aunt Mary paid for the medical bills.

In reply to a letter dated June 1910 from Chalivat's father in Paris, Clara said that she was unaware of the whereabouts of his son. She outlined the story of how she had befriended Albert and how he met and married her daughter Zintka. Clara had previously written to the Chalivats in France but had given the letter to Albert, who had not forwarded it. The communication made no mention of the reason that the couple split up, but merely observed that Albert was a cross between a hobo and a philosopher and that Zintka followed her intuition and made no attempt to adjust herself to her new relationship. She explained that since March, Zintka had been living in Seattle and employed by a Sportsman's Club called *The Nation of Lakotah*. She also assured Mr. and Mrs. Chalivat that their son always spoke of them both with the greatest affection and she wished that she could give them more satisfactory news.[6]

Having just moved to Seattle, where she was trying to find work, one night Zintka called in on one of Clara's friends, seeking help. Her friend Cora Eaton wrote of her concerns.

...Zintka came here tonight at nearly 10 p.m., ostensibly to make a call on me, ... She said she came with only two dollars on hand, two days ago and that she has exhausted her two dollars. She expected to go to work at once, - a big expectation, seems to me, in a big city, - and she says she got a position in a doctor's office, 'to sterilize his instruments'... but she has a very sore eye, and he told her to wait till the eye is better.

The eye looks serious to me. I am not an eye specialist, but I have seen several cases like it that went on to ulceration, with a long siege of several weeks with an eye salve and some medicine....

Then when I was seeing her to the door, she asked me for money. She asked for five dollars, but that looked like a big sum for her to pay back....

My dear, you have sympathy for all you have put up with all these years. It makes my blood boil when I realize it was not of your own choosing and that you have had to spend your life carrying out the whim of some one who does not even pay the cost in money, let alone in work and worrying....

Yours faithfully, Cora Smith Eaton.[7]

Clara's reply:

My dear friend:
Your letter filled me with great regret. Zintka went to Seattle with my full consent. She said it would be easier for her to work... I fitted her up with a very good wardrobe; ... I was sorry to give her so little but it was all I had... Zintka does not feel any obligation to tell the truth, and no shame when her untruth is discovered. She is not immoral, but

unmoral,... I have tried to make her live and learn and do according to my ideas. ... Even if I devoted myself wholly with regard to her it would not satisfy her or develop her as I would want to. Yet I do not blame her at all. She has been sinned against in being taken from her proper surroundings....

I am sincerely yours, Clara B. Colby.

Zintka did not last long with the Nation of Lakotah. She was back with Clara in July of 1910, once again having a relapse of her illness. Clara sold the piano to pay the medical bills, and she began divorce proceedings for Zintka. In late August, having recovered from illness, Zintka left once more; this time headed for South Dakota to search for her Indian relatives. In a letter to her friend Clara MacNaughton, Clara said that Zintka had left, and as a result, 'I feel I need have no more responsibility for her.' This comment turned out to be mostly true because this would be the last time that Zintka lived with her mother.

During all this time, while Clara was experiencing the difficulties of raising a teenage daughter from another culture, without the support of the person who adopted her, Leonard and Maud Colby were having problems in raising their son, Paul. Not yet sixteen years old, he had already run away from his home in Beatrice, and the first news about him appeared in the *Beatrice Sun* on January 20, 1909

HELD AS A BURGLAR
Young Colby Of Beatrice Under Arrest At El Paso, Texas
To visit his son, P. L. Colby, now confined in the county jail awaiting trial on the charge of burglary, Leonard W.

Colby of Beatrice, Neb., has arrived here to aid his boy, if possible. Young Colby was arrested about a month ago on the charge of burglarizing a restaurant of jewelry and clothing valued at $100. At that time he refused to divulge the names of his parents, but the arrival of his father here indicates the young man informed him of his plight.

Although he has already been indicted by the grand jury, young Colby, who, it seems, has knowingly drifted from pleasant environments to a jail cell, with the penitentiary doors swinging wide before him, will have the assistance of his father.

It would appear that young Colby's arrest in Texas was a sign of things to come, as shown by the report in the Beatrice Sun on May 16, 1909.

YOUNG COLBY ARRESTED

A dispatch from North Platte under date of May 14 says: The young son of General Colby of Beatrice was arrested here last night with another boy associate. They are charged with breaking into two cabooses in the Grand Island Union Pacific yards and stealing revolvers, clothing and several other articles. Both confessed shortly after their arrest. Colby, who is a lad of 16 or 17, seems unconcerned over the affair.

It seemed that Leonard would continue to have problems in raising sons, because a few years later, Clarence was also in trouble for stealing. In January 1912, he was sentenced to fifteen days in the county jail and fined $5 for stealing a watch belonging to a man employed as a janitor at the Paddock Theatre. In 1916, he was reported as being held in the jail awaiting a hearing on a charge of stealing a pump, valued at $86.

CHAPTER 22

AT THE FRONT WITH THE SUFFRAGETTES

ALTHOUGH THE WOMAN'S TRIBUNE was published as usual on March 6, 1909, after almost 26 years, the newspaper now looked in danger of ceasing publication altogether. Clara ceaselessly approached friends, family members, and anyone else that she thought might be interested in becoming a partner in the venture, all to no avail.

Having lost heart of being accepted as a full participant in the National American Woman's Suffrage Association, and feeling somewhat disheartened about the progress of the movement in America, she yearned to be involved again in the more aggressive campaign going on in Britain. There was a feeling that British suffragettes were close to success, and Clara wanted to be there when it happened.

In letters to her friends, Clara declared her enthusiasm to return to England. In response to this, she received encouragement to make the move. Ellen Sabin, President of the Milwaukee Downer College, wrote, 'I almost envy (but I won't let myself envy my talented friends) you the prospect of England again, with, too, a business to do there. These are stirring times in England, and one would like to know the power of the thought and feeling there stirring at first hand.'[1]

The reference to business was the possibility of being an independent journalist, writing for American and English publications about the suffrage cause in each country. Clara had already received the promise of a regular 'Report from London' article from the editor of the *Oregon Daily Journal,* and she also published articles in magazines like *The Englishwoman, Harper's Bazaar, Overland Monthly, Arena* and in the *Washington Herald.* She was also lobbying for government support as a delegate at some of the conferences coming up in the next twelve months. Newspapers across America reported the fact that Clara was leaving to join the suffragette cause, following reports that the suffrage bill had passed in the House of Commons and that success for woman suffrage was imminent.

GOING FAR TO AID THE SUFFRAGE CAUSE
Mrs. Clara Bewick Colby Will Leave Soon for Battle in England.
In the hope of being some aid in removing the shackles which hinder the absolute freedom and liberty of her sex, Mrs. Clara Bewick Colby will leave here to join her sister suffragettes in England. With them, she will struggle strenuously in the monster demonstrations for the suffrage

cause. Already the suffragettes have gained a tremendous following, and recently in the second reading before the House of Commons of the suffrage bill, it was passed by a majority of 110. But Premier Asquith declares that there will not be sufficient time for its consideration at the convened meeting of Parliament on November 16th. ....

It is Mrs. Colby's plan to be a moving factor in the big demonstration of Thursday, November 10th, under the auspices of the Women's Social and Political Union. It is anticipated that this will be one of the biggest events in suffrage history in England or otherwise.[2]

Clara sailed from Montreal on the White Star liner, the S.S. *Laurentic*, on October 29th and arrived in Liverpool precisely one week later. Transfers were faster in those days than today, with only half an hour allowed to clear customs and board the special limited train for London.

An account of her arrival in London, including the celebration of Guy Fawkes Day and a report of the Lord Mayor's procession to the Guildhall for his induction into office, was published in her first article in the *Oregon Sunday Journal* of November 27. She also described the situation regarding the progress of a suffrage law in the House of Commons by way of the Conciliation Bill. One hundred and nine votes had carried the Bill, and it should have moved on to the next stage, where it would become law. Although it would only give the ballot to a limited number of women based upon their marital status and property holdings, the suffragist movement supported it.

Emmeline Pankhurst, the leader of the Women's Social and Political Union, agreed to the idea and they declared a truce: all militant suffragette activities would cease until the fate of the Constitution Bill was clear. The Prime Minister, Herbert Asquith, however, was inclined to shelve the Conciliation Bill until after the next election, based on his understanding of how it might affect his party's votes.

Clara's next article, published in the *Oregon Journal* on December 4th, described the suffragettes making their four-teenth delegation to present their case to the Prime Minister. Sending a delegation to the Prime Minister was something that the WSPU had done ever since the Women's Sunday in Hyde Park two years before. Emmeline Pankhurst led 300 women from Caxton Hall to the House of Commons. Clara watched from the steps of St. Margaret's Church as thousands of people collected in front of the Parliament buildings.

The police came in full force, backed up by the mounted re-serves. She saw many women going away under police escort, but she was not near enough to see what was done to cause the arrest. This demonstration became known as Black Friday, mainly because of the way the police used force against the women. The conciliation committee undertook interviews with 135 demonstrators, nearly all of whom described acts of violence; 29 of which included details of sexual assault. Po-lice arrested four men and 115 women, although the following day, they dropped all charges.

Clara had previously written in her article that the Brit-ish press seemed to be ignoring any news about the suffrag-ist campaign, but now she said, 'The silence of the press has been broken.' The only thing was, now the press only spoke of the 'Suffragist Rioters,' and nothing about the police bru-tality. The front page of The *Daily Mirror* showed a suffrag-ette on the ground, who the newspaper inferred had fainted.

Miss Sylvia Pankhurst's eyewitness account of the situation was, 'A policeman struck her with all his force, and she fell to the ground. Then a tall, grey-haired man with a silk hat was seen fighting to protect her, but three or four police seized hold of him and bundled him away.'[3] With the response they received on Black Friday, the WSPU declared the end of the truce.

Four days later, on November 22nd, the suffragettes were again meeting at Caxton Hall, still hoping for a positive outcome from the Conciliation Bill. During the meeting, a white envelope was handed up to Mrs. Pankhurst by a messenger. After glancing at it, Mrs. Pankhurst announced that the Prime Minister had made his expected statement, and while it was being considered, the meeting would be suspended. The committee returned after about a half hour, and Mrs. Pankhurst read the message as the future of women's rights hang in the balance. The Prime Minister had promised a resolution... not before March, not for the next session, but for the next Parliament, and even this depended upon re-election for the government. His answer was a total shelving of the bill.

After a great outburst of anger and cheering rose, Mrs. Pankhurst announced that she would lead the delegation to the Prime Minister's door, since the House of Commons had risen. The suffragettes formed up in fours, and the march moved off at such speed that they reached Parliament Square within a quarter of an hour. The police and onlookers assumed that this was the usual march to the House, but at the last minute they turned down Parliament Street. The superintendent hurriedly signaled to a body of police to close the entrance to Downing Street, but they only had time to form a single cordon. The marchers maintained their pace, and under pressure against the center of the policemen, it broke, and the women rushed forward through the gap with cries of triumph. The report in the *Votes for Women* continued:

> *Against the gathering lines of police, the women charged again and again with reckless indifference to blows or the violent pushes that flung them to the ground. Indeed, the whole length of the street from the official residences down to the entrance was now one wild turmoil of struggling men and women, swaying this way and that, the women continually striving to advance, in most cases isolated, and the police continually thrusting them back. The banners were easily broken to pieces and became an extra danger. Every now and then, when a woman fell, those around fell on top of her, with a terrible result. Here I saw one of the most famous doctors rush against the police at the very front. Flung savagely back, she instinctively tidied her scarf and rushed again. Here a writer, equally famous, was caught bodily off her feet and dashed upon the pavement, but being an athlete as well as a writer, she fell upon her hands. There a hospital nurse almost succeeded in breaking the renewed line till she was caught by the throat and driven back again into the seething contest.[4]*

The women did manage to approach the Prime Minister in what some of the press called 'an assault.' One person shook him by the arm and cried, 'Mr. Asquith, how dare you?' Another cried out, 'Mr. Asquith, give us the Bill, the whole Bill, and nothing but the Bill! Take your veto off the Commons!' This confrontation was later known as 'the Battle of Downing

Street' and was one of the most violent struggles of the suffragette campaign. If the Prime Minister had only decided to meet with the delegation or any of the fourteen deputations they had organized to the House, then all this could have been avoided.

It would appear that the *Oregon Daily Journal* did not run any more Reports from London, so there was no description of the Battle of Downing Street from Clara Colby. Judging from the speaking engagements which followed, it would appear that Clara had aligned herself with a breakaway group from the WSPU calling themselves 'the Women's Freedom League.' It was a group which by 1911 had sixty branches and over 4,000 members. They also published their newspaper, *The Vote*, to which Clara contributed articles.

Like their sister organization, the WSPU, the Women's Freedom League met at Caxton Hall in Westminster. Clara found the place familiar because she had been there as guest speaker.[5]

Throughout 1911, Clara traveled through England, speaking at meetings and garden parties wherever suffragettes met. In May of 1911, Governor West appointed Clara as a delegate to represent Oregon at The International Congress of Women in Stockholm, starting on June 11, and later as a delegate at the Universal Races Congress, held at the University of London in July.[6]

One of her priorities was to be back in London for the June 17th Suffrage Procession, at which she was representing Washington DC. The article and pictures in the *New York Times* captured the astonishing sight that this event held for Londoners on that day.

TRIUMPHAL MARCH OF 40,000 WOMEN IS REMARKABLE SIGHT.
Suffrage Procession Is Five Miles Long and Includes Delegates From Europe, Britain and the Empire.

The woman's suffrage demonstration which took place recently was one of the most remarkable sights London has ever seen....

The procession was five miles long, and it took 2½ hours to pass a given point. Three hours after the head of the procession had left the Embankment, the last contingent wound into Piccadilly. There was a large crowd of deeply interested but undemonstrative spectators all along the route, and not the least wonderful part of the proceedings was the sympathetic behavior of this crowd.

Women of every class of society united in the common cause. Each part of the kingdom had its national contingent, and there were delegates from every country in Europe as well as the United States.

The procession was headed by Mrs. Drummond dressed in a green hunting costume and riding astride. She was followed by Joan of Arc in armor mounted on a white horse. Next came the 'prisoners' pageant,' comprising some 700 women each bearing a fluttering pennant, headed by Mrs. Pankhurst, Miss Christabel Pankhurst and Mrs. Pethick Lawrence, their fighting leaders.

The various overseas dominions and colonies came next, with New Zealand in the place of Honor, as the first country in the British empire to give women the vote. It was interesting to note the part taken in this section by the wives and other relatives of dominion premiers and other *men of distinction now in London for the coronation, who thus showed their sympathy with the movement.*

On reaching the Albert Hall, a meeting was held at which Mrs. Pankhurst presided. Miss Christabel Pankhurst, whose wonderful quality of voice made itself heard without effort all over the immense building, moved a resolution which was carried unanimously.

'Fighting,' observed Miss Pankhurst incidently, 'is a joy to us, and submission is a thing that we have forgotten all about. The triumph of the bill does not rest with the prime minister, but with us, and therefore our motto must be 'Forward and Conquer.' '[7]

Clara returned to the United States on the RMS *Cedric*, which arrived in New York on December 1, 1911. She went straight to Washington, where she stayed with her friend Clara Mac-Naughton. On December 12th, they jointly hosted an informal 'At Home,' which they announced in *The Washington Post*.

The Washington Herald reported that she was overflowing with enthusiasm and high hopes for the cause after a year's campaigning in England in the interest of woman suffrage and lecturing on Walt Whitman. In an interview, she said that in the opinion of thousands of English women, the one significant obstacle in the granting of political equality to their sex was Prime Minister Asquith. Most of the other men prominent in public life, she stated, had given assurances that they hold the suffragettes' demands to be just, and that they believe the putting of the ballot in woman's hands would result in the most significant step forward that representative government has taken in the last hundred years.[8]

Two interesting phases of the situation, Mrs. Colby said, are the refusal of women to make census records, and of those who are property holders, to pay taxes. On the night that the enumerators (census collectors) were scheduled to call at their homes, many women remained away. They gathered in groups of ten to twenty at specific houses, whose owners had declined to fill in the census blanks.

In England, the year 1911 was a national census year, and there is no mention of Clara Colby in the records.

CHAPTER 23

THE FRONT IN FIVE STATES AND THE CAPITAL

RETURNING TO THE UNITED States, Clara was quickly back on the speaker circuit, starting in Washington. Here, she lectured at the District Suffrage Association in the public library, at which she described the work of the English suffragettes and her observations on their campaign. She was 'engaged by the New Jersey Suffrage Association to make a tour of their State, speaking in a total of ten cities, the object being, of course, to rouse the whole State to an interest in suffrage at this especially critical time when suffrage legislation is pending in the State Legislature.' [1]

The most significant suffrage event during her stay in Washington was a mass meeting held at the Columbia Theater on March 31, 1912, for which Mrs. MacNaughton chaired the committee of arrangements and finance. The announced purpose of the meeting was to stimulate interest in the pending constitutional amendments for woman's suffrage in Wisconsin, Oregon, Ohio, and Kansas. Three Senators, five Congressmen, Mrs. Belva Lockwood, and Mrs. Clara Bewick Colby addressed the meeting. Senator Miles Poindexter chaired the meeting and, amid vigorous applause, he said that women are not losing any of their feminine charms because they are taking an active part in politics. Senator Poindexter introduced Mrs. Colby 'as a woman who had been on the firing line for many years.'

Taking the stage, Clara said that the women based their claims to equal suffrage on their natural rights. Mrs. Colby cited instances in which woman, by the decision of the United States Supreme Court, had been declared a citizen and could, therefore, vote.[2]

While in England, Clara had taken a great interest in the New Thought movement. She was influenced by her friend Frances Swiney, who was a writer, a theosophist and a supporter of New Thought. Now that she was back in America, Clara was to be found speaking at the New Thought Fellowship at Lockwood Hall. She was also promoted as being a recent speaker at the Higher Thought Center in London.

Clara left Washington for the long trip to California on April 6, 1912; stopping en route at Oregon to play an active part in the campaign to change that state's constitution. Without having a permanent home to go to, she stayed with friends while she campaigned in their locality. She spent May in Eugene, and June through August in Portland. The *Oregon Daily*

Journal of September 2nd expressed regret at the departure of Mrs. Colby for Kansas and Wisconsin to continue her campaign work.[3]

Clara had been engaged to organize the women of several towns and counties into active clubs and leagues, on behalf of the management of the state association. She spent a month in Kansas, where she spoke at more than fifty meetings in four weeks to canvass votes for changes to their state constitution. In October, she moved to her old home state of Wisconsin to do the same there. The referendums passed in Oregon and Kansas, which was gratifying for Clara after her five months campaigning in those states. She was not so happy about Wisconsin's nil change, but she did spend time with the Rev. Olympia Brown, planning a campaign in Washington. They spoke of the opportunity to address a Congressional hearing in the next term of Congress.

Returning to Washington, she spent the winter planning for the next appeal to Congress, which was to be a House Committee organized for January 31, 1913. Assisted by members of Congress from the nine equal-suffrage States, the Federal Woman's Equality Association secured the largest of the House committee rooms, which could accommodate up to 400 people. Once that was secured, suffragists from throughout the nation were called upon to join them in Washington and march to the Capitol to help make their appeal. The event achieved newspaper coverage nationwide, and Clara was reported both in the headline and as the leading speaker.

ASKS 'ARE WOMEN PEOPLE?'
Mrs. Clara B. Colby Points to Language of Constitution in Argument for Woman Suffrage.

Four hundred women from every section of the Union appeared before the House Committee on Presidential and Congressional Elections to appeal for the passage of the French bill, to give women the right to vote for Representatives in Congress.

Heading the petitioners was Rev Olympia Brown of Racine, Wis. President of the Federal Woman's Equality Association, and with them a dozen members of Congress from each of the nine equal-suffrage States.

Mrs. Clara B. Colby of Portland, Or. pleaded for a constitutional amendment prohibiting States from disenfranchising citizens on account of sex. Declaring that the constitution says the representatives shall be chosen by 'the people of the several States,' she asked, 'Are women people?' She added that American women would continue their 'earnest and dignified efforts to gain political freedom' as long as might be necessary to gain their purpose.[4]

Although Clara was using her usual argument that the constitution already gave the government the power to give women the vote, this was the first time she pleaded for a constitutional amendment to prohibit States from disenfranchising citizens on account of their sex. This was exactly the method by which women were given the vote in 1920.

Changes were taking place within the American suffrage movement at that time. A young suffragist called Alice Paul, who had spent two years working with the suffragettes in England, had returned to join the NAWSA as a member of the recently-revised Congressional Committee. This was the same committee which Clara headed until its disbandment in 1898.

The first of Miss Paul's projects with the NAWSA was the Woman Suffrage Procession in Washington on March 13th, the day before President Wilson's inauguration. Paul's militant approach to this event caused disagreements with the leaders of the NAWSA, resulting in Alice Paul forming a breakaway group. It was initially called the Congressional Union; later becoming the National Woman's Party. March 13th was a successful day for both the NAWSA and the CU, however, because the parade attracted 8,000 women to march, while the event attracted half a million spectators – creating greater awareness for the cause of woman suffrage.

Reports of the militant activities of the English suffragettes became a controversial issue among American suffragists, with some of the leaders condemning what they saw as Clara's support for a similar approach in the United States. She merely approved of what the English women had been driven to, as was reported by the *Washington Post*.

AID US SUFFRAGISTS

Giving the militant window-smashing English suffragettes credit for many of the suffrage victories in the United States and other countries, Mrs. Clara Bewick Colby yesterday afternoon addressed a largely attended meeting of the Federal Woman's Equality Association at the New Ebbitt and told of personal experiences in London suffrage campaigns.

'The English women have been driven to their militant methods, and we should not blame them.' Said Mrs. Colby. 'They always stop at the actual taking of life, but they have had the fact hammered into them that Englishmen never got any reforms without committing violence. I believe in

peace, and I would not advocate the militant methods for the United States, but we must realize that the work done in England has had an effect in America.'

Mrs. Colby criticized as 'foolish and inane' the arguments advanced last week by anti-suffragists before the House committee on the election of President, Vice President and representatives against Representative French's bill giving women the right to vote for members of the House.[5]

Another opportunity came on April 21, 1913, when Congressmen from equal suffrage states and members of the Woman's Federal Equality Association presented arguments to the Senate Committee on Suffrage. They urged the necessity and justice of the proposed amendment to the Constitution of the United States. 'Mrs. Colby made the closing argument. She stated that the only point that the anti-suffragists have made is that the States would resent the passage of a resolution for woman suffrage by the Federal Congress.'[6] This statement was an observation regarding the strong opinions that arose about States' rights, and it was a factor that was only overcome by the passing of the Nineteenth Amendment. This amendment prohibited States from disenfranchising citizens on account of sex.

The Woman's Equality Association WEA viewed Clara as a frontline fighter who could be sent into campaign whenever a suffrage proposal was put on the ballot. So, in 1913, it was the turn of Michigan. Just as she had been campaigning in Oregon, Kansas, and Wisconsin the previous year, she was sent to tour Michigan from March until April 8th. Michigan did not favor equal suffrage, and it would be another five years before the amendment passed to allow women to vote in Michigan.

Wherever she went, Clara was always writing. During her travels in Michigan, she wrote the following article, which appeared in the English newspaper, *The Vote.*

Our readers will be interested in further news just to hand from our good friend Mrs. Bewick Colby. She writes: 'I have been spending the winter at Washington working in the interests of our Federal Suffrage Bill. A sub-committee was appointed to investigate the Constitutional points involved in the Bill and report early in the Session of Congress beginning on April 7. This has given our movement a Congressional standing it has not had for twenty years. Then, also, the old and long-continued work for a constitutional amendment prohibiting the States from disenfranchising women on account of sex – which, if it is passed by both Houses of Congress by a two third vote would then have to be adopted by three-fourths of the State Legislatures before it became a part of the Constitution – is likely to have good attention from this Congress. The Democratic Party now in power, of which not many years ago not a member could be found to say he was favorable, has made our Committee on Women Suffrage to the Senate an important committee for the first time. Heretofore it has been what is called a minority committee – given to the minority party because they had to give them something! While the Republicans were in power, we always had a Democrat chairman who was unfavorable, and we could not get any report. Now the Democrats are in power they have given us a good committee of nine, of which, the majority are in favor of equal

Suffrage and the chairman, a Democrat from Colorado, is one of our strongest and wisest supporters.

I am writing this in Michigan, where I came to help until the vote is taken in April. You remember we celebrated a victory in Michigan last November, but after a whole month's holding back some of the returns, during which time they were evidently changed by fraud, the women were counted out by 762 votes, although over 236,000 had been cast in their favor. Now they have it re-submitted and are doing their best to prevent fraud at the next election.[7]

During all this time of campaigning and traveling, Clara had almost no contact with Zintka and had little knowledge of where she was and what she was doing. In a copy of a letter from Clara to Zintka dated May 26, 1913, she says, 'I was glad to hear from you after so long a time. You have not told me whether you got the Testament and Psalms I sent you for your birthday or the Christmas book. My dear, you should tell me more about yourself and your husband. ... With love and best wishes, I am always your affectionate mother, Clara Bewick Colby.'[8]

The revelation that Zintka had married was a bit premature. The *Santa Ana Register* of June 4, 1913, revealed that a marriage license was issued to Robert J. Keith of Santa Ana and Princeton Davis of Oregon, probably on March 31st (Princeton being the name under which Zintka worked at Pathe´). Further information published in the *Los Angeles Times* on October 7, 1913, revealed more about how Zintka had become Mrs. Robert J. Keith.

In 1912, she had married Charles B. Davis, a Cherokee Indian with whom she had been working at the Pathe´ motion including that of Clara Bewick Colby. Unfortunately, there is no trace of these recordings.

Just like her first trip to Europe, when she studied and wrote about the City of Glasgow, she followed up the Budapest conference by visiting with local people that she had met. She wrote articles about Budapest and Hungary, upon which she based lectures whenever the opportunity arose.

Clara's article, 'The Child in Hungary,' described the unique model of child protection that existed in Hungary at that time. Every child, as a future citizen, had a claim upon the State, a claim which was not affected by the conditions under which the child came into existence, or the fortunes of its parents. Indicative of the importance of this child care program was the fact that the chief director was a Minister in the Government.[3]

While she was attending the conference in Budapest, word came through that Governor West had named Mrs. Colby as Oregon's delegate to the International Peace Congress, being held in The Hague in August.

The world was just one year away from the outbreak of World War One, which should have meant that a conference about peace would have great meaning. Judging by the newspaper reports of the day, the 1913 Congress at The Hague achieved very little, compared to the previous Hague Conventions of 1899 and 1907. *The Globe* newspaper in London summed up what many may have been thinking in their article of August 22, 1913.

There is something almost pathetic about the proceedings of the Peace Congress at The Hague. ...we are very much afraid that despite the amiable idealists of the Peace Congress, this state of things will last as long as human nature.

Sadly, the 1913 Peace Congress produced no positive results, and the rest is history.

When Clara arrived back in London on September 13th, she was broke. The one thing she could always count on was her network of friends; sometimes without having to ask, someone would give her enough money to get by. On this occasion, Clara had tea with her friend Mrs. Cox, who gave her five shillings for what she called her literature lesson, a sum which met all Clara's expenses including her board until the following Friday. In the next few days, she waited patiently to receive some promised payments in the mail. Nothing arrived. Having committed herself to give a lecture in Cheltenham and not having the train fare, Clara returned to Mrs. Cox to borrow one pound, who was more than willing to oblige.

Clara then took the now familiar trip down to the county where she was born, and on October 3rd she spoke to a full audience in the Cheltenham Town Hall about the International Woman's Alliance in Budapest. Since this was a fee-paying lecture, she was now in a position to be able to pay her way to the next engagement, which was in Belfast. She took the overnight sailing to Ireland and was at a friend's house for breakfast.

The Irishwoman's Suffrage Foundation had arranged for Clara to speak to their members at the Imperial Picture Palace on October 20th. Again, she spoke about the conference in Budapest. *The Irish Citizen* also interviewed Clara on the progress of the suffrage campaign in the United States.

will show the merits of this measure, which asks of Congress what it can give directly without sending women to ask their freedom from every man in the States. Mrs. Clara Bewick Colby, corresponding secretary, will base her plea on women's rights under the old common law of England, which has been called the storehouse of our liberties. Representative Burton L. French, of Idaho, who introduced the bill, will argue that it is within the power of Congress under the Constitution to pass such an act.[9]

The woman suffrage amendment was defeated in the House, however, newspapers across the country ran a report that said of the women:

Although their objects are often defeated, their zeal always wins. The newest proposition has just been submitted by Mrs. Clara Bewick Colby. She says the women still have another chance and that is this: Get some woman to go to the polls and try to vote. If the officials refused, she would sue and bring a test case before the supreme court. Then the highest court would have to decide whether a woman is a citizen.[10]

In spite of her busy schedule and the fact that she was actually earning money during 1914, Clara was feeling restless. She was frustrated at being tied down to her activities in Washington. Clara wrote to her sister Mary, who was living in Palo Alto, sounding downcast about her situation. This was compounded no doubt by the outbreak of war in Europe.

Oh, I should enjoy being there with you. I seem to have half my heart in England and the other half on the Pacific

Coast, so I do not know which to give up. I was planning to make lecture arrangements across the water for November and December and had some already arranged in Scotland, but these, of course, must now be given up. Did you ever know such a muddle as the men have got this round world into? [11]

Zintka stood on another pedestal and represented Sacajawea, dressed in a white leather, fringed dress, rented from Goldstein Costumes on Market Street. At that moment, mother and daughter were finally a team together, working in the cause that had dominated Clara's life. It must have been a gratifying moment for them both, even though their relationship had been declining for several years.

Following the end of the Exposition, Clara received an acknowledgment from the event organizers, expressing their appreciation of the Congress. The letter stated that in terms of attendance it was one of the largest convention special days, with 56,255 people entering on that day.

Over the next week, Clara and Zintka stayed with friends in San Francisco and with her sister Mary in Palo Alto. Mary was at that time hosting Violet Bates, a second cousin visiting from England.[5]

Zintka was back home in Hanford by August 3rd, when she wrote to say that Clyde had malaria and the baby had the chicken pox. Further bad news came to Clara before she left California, informing her that her brother William had died back in Madison. He died from complications arising from an accident two years previously, when a horse had kicked him. Clara had planned to return east via Wisconsin, so she was able to spend some time with her sister-in-law Jennie before moving on to Racine, Wisconsin, where her friend Olympia Brown had arranged for Clara to give several lectures in that city.

When Clara returned to Washington, she was homeless, but luckily her friend Belva Lockwood was moving South for the winter, leaving a spot free. Clara moved into the second floor front bedroom of Belva's house at 304 Indiana Avenue NW. Before she could get settled in, the New Jersey suffrage union hired Clara to support their campaign for the woman suffrage proposition, in Asbury Park.

The situation would be to join a group of suffragists who were speaking from the back of autos gaily decorated in the national colors: the violet, green and white of the Woman's Political Union and the golden yellow of the suffrage society. The news reporter declared that Mrs. Colby was a very interesting speaker, who, 'had never spoken thru a megaphone before, but she said she had experience in speaking with the ballot and knows how to do it.'[6]

As Belva Lockwood operated a rooming house in her large home, it was happenstance that one of Clara's new neighbors was Dr. Mary Walker, the Civil War surgeon who had won the Medal of Honor for her efforts to treat the wounded during the Civil War. More recently, she had become involved in the campaign for woman suffrage, and she had testified at some of the same House committees as Clara. She was mainly well known for her opinions on dress reform and frequently dressed in men's clothes.

During that winter, a severe flu epidemic was raging and many tenants in the building were seriously sick. Clara made herself a nurse and friend to each one of them, visiting them all daily, attending to whatever needs with which she could help. Eventually, she caught the disease too.[7]

She was always on the go, organizing meetings for the Woman's Press Association, the Federal Suffrage Association, the Washington Secular League, and speaking at the New Thought Centre. In November of 1915, Clara's fourth winter course of lectures began at the Oxford Hotel every Wednesday at 4 and 8 pm. They started with a story of the life and achievements of Elizabeth Cady Stanton, celebrating the 100th anniversary of her birth. The range of subjects that she spoke on was extraordinary, including the works of a Bengali Nobel prize winner; the study of Emerson's self-reliance; 'Ecce Mater,' meaning woman's rightful place in Christian teaching, and the life of Florence Nightingale.

During the year that followed the Panama-Pacific Exposition, Zintka kept in touch with her mother, although there was not much good news in her correspondence. In January of 1916, she wrote that her husband had been seriously sick, taken to hospital, and although he had survived, they received doctors and hospital bills of $350. On top of that, she reported that her children were both sick, and she had sent her oldest to Los Angeles in the care of an Indian lady. The following month, she wrote again to say that the baby had died. She closed with, 'Well mother dear, I will close for this time. Will write again as soon as I know where and what the address is of my brother-in-law in Oakland. With lots of love, God bless you. Affectionately, your daughter Zintka.'

The last big event of that winter was the hearing on the two suffrage bills, which came before the House committee on March 27, 1916. Clara's argument, which had been endorsed by several constitutional lawyers, was the same simple proposition that a woman's rights as a citizen gave her the right to vote. In the Washington Herald, she said, 'We maintain that women have the right to vote under the original constitution, and this constitution need not be amended. Congress can bring this right into activity. We are asking that it do so.'[8]

This was the last time in a record of over 20 years that Clara had been addressing Congressional hearings. An indication of the respect she received was shown in a letter from the Chairman of the Committee on Woman Suffrage, 64th Congress:

Mrs. Colby's presentation of the Federal Suffrage law to these committees was such as to receive the unstinted praise of the Senators and Representatives who heard her strong and logical arguments irrespective of the individual views held. She has contributed largely to the cause of equal suffrage for woman, and her work and words will be of lasting benefit to the outcome of woman's suffrage.[9]

During these last months in Washington, Clara had struggled to earn enough money from her lectures to be able to buy food. She noted in her diary that she 'was quite bad with grippe' (influenza) and had no appetite. She would get out of bed to go and lecture, but went straight back to bed afterward. In February, she wrote that 'for two weeks my face was so blotched with cold sores that I could not go to the Capitol. At last, Feb. 18 & 19, I went up – saw Judge Raker and Senator Lee.'[10] She understood that she could not afford to live in Washington and that as soon as the hearings were over, she would need to move to Oregon, where the climate and the cost of living would be more favorable. Her diary states, 'It seems to be the voice of the Spirit that I go to Oregon this spring.'

When she left Washington in May, the tenants of the different rooms stood together at the head of the stairs, all in tears as she bade them goodbye to go to the train. She planned on stopping in Madison at the home of one of her stepsisters, to visit with family members in town and out at Windsor. By the time she reached Portland, she must have partly recovered from her sickness because she spoke to members of the Woman's Political Science club on June 13th about her recent activities in lobbying Congress.

Her final destination was Eugene, where she planned to rent a room in the town she had grown to love during her Oregon campaign. She sounded quite positive when she wrote from Eugene to her friend Belva Lockwood, saying that she was already planning her return to Washington for the next winter's work with Congress. She outlined her viewpoint on the Federal Suffrage bill as compared to the constitutional amendment on which the NAWSA was working. Compared to the way that competing suffragists had criticized Clara for being divorced and adopting an Indian child, Clara was quite praiseworthy in her letter when referring to Carrie Chapman Catt:

> *I think Mrs. Catt is making a very dignified and able campaign for the amendment, and as Senator Thomas says he will call up the amendment when Mrs. Catt so advises him. I think it would be a dreadful thing – historically – for the amendment to pass before our Federal Suffrage bill, as it would stamp on the history of the U.S. for evermore that women had no rights originally in this republic and that men had to give them their citizen's rights.*[11]

Olympia Brown was not as positive as Clara sounded in her letter to Belva Lockwood, and she recognized that Clara might be seriously ill.

After reading your last letter, I felt quite worried about your health. I had supposed your ailments were temporary and that on getting to Oregon the change of scene and improvement of conditions would bring you out all right. Being taken by pneumonia suggests a weakened condition of the system which has been created by the hardships you endured last winter.[12]

Clara wrote back in a rare negative manner, 'I do not see how I am going to make it.' Mary's daughter Eva, who was in Eugene to be of assistance to her aunt, called her mother one night to say that Clara had suffered a complete relapse of pneumonia. Mary drove to Eugene and stayed with Clara for several days to nurse her back to health. When Clara did not respond and having patients back in Palo Alto, Mary decided to bundle Clara in the back seat of the car and drive her back to Palo Alto. She arrived home at 758 Waverley Street on September 1st. Clara then struggled to overcome her sickness. This fight for life was to be her last campaign, and she passed away on September 7, 1916.

Thus ended a life of untiring and heroic endeavor. Mrs. Colby's courage was wonderful, and it helped her to defy and overcome the most adverse circumstances. She had great sorrows, but she never paraded them. Indeed, she seldom spoke of them, even to her most intimate friends. She suffered great injustice, but she never complained. Always cheerful, always hopeful, she 'left the things that were behind, and pressed forward to the things that were before.'[13]

Following a small service at Dr. Mary White's home, Clara's body was cremated and her ashes sent home to Wisconsin. A small gravestone marks the spot amid the Windsor Congregational Cemetery, along with her mother and father and other members of the Bewick family.

Clara had turned 70 on August 5th, when the campaign which she had fought for all her life was very close to success. It was less than four years later that the Nineteenth Amendment came into effect, on August 18, 1920, giving all American women the right to vote. Just as Clara's mother and father were never to be the beneficiaries of the farm which they pioneered in Wisconsin, so it was with Clara. She was a pioneer of the woman suffrage movement, and her work opened the doors of opportunity for others to walk through and claim the goal from which all American women benefit today.

EPILOGUE

THE DEATH OF CLARA Bewick Colby was widely reported in newspapers across the United States. Her friend, Olympia Brown, wrote a tribute to Clara, which was printed in the Wisconsin newspapers.

The many friends of Mrs. Clara Bewick Colby have been surprised to learn of her death, which occurred at the home of her sister, Dr. Mary B. White, in Palo Alto, Calif., on Sept. 7.

Perhaps few have realized what the death of Mrs. Colby means to the Woman's Suffrage cause, and what sacrifices she has made to promote its interests. Her death, while directly attributable to pneumonia, was primarily caused by the labors she performed and privations she endured during her stay in Washington last winter. Not only was this a winter of strenuous work, but in addition to her usual vocations, writing and lecturing, and attending meetings, she also gave considerable time and energy to caring for sick friends. It so chanced that in the house where she lived there was considerable sickness; some of the cases appealed to her sympathies, and as usual she made their cases her own, visiting them daily and ministering to their wants.

Probably in all that galaxy of heroic women who have championed the rights of women since 1848, there is not one that has made more personal sacrifices than Mrs. Colby. She has given her time and wonderful energy for years without money and without price, and through all, she has always been cheerful, charitable, and hopeful. Even when things looked the darkest, she could see a great accomplishment just ahead, and with untiring zeal and ceaseless labor, she strove for the attainment of her ideal. ...

Her going will leave a great gap in the ranks of suffrage workers and will add one more to the list of noble women who have given their all and sacrificed their lives to emancipate the women of the United States.[1]

A memorial service eulogizing the life and work of Mrs. Colby was held at All Souls Unitarian Church in Washington on December 17, 1916. *The Washington Post* reported that many prominent civic leaders addressed the group and said that other suffrage leaders regarded Mrs. Colby as one of the greatest pioneers of the movement for the women's vote. A total of seven organizations, from the fields of suffrage, peace, religion, new thought, her university alumni, and the press association, all sent representatives who delivered addresses to those attending. Notable by their absence was any representative from the NAWSA, for whom Clara had performed so much work, over so many years.

Olympia Brown went on to publish *Democratic Ideals: a Memorial Sketch of Clara B. Colby* in 1917. In this, she reprinted the letters she had received from those who remembered Clara, including the following:

Dear Mrs. Brown
When the history of the struggle of the women of the United States for suffrage shall have been written, it will contain a record of Clara Bewick Colby, who as a citizen, as the corresponding secretary of the Federal Suffrage Association, as a lecturer, did heroic work in behalf of the cause of suffrage. She was earnest in her purpose, intense in her convictions, capable in all she undertook.
Hon. Burton L. French
House of Representatives.

Dear Mrs. Brown
I knew Mrs. Colby for twenty years, and I never heard her make an unkind criticism of a fellow worker. She was wholly unselfish, single-minded, without desire for personal glory. Woman suffrage never had a more earnest, sincere, and devoted advocate. With her, it was a vital, fundamental principle for which no labor was too hard, no sacrifice too great. Her courage was sublime. She never waited for money or other assistance when an opportunity offered to advance her cause but went forward with dauntless faith that in some way the means would be provided. It was in this spirit that she carried through to success a congress of

the Federal Suffrage Association in San Francisco during the Pan Pacific Exposition in 1915.
                    Ida Husted Harper
                Biographer of Susan B. Anthony.

My dear Mrs. Brown
I take it as a privilege to write you a few words in regard to Mrs. Colby and her work in behalf of the Federal Suffrage law in relation to the election of members of Congress as it has come under my observation. ...

Her work brought her before the various committees of the House and Senate – in particular, the House Committee on Judiciary and the Committee on Election of President, Vice President and Representatives in Congress, and the Judiciary and Woman's Suffrage Committee of the Senate. ...

It would be hard for me to express my full consideration of the noble and splendid work done by our friend in this cause – so near and dear to her. It had become her life work and had she been spared; she would have been given the privilege of seeing her desires fully realized – for it certainly will be a reality ere long.

Being much impressed with your work, I wish you every success. Believe me, I am,
                    Yours very truly
                    Hon. John E. Raker
                House of Representatives.

LEONARD AND ZINTKA

By the time of Clara's death, no other member of the family had maintained contact with Zintka, so it is likely that she learned of her mother's departure from the newspapers. She was still in the San Francisco area in 1916, but the 1920 census shows that she had moved to live with her in-laws in Hanford, California. This was the period when Spanish influenza was sweeping across America, and when the census was taken, Zintka was already infected. She died on February 14, 1920, and was buried in the local cemetery in Hanford, where she lay until 1991. It was then that Renee Sansom Flood (author of Lost Bird of Wounded Knee), working with the Wounded Knee Survivors Association, returned Zintka Lanuni to her final resting place at the Wounded Knee Memorial Gravesite in South Dakota.

Leonard continued to prosper, and there is no evidence that he was again investigated or charged with any fraud. He died on November 15, 1924, after a long illness. A few months later, Maud responded to a letter from Stevenson Bewick, who was compiling the Bewick Family History. In it she revealed what little she knew about Zintka.

January 6, 1925
The last we heard of Zintka was about ten years ago when a sensational write-up about her in a Los Angeles paper was sent to us. According to this write-up, she claimed that General had just died and left her his entire 'fortune,' and it seems that she had run bills of all sorts on the strength of the 'fortune' that she inherited, and when payment was not forthcoming some of her creditors began an investiga-

*tion. ... This is the last we ever heard, and I have no idea as
to her present whereabouts. ...*

*Clarence died two years ago today. He became very
ill of pneumonia; we had him cared for at the Lutheran
Hospital in this city. ... We buried him January 10, 1923, in
what is called 'The Old Cemetery' where Grandfather and
Grandmother Chilton are buried. ...*

*Clarence was a keen disappointment; his was a case of
arrested development – he had the mind of a twelve-year-
old child. He worked as a farm hand or as a common la-
borer on the streets, and he supplied his own wants largely.
He needed to be looked after to keep him from vicious and
demoralizing companions; the drink was his besetting sin.
He was about forty years of age at the time of his death,
and of course, was never married.*
With good wishes for the New Year, I am,

Yours sincerely,
Marie M. Colby

*P.S. I believe you would be interested to learn something of
the splendid work General did the last eighteen years of his
life. He joined the Christian Church the day he was sixty
years old and was one of the most faithful attendants from
that time on. He was substitute Sunday School teacher for
several years, and about six years ago took the 'Business
Man's Bible Class' as teacher, and from an enrollment of
about a dozen the class increased until he had ninety enrolled at the time of his death.*[2]

It would appear that Leonard finally made the religious con-
version that Clara and grandmother Chilton had always hoped

would happen. Maud lived on in Beatrice until June 10, 1942, where she died at age 78.

VICTORY FOR THE CAMPAIGN

When Clara Colby started her work for woman suffrage, only the Wyoming Territory gave women the right to vote. At the point when she died, twelve states and the Alaska Territory had given women the vote and another fifteen states had advanced their legislation, which would result in those states giving women the vote before the Nineteenth Amendment came into force. Towards the end of Clara's life, the support in Congress for woman suffrage had grown significantly. In October 1915, President Woodrow Wilson voted in favor of woman suffrage in his home state of New Jersey, the first indication that his position was changing. (New Jersey was the state where Clara had campaigned after returning from California.) By 1918, President Wilson fully supported a federal amendment to prohibit both states and the federal government from denying the right to vote based on sex. The Amendment passed the House on May 21, 1919, and on June 4, 1919, it was voted on by the Senate. To become law, the Amendment had to be ratified by at least 36 states, and this was finally achieved when Tennessee ratified on August 18, 1920. The Nineteenth Amendment became official on August 26, 1920

The suffrage leaders who were most prominent when the Amendment came into law were in effect the leaders of the movement at that time. Carrie Chapman Catt had served as the president of the NAWSA from 1900 to 1904 and from 1915 to 1920, and she has gained most acclaim, apart from the founders, Susan B. Anthony and Elizabeth Cady Stanton. The young leaders of the National Woman's Party, Alice Paul and Lucy Burns, also received accolades as being crucial to the success of the movement—even though they only returned to America in 1912.

It took the efforts of thousands of women to build the movement which resulted in the ultimate success of the Nineteenth Amendment, but few can match the lifelong dedication shown by Clara Bewick Colby in her work, particularly considering her adverse circumstances and overwhelming difficulties.

Notes

Chapter 1

1. *Riding the Cars*, an essay by Clara Bewick. Wisconsin Historical Society, WHS.
2. *The Bewick Family History*, written by SCL Bewick. WHS
3. Ibid.
4. Notes from Violet Bates. Violet Bates was a granddaughter of Walter Medhurst and great-aunt of the author. Hillier family papers.
5. *Bewick Family History*. WHS
6. New York Passenger Lists
7. *The Morning Chronicle*. 18 July 1846
8. Clara Bewick Colby papers. WHS
9. From her essay *Reminiscence*. WHS

Chapter 2

1. Port of New York passenger records.
2. *The Bewick Family history*. WHS
3. Ibid.
4. Ibid.
5. Clara Colby's essay, *Trip to America* WHS
6. *Riding the Cars*. WHS

Chapter 3

1. *Concerning Farmers' Wives*, by Clara B. Colby. WHS
2. Clara Colby's notes regarding the death of her mother. WHS
3. *The Bewick Family history* WHS
4. Ibid.
5. Ibid.
6. Clara B. Colby papers WHS

Chapter 4

1. *Democratic Ideals* by Olympia Brown.
2. Ibid.
3. *The Bewick Family History.* WHS
4. *A Plea for the English Government.* WHS
5. Clara B. Colby papers, WHS
6. Address in the 1868 Madison City Directory.
7. *State Journal.* November 14, 1868
8. State Journal. June 5, 1869
9. *Lost Bird of Wounded Knee*, by Renee Sansom Flood. Scribner 1995.

Chapter 5

1. *Democratic Ideals.* Olympia Brown
2. Clara B. Colby papers, WHS
3. *Democratic Ideals.* Olympia Brown
4. *State Journal.* June 21, 1870
5. Clara B. Colby papers, WHS
6. Ibid.
7. Letter from Grandmother. Clara B. Colby papers, WHS
8. Ibid.
9. Ibid.

9. *The Boston Globe*, November 18, 1895

10. Letter from Susan B. Anthony to Clara dated December 13, 1895. Huntington Library, California.

11. *The Woman's Tribune*, June 13, 1896.

12. WHS

Chapter 14

1. *Nebraska State Journal*, January 1, 1897

2. *The Woman's Tribune*, July 9, 1898.

3. *Kansas City Journal*, July 10, 1898. Also the *Aberdeen People's Journal*, Scotland. July 16, 1898

4. *The Woman's Tribune*, June 25, 1898.

5. *Arkansas Democrat*, December 28, 1898

6. *Nebraska State Journal*, January 19, 1899.

7. *Beatrice Daily Sun*, June 9, 1906.

8. *Lost Bird of Wounded Knee*, by Renee Sansom Flood. Scribner 1995.

Chapter 15

1. *Democratic Ideals*, by Olympia Brown. 1917

2. *The Woman's Tribune*, October 21, 1899.

3. Ibid.

4. *The Woman's Tribune*, August 12, 1899.

5. *The Woman's Tribune*, Nov4, 1899.

6. November 20, 1899. Clara B. Colby papers, WHS

Chapter 16

1. *The Woman's Tribune*, July 28, 1900

2. The Oxford Dictionary of Biography.

3. *The Woman's Tribune*, May 25 and June 15, 1901

4. *The Woman's Tribune*, July 27, 1901.
5. *The Woman's Tribune*, September 21, 1901.
6. *The Nebraska State Journal.* April 14, 1901.
7. *The Woman's Tribune*, January 18, 1902.
8. *The Woman's Tribune*, July 5, 1902
9. *The Woman's Tribune,*July 12, 1902
10. ibid.
11. *The Los Angeles Times.* April 30, 1902
12. *The Woman's Tribune,* November 8, 1902

Chapter 17

1. *The Nebraska State Journal.* December 8, 1903.
2. *Beatrice Daily Sun,* December 19, 1903
3. Letter to herself. August 11, 1903 WHS.
4. Letter from Leonard to Clara. August 16, 1903. WHS
5. Letter from Clara to Leonard. August 22, 1903. WHS
6. Diary notes for August. WHS
7. Letter from Leonard to Clara. September 30, 1903.
8. Undated letter from Zintka to Clara. WHS.
9. Hand written undated letter from Zintka to Miss Peabody. WHS.
10. Letter from Leonard to Clara. June 1, 1904. WHS
11. Letter from Clara. September 28 1904. WHS

Chapter 18

1. *The Washington Post.* December 18, 1904.
2. *Beatrice Daily Sun.* February 3, 1905.
3. *The Washington Times.* January 31, 1904.
4. Letter from the Indian Service. WHS
5. Letter from Montgomery. WHS.
6. *The Woman's Tribune,* March 31, 1906

7. *Beatrice Daily Sun.* March 31, 1906
8. Letter from Chemawa to Clara Colby. WHS.
9. *Beatrice Daily Sun.* June 15, 1906.
10. *Lincoln Daily Star.* June 16, 1906

Chapter 19

1. Letter to Leonard from Clara, January 1, 1907. WHS
2. Letter from Clara to Leonard dated December 22, 1907. WHS.
3. Letter from Leonard to Clara dated December 26, 1907. WHS.
4. *Beatrice Daily Sun.* April 2 1908
5. *The Lincoln Star.* November 29, 1987.

Chapter 20

1. *The Woman's Tribune,* August 8, 1908.
2. *Gloucestershire Echo.* July 27, 1908
3. *The Woman's Tribune,* December 12, 1908.
4. *Evening Star.* October 14, 1908.
5. Letter from Carrie Catt to Clara Dated November 28, 1908. WHS
6. Letter from Carrie Catt to Clara Dated December 14, 1908. WHS

Chapter 21

1. Letter to Clara. August 8, 1908.
2. Letter to Clara from Zintka. December 28, 1908. WHS.
3. *Beatrice Daily Sun.* May 4, 1909
4. *Beatrice Daily Sun.* May 23, 1909
5. Letter from Leonard to Clara, dated May 11, 1909. WHS
6. From a reply to M. Chalivat's letter dated June 28, 1909. WHS
7. Letter from Dr. Clara Smith Eaton March 9, 1910

Chapter 22

1. Letter from Ellen Sabin. March 22, 1910
2. *The Oregon Daily Journal.* October 23, 1910
3. *Votes for Women.* November 25, 1910. See the illustration from *The Daily Mail's* front page.
4. *Votes for Women.* November 25, 1910. The Battle of Downing Street.
5. *The Vote.* May 6, 1911
6. *Statesman Journal.* May 16, 1911
7. *New York Times.* June 1911. See the illustration of the march from *The New York Times.*
8. *The Washington Herald.* December 7, 1911.

Chapter 23

1. *The Courier News*, Bridgewater, NJ. February 27, 1912
2. *Washington Herald.* April 1, 1912
3. *Oregon Daily Journal.* September 2, 1912
4. *The Boston Globe.* January 31, 1913.
5. *Washington Post.* February 7, 1913
6. *Washington Herald.* April 22, 1913.
7. *The Vote.* England. April 18, 1913
8. Letter from Clara to Zintka. WHS.
9. *The Lincoln Star.* October 3, 1913.
10. *Los Angeles Times.* October 7, 1913.

Chapter 24

1. *The Oshkosh Northwestern.* May 14, 1913
2. *Oregon Daily Journal.* July 27, 1913.
3. From her article *The Child in Hungary.* WHS
4. *Irish Citizen.* November 8, 1913

5. From Clara's diary. Annie Kenney was a victim of forced feeding when in prison on hunger strike. WHS

6. Clara's diary. WHS.

7. *Democratic Ideals*, By Olympia Brown. 1917.

8. *Hamilton Evening Journal*, Hamilton Ohio. March 24, 1914.

9. *Washington Post*, December 17, 1914

10. *Lincoln Journal Star.* January 27, 1915.

11. Letter from Clara to Mary dated August 14, 1914. WHS.

Chapter 25

1. Letter from Alfred Hazlett dated March 18, 1915. WHS

2. *Lost Bird of Wounded Knee,* by Renee Sansom Flood. Scribner 1995

3. *San Francisco Chronicle.* July 11, 1915.

4. A letter from Ida Husted Harper in Democratic Ideals by Olympia Brown.

5. Violet Bates was also a great aunt of the author who came to live at his childhood home.

6. *Asbury Park Press.* October 19, 1915.

7. *Democratic Ideals*, by Olympia Brown.

8. *The Washington Herald.* March 25 1916.

9. Letter from John E. Raker to Olympia Brown dated October 9, 1917. WHS.

10. Clara's 1915 diary. WHS.

11. Letter from Clara to Belva Lockwood dated July 17, 1916. WHS.

12. Letter from Olympia Brown to Clara dated August 8, 1916. WHS.

13. *Democratic Ideals*, by Olympia Brown. 1917

Epilogue

1. *The Journal Times.* Racine. September 14, 1916.

2. Clara B. Colby papers. WHS.

Bibliography

Books

Anthony, Katherine. *Susan B. Anthony: Her Personal History and Her Era*. (Doubleday & Co. 1975)

Armitage, Susan, and Jameson, Elizabeth. *The Women's West*. (University of Oklahoma Press. 1987)

Brown, Olympia. *Democratic Ideals. A Memorial Sketch of Clara B. Colby*. (Washington, D.C. Federal Suffrage Association. 1917)

Danky, James P. and Wiegand, Wayne W. *Women in Print*. (Madison. University of Wisconsin Press. 2006)

Debo, Angie. *A History of the Creek Indians. The Road to Disappearance*. (University of Oklahoma Press. 1979)

Dobbs, Hugh J. *History of Gage County, Nebraska*. Article on General Leonard Wright Colby. (Lincoln. Western Publishing and Engraving. 1918)

Edgerly, Lois Stiles. *Give Her This Day: A Daybook of Women's Words*. (Tilbury House Publishing. 1990)

Gordon, Ann D., Editor. *The selected papers of Elizabeth Cady Stanton and Susan B. Anthony, Vol 6. An Awful Hush*. (New Brunswick, N.J. Rutgers University Press 2013)

Harper, Ida Husted. *A Brief History of the Movement for Woman Suffrage in the United States*. (New York, NWS Publishing. 1919)

Harper, Ida Husted. *The Life and Work of Susan B. Anthony*. 2 volumes. (Bowen-Merrill Company. 1898)

Holliday, John. *Mission to China: How an Englishman Brought the West to the Orient.* The biography of Clara B. Colby's great uncle, the Rev Dr. Walter Henry Medhurst. (Stroud, Gloucestershire. Amberley Publishing. 2016)

Pappas, Christine. *More Notable Nebraskans.* (Lincoln. Media Productions and Marketing. 2001)

Reeves, Winona Evans. *The Blue Book of Nebraska Women.* (Missouri Printing and Publishing Company. 1916)

Sansom Flood, Renee. *Lost Bird of Wounded Knee. Spirit of the Lakota.* (New York, Scribner.1995)

Watson, Martha, Author. *A voice of their own. The woman suffrage press,* 1840-1910 (Tuscaloosa. University of Alabama Press 1991)

Stanton, Elizabeth Cady. *The Woman's Bible.* Unabridged republication of two volumes. (CreateSpace Independent Publishing. 2011)

Swiney, Frances. *The Awakening of Women.* (London. William Reeves. 1908)

Articles, Essays, and Dissertations.

Bloomberg, Kristin Mapel. *How Shall we Make Beatrice Grow.* (History, Nebraska. 2011)

Colby, Clara Bewick. *Concerning Farmers Wives.* (Boston. New England Publishing Company. 1881)

Colby, Clara Bewick. *The Ballot and Bullet Theory.* Memorial Library, University of Wisconsin, Madison.

Colby, Clara Bewick *Margaret Fuller – Greatest of American Women.* (The Englishwoman. 1911)

Colby, Clara Bewick. *Elizabeth Cady Stanton.* (Arena Magazine, Volume 29. 1903)

About the Author

John Holliday grew up in England but spent much of his life as a business entrepreneur in Canada and Australia. John's interest in writing arose when he decided to write a memoir of his business life. That experience led to a decision to write *Mission to China: How an Englishman Brought the West to the Orient*, published initially in England, followed by a Chinese edition in Taiwan.

Mission to China is a biography of Walter Medhurst, John's 2nd great grandfather, and a famous missionary to China. During the research of the book, John became aware of the extraordinary life of Clara Colby, whose grandmother was Walter Medhurst's sister, and he became determined that this should be his next book.

John lives with his wife Colleen in Queensland, Australia.

CPSIA information can be obtained
at www.ICGtesting.com
Printed in the USA
FSHW021647081219
64670FS